© 1998 By Frank J. Fabozzi Associates
New Hope, Pennsylvania

This publication is designed to provide accurate and authoritative information in regard to the subject matter covered. It is sold with the understanding that the publisher is not engaged in rendering legal, accounting, or other professional services.

ISBN: 1-883249-37-6

Printed in the United States of America

Table of Contents

Contributing Authors   iv

1. **Investment Management:**
   An Architecture for the Equity Market   1
   Bruce I. Jacobs and Kenneth N. Levy

2. **Investment Analysis:**
   Profiting from a Complex Equity Market   21
   Bruce I. Jacobs and Kenneth N. Levy

3. **Medium and Small Capitalization Indexing**   37
   George U. Sauter

4. **Enhanced Equity Indexing**   51
   John S. Loftus

5. **The Active versus Passive Debate:**
   Perspectives of an Active Quant   67
   Robert C. Jones

6. **Factor-Based Approach to Equity Portfolio Management**   87
   Frank J. Fabozzi

7. **Dividend Discount Models**   107
   William J. Hurley and Frank J. Fabozzi

8. **Normal Portfolios: Construction of Customized Benchmarks**   127
   Jon A. Christopherson

9. **Equity Style: What It Is and Why It Matters**   143
   Jon A. Christopherson and C. Nola Williams

10. **Fundamental Factors in Equity Style Classification**   163
    David R. Borger

11. **Value-Based Equity Strategies**   183
    Gary G. Schlarbaum

12. **The Use of Derivatives in Managing Equity Portfolios**   201
    Roger G. Clarke, Harindra de Silva, and Greg M. McMurran

13. **Implementing Investment Strategies:**
    The Art and Science of Investing   235
    Wayne H. Wagner and Mark Edwards

Index   251

Contributing Authors

David R. Borger	Wilshire Asset Management
Jon A. Christopherson	Frank Russell Company
Roger G. Clarke	Analytic/TSA Global Asset Management
Harindra de Silva	Analytic/TSA Global Asset Management
Mark Edwards	Plexus Group
Frank J. Fabozzi	Yale University
William J. Hurley	The Royal Military College of Canada
Bruce I. Jacobs	Jacobs Levy Equity Management
Robert C. Jones	Goldman Sachs Asset Management
Kenneth N. Levy	Jacobs Levy Equity Management
John S. Loftus	Pacific Investment Managment Company
Greg M. McMurran	Analytic/TSA Global Asset Management
George U. Sauter	The Vanguard Group
Gary G. Schlarbaum	Miller, Anderson & Sherrerd, LLP
Wayne H. Wagner	Plexus Group
C. Nola Williams	Frank Russell Company

Chapter 1

Investment Management: An Architecture for the Equity Market

Bruce I. Jacobs, Ph.D.
Principal
Jacobs Levy Equity Management

Kenneth N. Levy, CFA
Principal
Jacobs Levy Equity Management

INTRODUCTION

Anyone who has ever built a house knows how important it is to start out with a sound architectural design. A sound design can help ensure that the end product will meet all the homeowner's expectations — material, aesthetic, and financial. A bad architectural design, or no design, offers no such assurance and is likely to lead to poor decision-making, unintended results, and cost overruns.

It is equally important in building an equity portfolio to start out with some framework that relates the raw materials — stocks — and the basic construction techniques — investment approaches — to the end product. An architecture of equity management that outlines the basic relationships between the raw investment material, investment approaches, potential rewards and possible risks, can provide a blueprint for investment decision-making.

We provide such a blueprint in this chapter. A quick tour of this blueprint reveals three building blocks — a comprehensive core, static style subsets, and a dynamic entity. Investment approaches can also be roughly categorized into three groups — passive, traditional active, and engineered active. Understanding the market's architecture and the advantages and disadvantages of each investment approach can improve overall investment results.

The authors thank Judith Kimball for her editorial assistance.

Exhibit 1: Equity Market Architecture

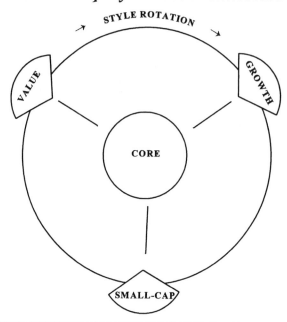

AN ARCHITECTURE

Exhibit 1 provides a simple but fairly comprehensive view of the equity market.[1] The heart of the structure, the core, represents the overall market. Theoretically, this would include all U.S. equity issues. (Similar architectures can be applied to other national equity markets.) In line with the practice of most equity managers, a broad-based equity index such as the S&P 500 or (even broader) the Russell 3000 or Wilshire 5000, may proxy for the aggregate market.

For both equity managers and their clients, the overall market represents a natural and intuitive starting place. It is the ultimate selection pool for all equity strategies. Furthermore, the long-term returns offered by the U.S. equity market have historically outperformed alternative asset classes in the majority of multi-year periods. The aim of most institutional investors (even those that do not hold core investments per se) is to capture, or outdo, this equity return premium.

The core equity market can be broken down into subsets that comprise stocks with similar price behaviors — large-cap growth, large-cap value, and small-cap stocks. In Exhibit 1, the wedges circling the core represent these style subsets. The aggregate of the stocks forming the subsets equals the overall core market.

---

[1] See also Bruce I. Jacobs and Kenneth N. Levy, "How to Build a Better Equity Portfolio," *Pension Management* (June 1996), pp. 36-39.

Exhibit 2: Small-Cap Stocks May Outperform Large-Cap in Some Periods and Underperform in Others

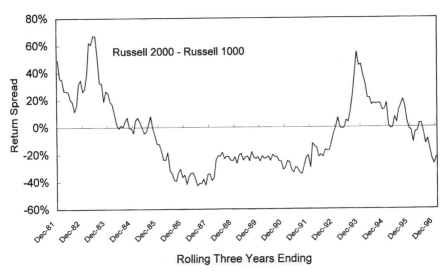

One advantage of viewing the market as a collection of subsets is the ability it confers upon the investor to "mix and match." Instead of holding a core portfolio, for example, the investor can hold market subsets in market-like weights and receive returns and incur risks commensurate with those of the core. Alternatively, the investor can depart from core weights to pursue returns in excess of the core market return (at the expense, of course, of incremental risk). Investors who believe that small-cap stocks offer a higher return than the average market return, for example, can overweight that subset and underweight large-cap value and growth stocks.

Over time, different style subsets can offer differing relative payoffs as economic conditions change. As Exhibit 2 shows, small-cap stocks outperformed large-cap stocks by 60 percentage points or more in the rolling 3-year periods ending in mid-1983 and by 45 to 55 percentage points in late 1993. But small cap underperformed by 20 to 40 percentage points in the rolling 3-year periods between early 1986 and December 1991.[2] Exhibit 3 shows that large-cap growth stocks outperformed large-cap value stocks by 30 to 40 percentage points in the rolling 3-year periods from mid-1991 to mid-1992 but underperformed by 20 to 35 percentage points in every rolling 3-year period from mid-1983 through 1986.[3]

---

[2] Exhibit 2 uses the Frank Russell 1000 (the largest stocks in the Russell 3000) as the large-cap index and the Russell 2000 (the smallest stocks in the Russell 3000) as the small-cap index.

[3] Exhibit 3 uses the Russell 1000 Growth and the Russell 1000 Value as the growth and value indexes; these indexes roughly divide the market capitalization of the Russell 1000. Results are similar using other indexes, such as the Wilshire and S&P 500/BARRA style indexes.

Exhibit 3: Large-Cap Growth Stocks Outperform Large-Cap Value in Some Periods and Underperform in Others

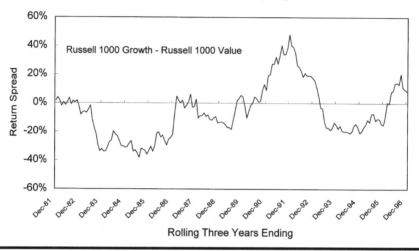

Just as some investors attempt to time the market by buying into and selling out of equities in line with their expectations of overall market trends, investors can attempt to exploit the dynamism of style subsets by rotating their investments across different styles over time, in pursuit of profit opportunities offered by one or another subset as market and economic conditions change.[4] The curved lines connecting the style wedges in Exhibit 1 represent this dynamic nature of the market.

The equity core and its constituent style subsets constitute the basic building blocks — the equity selection universes — from which investors can construct their portfolios. Another important choice facing the investor, however, is the investment approach or approaches to apply to the selection universe. Exhibit 4 categorizes possible approaches into three groups — traditional, passive, and engineered. Each of these approaches can be characterized by an underlying investment philosophy and, very generally, by a level of risk relative to the underlying selection universe.

TRADITIONAL ACTIVE MANAGEMENT

Traditional investment managers focus on "stock picking." In short, they hunt for individual securities that will perform well over the investment horizon. The search includes in-depth examinations of companies' financial statements and investigations of companies' managements, product lines, facilities, etc. Based on the findings of these inquiries, traditional managers determine whether a particular firm is a good "buy" or a better "sell."

[4] See Bruce I. Jacobs and Kenneth N. Levy, "High-Definition Style Rotation," *Journal of Investing* (Fall 1996), pp. 14-23.

Exhibit 4: Equity Investment Approaches

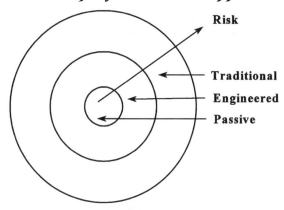

The search area for traditional investing may be wide — the equivalent of the equity core — and may include market timing that exploits the dynamism of the overall market. Because in-depth analyses of large numbers of securities are just not practical for any one manager, however, traditional managers tend to focus on subsets of the equity market. Some may hunt for above-average earnings growth (growth stocks), while others look to buy future earnings streams cheaply (value stocks); still others beat the grasses off the trodden paths, in search of overlooked growth and/or value stocks (small-cap stocks). Traditional managers have thus fallen into the pursuit of growth, value, or small-cap styles.

Traditional managers often screen an initial universe of stocks based on some financial criteria, thereby selecting a relatively small list of stocks to be followed closely. Focusing on such a narrow list reduces the complexity of the analytical problem to human (i.e., traditional) dimensions. Unfortunately, it may also introduce significant barriers to superior performance.

Exhibit 5 plots the combinations of breadth and depth of insights necessary to achieve a given investment return/risk level.[5] Here the breadth of insights may be understood as the number of independent insights — i.e., the number of investment ideas or the number of stocks. The depth, or goodness, of insights is measured as the *information coefficient* — the correlation between the return forecasts made for stocks and their actual returns. Note that the goodness of the insights needed to produce the given return/risk ratio starts to increase dramatically as the number of insights falls below 100; the slope gets particularly steep as breadth falls below 50.

---

[5] The plot reflects the relationship:

$$IR = IC \times \sqrt{BR}$$

where *IC* is the information coefficient (the correlation between predicted and actual returns), *BR* the number of independent insights, and IR (in this case set equal to one) the ratio of annualized excess return to annualized residual risk. See Richard C. Grinold and Ronald N. Kahn, *Active Portfolio Management* (Chicago, IL: Probus Publishing, 1995), Chapter 6.

Exhibit 5: Combination of Breadth (Number) of Insights and Depth, or "Goodness," of Insights Needed to Produce a Given Investment Return/Risk Ratio

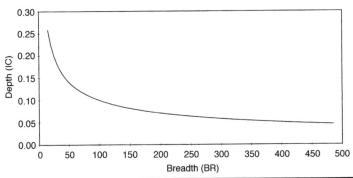

Traditional investing in effect relies on the ability of in-depth research to supply information coefficients that are high enough to overcome the lack of breadth imposed by the approach's fairly severe limitations on the number of securities that can be followed. As Exhibit 5 shows, however, the level of information coefficients required at such constricted breadth levels constitutes a considerable hurdle to superior performance. The insights from traditional management must be very, very good to overcome the commensurate lack of breadth.[6]

Furthermore, lack of breadth may also have detrimental effects on the depth of traditional insights. While reducing the range of inquiry makes tractable the problem of stock selection via the labor-intensive methods of traditional active management, it is also bound to result in potentially relevant (and profitable) information being left out. Surely, for example, the behavior of the growth stocks not followed by traditional growth managers — even the behavior of value stocks outside the growth subset — may contain information relevant to the pricing of those stocks that do constitute the reduced traditional universe.

Another inherent weakness of traditional investment approaches is their heavy reliance on subjective human judgments. An ever-growing body of research suggests that stock prices, as well as being moved by fundamental information, are influenced by the psychology of investors. In particular, investors often appear to be under the influence of cognitive biases that cause them to err systematically in making investment decisions.[7]

---

[6] Market timing strategies are particularly lacking in breadth, as an insight into the market's direction provides only one investment decision. Quarterly timing would produce four "bets" a year — a level of diversification few investors would find acceptable. Furthermore, unless timing is done on a daily basis or the timer is prodigiously skilled, it would take a lifetime to determine whether the results of timing reflect genuine skill or mere chance.

[7] See, for example, Daniel Kahneman and Amos Tversky, "Prospect Theory: An Analysis of Decision Under Risk," *Econometrica* (Number 2, 1979), pp. 263-292, and Richard H. Thaler (ed.), *Advances in Behavioral Finance* (New York, NY: Russell Sage Foundation, 1993).

Kenneth Arrow, for example, finds that investors tend to overemphasize new information if it appears to be representative of a possible future event; thus, if investors perceive a firm's management to be "good," and the firm has recently enjoyed high earnings, they will tend to place more reliance on the higher than the lower earnings estimates provided by analysts.[8] Robert Shiller finds that investors are as susceptible as any other consumers to fads and fashions — bidding up prices of "hot" stocks and ignoring out-of-favor issues.[9] We describe below four common cognitive errors that investors may fall prey to.

Cognitive Errors
Loss Aversion (The "Better Not Take the Chance/ What the Heck" Paradox)

Investors exhibit risk-averse behavior with respect to potential gains: faced with a choice between (1) a sure gain of $3,000 and (2) an 80% chance of gaining $4,000 or a 20% chance of gaining nothing, most people choose the sure thing, even though the $3,000 is less than the expected value of the gamble, which is $3,200 (80% of $4,000). But investors are generally risk-seeking when it comes to avoiding certain loss: faced with a choice between (1) a sure loss of $3,000 and (2) an 80% chance of losing $4,000 or a 20% chance of losing nothing, most people will opt to take a chance. It's only human nature that the pain of loss exceed the glee of gain, but putting human nature in charge of investment decision-making may lead to suboptimal results. Shirking risk leads to forgone gains. Pursuing risk in avoidance of loss may have even direr consequences ("digging a deeper hole"), as recent episodes at Barings and Daiwa have demonstrated.

Endowment Effect (The "Pride in Ownership" Syndrome)

The price people are willing to pay to acquire an object or service is often less than the price they would be willing to sell the identical object or service for if they owned it. Say you bought a stock last year and it's quadrupled in price. If you won't buy more because "it's too expensive now," you should sell it. If you won't sell it because you were so brilliant when you bought it, you're sacrificing returns for pride in ownership.

The Gambler's Fallacy ("Hot Streaks, Empty Wallets")

Is it more likely that six tosses of a coin will come up HTTHTH or HHHTTT? Most people think the former sequence is more typical than the latter, but in truth both are equally likely products of randomness. In either case, the probability of the next flip of the coin turning up heads, or tails, is 50%. Market prices, too, will display patterns. It's easy to interpret such patterns as persistent trends, and tempt-

---

[8] Kenneth J. Arrow, "Risk Perception in Psychology and Economics," *Economic Inquiry* (Number 1, 1982), pp. 1-8.

[9] Robert J. Shiller, "Stock Prices and Social Dynamics," *Brookings Papers on Economic Activity* (Number 2, 1984), pp. 457-510.

ing to trade on them. But if the latest "hot streak" is merely a mirage thrown up by random price movements, it will prove an unreliable guide to future performance.

Confirmation Bias ("Don't Confuse Me with the Facts")

People search for and place more reliance upon evidence that confirms their preconceived notions, ignoring or devaluing evidence that refutes them. Four cards lie on a table, showing A, B, 2, and 3: What is the fewest number of cards you can turn over to confirm or refute that every card with a vowel on one side has an even number on the other side? Most people choose A, then 2. An odd number or a letter on the reverse of A would refute the conjecture. The 2, however, can merely confirm, not refute; the presence of a vowel on the reverse would confirm, but anything else would simply be immaterial. The correct choice is to turn A, 3, and B. A vowel on the reverse of 3 can refute, as can a vowel on the reverse of B. Investment approaches that do not have a method of systematically searching through all available evidence without prejudice, in order to find the exceptions that disprove their rules, may leave portfolios open to blindsiding and torpedo effects.

Investors susceptible to these biases will tend to take too little (or too much) risk; to hold on to an investment for too long; to see long-term trends where none exist; and to place too much reliance on information that confirms existing beliefs. As a result, the performances of their portfolios are likely to suffer.

The reliance of traditional investment management on the judgments of individual human minds makes for idiosyncrasies of habit that work to the detriment of investment discipline, and this is true at the level of the investment firm as well as the individual at the firm. It may be difficult to coordinate the individual mindsets of all analysts, economists, investment officers, technicians, and traders, and this coordination is even harder to achieve when subjective standards for security analysis differ from individual to individual.

Constructing Portfolios

The qualitative nature of the outcome of the security evaluation process, together with the absence of a unifying framework, can give rise to problems when individual insights into securities' performances are combined to construct a portfolio. However on target an analyst's buy or sell recommendations may be, they are difficult to translate into guidelines for portfolio construction. Portfolio optimization procedures require quantitative estimates of relevant parameters — not mere recommendations to buy, hold, or sell.

The traditional manager's focus on stock picking and the resulting ad hoc nature of portfolio construction can lead to portfolios that are poorly defined in regard to their underlying selection universes. While any particular manager's portfolio return may be measured against the return on an index representative of an underlying equity core or style subset, that index does not serve as a "benchmark" in the sense of providing a guideline for portfolio risk. Traditional portfolios' risk-return profiles may thus vary greatly relative to those of the underlying selection universe.

As a result, portfolios do not necessarily fit into the market's architecture. A traditional value manager, for example, may be averse to holding certain sectors, such as utilities. Not only will the portfolio's returns suffer when utilities perform well, but the portfolio will suffer from a lack of "integrity" — of wholeness. Such a portfolio will not be representative of the whole value subset. Nor could it be combined with growth and small-cap portfolios to create a core-like holding.

Because the relationship between the overall equity market and traditional managers' style portfolios may be ambiguous, "value" and "growth," "small-cap" and "large-cap" may not be mutually exclusive. Value portfolios may hold some growth stocks, or growth portfolios some value stocks. There is no assurance that a combination of style portfolios can offer a market-like or above-market return at market-like risk levels.

Because of their heavy reliance on human mind power and subjective judgment, traditional approaches to investment management tend to suffer from a lack of breadth, a lack of discipline, and a resulting lack of portfolio integrity. Traditional management, while it may serve as well as any other approach for picking individual stocks, suffers from severe limitations when it comes to constructing portfolios of stocks. Perhaps it is for this reason that traditionally managed portfolios have often failed to live up to expectations.

PASSIVE MANAGEMENT

The generally poor performance of traditional investment management approaches helped to motivate the development, in the late 1960s and the 1970s, of new theories of stock price behavior. The efficient market hypothesis and random walk theory — the products of much research — offered a reason for the meager returns reaped by traditional investment managers: stock prices effectively reflect all information in an "efficient" manner, rendering stock price movements random and unpredictable. Efficiency and randomness provided the motivation for passive investment management; advances in computing power provided the means.

Passive management aims to construct portfolios that will match the risk/return profiles of underlying market benchmarks. The benchmark may be core equity (as proxied by the S&P 500 or other broad index) or a style subset (as proxied by a large-cap growth, large-cap value, or small-cap index). Given the quantitative tools at its disposal, passive management can fine-tune the stock selection and portfolio construction problems in order to deliver portfolios that mimic very closely both the returns and risks of their chosen benchmarks.

Passive portfolios, unlike traditional portfolios, are disciplined. Any tendencies for passive managers to succumb to cognitive biases will be held in check by the exigencies of their stated goals — tracking the performances of their underlying benchmarks. Their success in this endeavor also means that the resulting portfolios will have integrity. A passive value portfolio will behave like its underlying selection universe, and a combination of passive style portfolios in market-like weights can be expected to offer a return close to the market's return at a risk level close to the market's.

As the trading required to keep portfolios in line with underlying indexes is generally less than that required to "beat" the indexes, transaction costs for passive management are generally lower than those incurred by active investment approaches. As much of the stock selection and portfolio construction problem can be relegated to fast-acting computers, the management fees for passive management are also modest. For the same reason, the number of securities that can be covered by any given passive manager is virtually unlimited; all the stocks in the selection universe can be considered for portfolio inclusion.

Unlike traditional management, then, passive management offers great breadth. Breadth in this case doesn't count for much, however, because passive management is essentially insightless. Built on the premise that markets are efficient, hence market prices are random and unpredictable, passive management does not attempt to pursue or offer any return over the return on the relevant benchmark. Rather, its appeal lies in its ability to deliver the asset class return or to deliver the return of a style subset of the asset class. In practice, of course, trading costs and management fees, however modest, subtract from this performance.

An investor in pursuit of above-market returns may nevertheless be able to exploit passive management approaches via style subset selection and style rotation. That is, an investor who believes value stocks will outperform the overall market can choose to overweight a passive value portfolio in expectation of earning above-market (but not above-benchmark) returns. An investor with foresight into style performance can choose to rotate investments across different passive style portfolios as underlying economic and market conditions change.

ENGINEERED MANAGEMENT

Engineered management recognizes that markets are reasonably efficient in digesting information and that stock price movements in response to unanticipated news are largely random. It also recognizes, however, that significant, measurable pricing inefficiencies do exist, and it seeks to deliver incremental returns by modeling and exploiting these inefficiencies. In this endeavor, it applies to the same company fundamental and economic data used by traditional active management many of the tools that fostered the development of passive management, including modern computing power, finance theory, and statistical techniques — instruments that can extend the reaches (and discipline the vagaries) of the human mind.

Engineered approaches use quantitative methods to select stocks and construct portfolios that will have risk/return profiles similar to those of underlying equity benchmarks but offer incremental returns relative to those benchmarks, at appropriate incremental risk levels. The quantitative methods used may range from fairly straightforward to immensely intricate. In selecting stocks, for example, an engineered approach may use something as simple as a dividend discount model. Or it may employ complex multivariate models that aim to capture the complexities of the equity market.[10]

The engineered selection process can deal with and benefit from as wide a selection universe as passive management. It can thus approach the investment problem with an unbiased philosophy, unhampered, as is traditional management, by the need to reduce the equity universe to a tractable subset. At the same time, depending upon the level of sophistication of the tools it chooses to use, engineered management can benefit from great depth of analysis — a depth similar to that of traditional approaches. Multivariate modeling, for example, can take into account the intricacies of stock price behavior, including variations in price responses across stocks of different industries, economic sectors, and styles.

Because engineered management affords both breadth and depth, the manager can choose a focal point from which to frame the equity market, without loss of important "framing" information. Analysis of a particular style subset, for example, can take advantage of information gleaned from the whole universe of securities, not just stocks of that particular style (or a subset of that style, as in traditional management). The increased breadth of inquiry should lead to improvements in portfolio performance vis-a-vis traditional style portfolios.

Engineering Portfolios

Engineered management utilizes all the information found relevant from an objective examination of the broad equity universe to arrive at numerical estimates for the expected returns and anticipated risks of the stocks in that universe. Unlike the subjective outcomes of traditional management, such numerical estimates are eminently suitable for portfolio construction via optimization techniques.[11]

The goal of optimization is to maximize portfolio return while tying portfolio risk to that of the underlying benchmark. The portfolio's systematic risk should match the risk of the benchmark. The portfolio's residual risk should be no more than is justified by the expected incremental return. Risk control can be further refined by tailoring the optimization model so that it is consistent with the variables in the return estimation process.

The quantitative nature of the stock selection and portfolio construction processes imposes discipline on engineered portfolios. With individual stocks defined by expected performance parameters, and portfolios optimized along those parameters to provide desired patterns of expected risk and return, engineered portfolios can be defined in terms of preset performance goals. Engineered managers have little leeway to stray from these performance mandates, hence are less likely

---

[10] See Bruce I. Jacobs and Kenneth N. Levy, "Investment Analysis: Profiting from a Complex Equity Market," Chapter 2 in this book.

[11] See also Bruce I. Jacobs and Kenneth N. Levy, "Engineering Portfolios: A Unified Approach," *Journal of Investing* (Winter 1995).

than traditional managers to fall under the sway of cognitive errors. In fact, engineered strategies may be designed to exploit such biases as investor overreaction (leading to price reversals) or investor herding (leading to price trends).

The discipline of engineered management also helps to ensure portfolio integrity. The style subset portfolios of a given firm, for example, should be non-overlapping, and the style subset benchmarks should in the aggregate be inclusive of all stocks in the investor's universe. Value portfolios should contain no growth stocks, nor growth portfolios any value stocks. The underlying benchmarks for value and growth portfolios, or large and small-cap portfolios, should aggregate to the equity core.

Engineering should reduce, relative to traditional management, portfolio return deviations from the underlying core or subset benchmark, while increasing expected returns relative to those available from passive approaches. While judicious stock selection can provide excess portfolio return over a passive benchmark, optimized portfolio construction offers control of portfolio risk.

Exhibit 6 compares the relative merits of traditional, passive, and engineered approaches to portfolio management. Traditional management offers depth, but strikes out with lack of breadth, susceptibility to cognitive errors, and lack of portfolio integrity. Passive management offers breadth, freedom from cognitive error, and portfolio integrity, but no depth whatsoever. Only engineered management has the ability to construct portfolios that benefit from both breadth and depth of analysis, are free of cognitive errors, and have structural integrity.

MEETING CLIENT NEEDS

A broad-based, engineered approach offers investment managers the means to tailor portfolios for a wide variety of client needs. Consider, for example, a client that has no opinion about style subset performance, but believes that the equity market will continue to offer its average historical premium over alternative cash and bond investments. This client may choose to hold the market in the form of an engineered core portfolio that can deliver the all-important equity market premium (at the market's risk level), plus the potential for some incremental return consistent with the residual risk incurred.

Exhibit 6: Comparison of Equity Investment Approaches

	Traditional	Passive	Engineered
Depth of Analysis	Yes	No	Simple — No Complex — Yes
Breadth of Analysis	No	Yes	Yes
Free of Cognitive Error	No	Yes	Yes
Portfolio Integrity	No	Yes	Yes

Alternatively, the client with a strong belief that value stocks will outperform can choose from among several engineered solutions. An engineered portfolio can be designed to deliver a value-benchmark-like return at a comparable risk level or to offer, at the cost of incremental risk, a return increment above the value benchmark. Traditional value portfolios cannot be designed to offer the same level of assurance of meeting these goals.

With engineered portfolios, the client also has the ability to fine-tune bets. For example, the client can weight a portfolio toward value stocks while retaining exposure to the overall market by placing some portion of the portfolio in core equity and the remainder in a value portfolio, or by placing some percentage in a growth portfolio and a larger percentage in a value portfolio. Exposures to the market and to its various subsets can be engineered. Again, traditional management can offer no assurance that a combination of style portfolios will offer the desired risk-return profile.

Expanding Opportunities

The advantages of an engineered approach are perhaps best exploited by strategies that are not constrained to deliver a benchmark-like performance. An engineered style rotation strategy, for example, seeks to deliver returns in excess of the market's by forecasting style subset performance. Shifting investment weights aggressively among various style subsets as market and economic conditions evolve, style rotation takes advantage of the historical tendency of any given style to outperform the overall market in some periods and to underperform it in others. Such a strategy uses the entire selection universe and offers potentially high returns at commensurate risk levels.

Allowing short sales as an adjunct to an engineered strategy — whether that strategy utilizes core equity, a style subset, or style rotation — can further enhance return opportunities. While traditional management focuses on stock picking — the selection of "winning" securities — the breadth of engineered management allows for the consideration of "losers" as well as "winners." With an engineered portfolio that allows shorting of losers, the manager can pursue potential mispricings without constraint, going long underpriced stocks and selling short overpriced stocks.

In markets in which short selling is not widespread, there are reasons to believe that shorting stocks can offer more opportunity than buying stocks. This is because restrictions on short selling do not permit investor pessimism to be as fully represented in prices as investor optimism. In such a market, the potential candidates for short sale may be less efficiently priced, hence offer greater return potential, than the potential candidates for purchase.[12]

Even if all stocks are efficiently priced, however, shorting can enhance performance by eliminating constraints on the implementation of investment

---

[12] See, for example, Bruce I. Jacobs and Kenneth N. Levy, "20 Myths About Long-Short," *Financial Analysts Journal* (September/October 1996).

insights. Consider, for example, that a security with a median market capitalization has a weighting of approximately 0.01% of the market's capitalization. A manager that cannot short can underweight such a security by, at most, 0.01% relative to the market; this is achieved by not holding the security at all. Those who do not consider this unduly restrictive should consider that placing a like constraint on the maximum portfolio overweight would be equivalent to saying the manager could hold, at most, a 0.02% position in the stock, no matter how appetizing its expected return. Shorting allows the manager free rein in translating the insights gained from the stock selection process into portfolio performance.

Long-Short Portfolios

If security returns are symmetrically distributed about the underlying market return, there will be fully as many unattractive securities for short sale as there are attractive securities for purchase. Using optimization techniques, the manager can construct a portfolio that balances equal dollar amounts and equal systematic risks long and short. Such a long-short balance neutralizes the risk (and return) of the underlying market. The portfolio's return — which can be measured as the spread between the long and short returns — is solely reflective of the manager's skill at stock selection.[13]

Not only does such a long-short portfolio neutralize underlying market risk, it offers improved control of residual risk relative even to an engineered long-only portfolio. For example, the long-only portfolio can control risk relative to the underlying benchmark only by converging toward the weightings of the benchmark's stocks; these weights constrain portfolio composition. Balancing securities' sensitivities long and short, however, eliminates risk relative to the underlying benchmark; benchmark weights are thus not constraining. Furthermore, the long-short portfolio can use offsetting long and short positions to fine-tune the portfolio's residual risk.

In addition to enhanced return and improved risk control, an engineered long-short approach also offers clients added flexibility in asset allocation. A simple long-short portfolio, for example, offers a return from security selection on top of a cash return (the interest received on the proceeds from the short sales). However, the long-short manager can also offer, or the client initiate, a long-short portfolio combined with a position in derivatives such as stock index futures. Such an "equitized" portfolio will offer the long-short portfolio's security selection return on top of the equity market return provided by the futures position; choice of other available derivatives can provide the return from security selection in combination with exposure to other asset classes. The transportability of the long-short portfolio's return offers clients the ability to take advantage of a manager's security selection skills while determining independently the plan's asset allocation mix.

---

[13] See Bruce I. Jacobs and Kenneth N. Levy, "The Long and Short on Long-Short," *Journal of Investing* (Spring 1997), pp. 73-86.

THE RISK-RETURN CONTINUUM

The various approaches to investment management — as well as the selection universes that are the targets of such approaches — can be characterized generally by distinct risk-return profiles. For example, in Exhibit 1, risk levels tend to increase as one moves from the core outward toward the dynamic view of the market; expected returns should also increase. Similarly, in Exhibit 4, risk can be perceived as increasing as one moves from passive investment management out toward traditional active management; expected returns should also increase.

Where should the investor be along this continuum? The answer depends in part on the investor's aversion to risk. The more risk-averse the investor, the closer to core/passive the portfolio should be, and the lower its risk and expected return. Investors who are totally averse to incurring residual risk (that is, departing from benchmark holdings and weights) should stick with passive approaches. They will thus be assured of receiving an equity market return at a market risk level. They will never "beat" the market.

Less risk-averse investors can make more use of style subsets (static or dynamic) and active (engineered or traditional) approaches. With the use of such subsets and such approaches, however, portfolio weights will shift away from overall equity market weights. The difference provides the opportunity for excess return, but it also creates residual risk. In this regard, engineered portfolios, which control risk relative to underlying benchmarks, have definite advantages over traditional portfolios.

The optimal level of residual risk for an investor will depend not only on the investor's level of aversion to residual risk, but also on the manager's skill. Skill can be measured as the manager's information ratio, or IR — the ratio of annualized excess return to annualized residual risk. For example, a manager that beats the benchmark by 2% per year, with 4% residual risk, has an IR of 2%/4%, or 0.5.

Grinold and Kahn formulate the argument as follows:[14]

$$\omega^* = \frac{IR}{2\lambda}$$

where ω^* equals the optimal level of portfolio residual risk given the manager's information ratio and the investor's level of risk aversion, λ. Increases in the manager's IR will increase the investor's optimal level of residual risk and increases in the investor's risk-aversion level will reduce it.

Exhibit 7 illustrates some of the trade-offs between residual risk and excess return for three levels of investor aversion to residual risk and two levels of manager skill. Here the straight lines represent the hypothetical continuum of portfolios (defined by their residual risks and excess returns) that could be offered

---

[14] Grinold and Kahn, *op. cit.*

by a highly skilled manager with an *IR* of 1.0 and a good manager with an *IR* of 0.5.[15] The points H, M, and L represent the optimal portfolios for investors with high, medium, and low aversions to residual risk. The point at the origin, P, with zero excess return and zero residual risk, may be taken to be a passive strategy offering a return and a risk level identical to the benchmark's.

Several important observations can be made from Exhibit 7. First, it is apparent that greater tolerance for risk (a lower risk aversion level) allows the investor to choose a portfolio with a higher risk level that can offer a higher expected return. Second, the more highly skilled the manager, the higher the optimal level of portfolio residual risk, and the higher the portfolio's expected excess return, whatever the investor's risk-aversion level. In short, higher excess returns accrue to higher-risk portfolios and to higher-*IR* managers.

Exhibit 7: Risk and Return Change with Investor Risk and Manager Skill

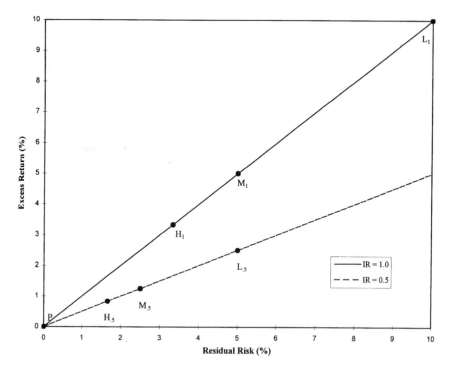

---

[15] In reality, no manager will offer a strategy for each possible risk/return combination. Furthermore, although *IR* is a linear function of residual risk when liquidity is unlimited and short selling unrestricted, in the real world *IR* will begin to decline at high levels of residual risk.

Exhibit 8: Sacrifice in Return from Overestimating Investor Risk Aversion

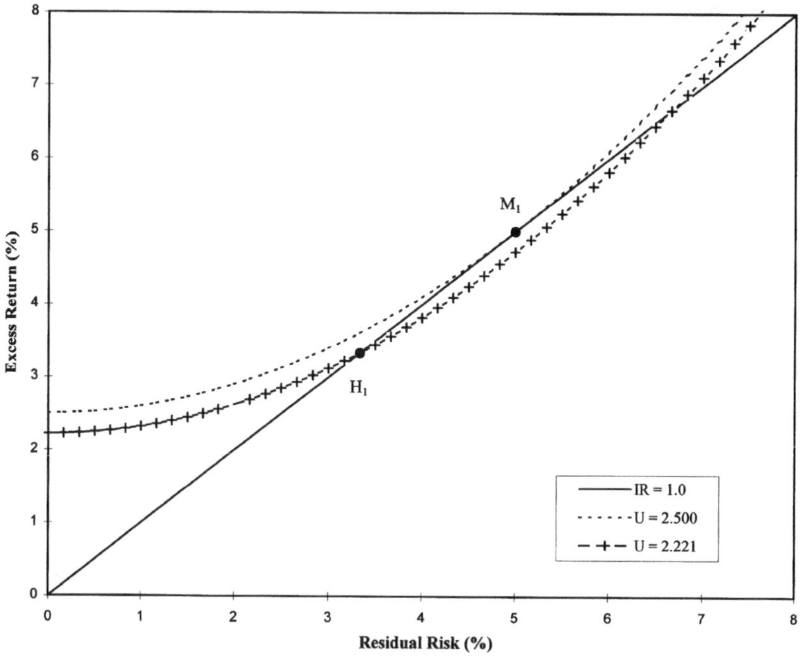

Within this framework, an investor who takes less than the optimal level of residual risk or who selects less than the best manager will sacrifice return.[16] Exhibit 8, for example, shows the decrease in return and utility (U) that results when an investor overestimates risk aversion. Here, an investor with a highly skilled manager, who actually has a medium level of risk aversion (M_1), chooses a portfolio suitable for an investor with a high level of risk aversion (H_1). The investor give-up in return can be measured as the vertical distance between M_1 and H_1. In somewhat more sophisticated terms, the higher-risk portfolio corresponds to a certainty-equivalent return of 2.500% and the less risky portfolio to a certainty-equivalent return of 2.221%, so the investor who overestimates his or her level of risk aversion and therefore chooses a suboptimal portfolio sacrifices 0.279 percentage points.

Exhibit 9 illustrates the return give-up that results when an investor with medium risk aversion uses a less skilled manager (IR of 0.5) rather than a higher-skill manager (IR of 1.0). Here the give-up in certainty-equivalent return between portfolio M_1 and portfolio $M_{.5}$ amounts to 1.875 percentage points. Choice of manager can significantly affect portfolio return.

---

[16] See also Bruce I. Jacobs and Kenneth N. Levy, "Residual Risk: How Much is Too Much?" *Journal of Portfolio Management* (Spring 1996).

Exhibit 9: Sacrifice in Return from Using Less Skillful Manager

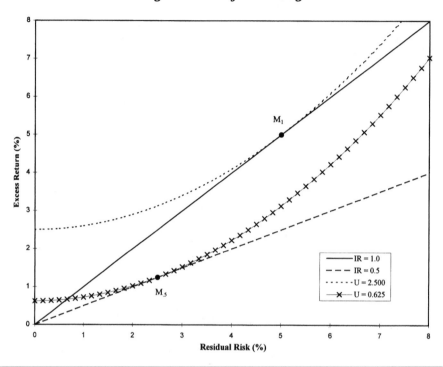

Suppose an investor finds a highly skilled manager ($IR = 1$), but that manager does not offer a portfolio with a risk level low enough to suit the investor's high level of risk aversion. A less skilled ($IR = 0.5$) manager, however, offers portfolios H$_{.5}$ and M$_{.5}$, which do provide about the right level of residual risk for this investor.

The investor might try to convince the $IR = 1$ manager to offer a lower-risk portfolio. If that fails, however, is the investor constrained to go with the less skilled manager? No. The investor can instead combine the highly skilled manager's H$_1$ portfolio with an investment in the passive benchmark portfolio P, reducing risk and return along the $IR = 1$ manager frontier. Such combination portfolios will offer a higher return than the portfolios of the less skilled manager, at a level of residual risk the investor can live with.

Finally, the manager's investment approach may affect the investor's optimal level of portfolio risk. Because engineered strategies control portfolio systematic and residual risk relative to the benchmark and take only compensated risks, they offer more assurance than traditional active strategies of achieving a return commensurate with the risk taken. Investors may feel more comfortable taking more risk with engineered portfolios, where risk and expected return are rigorously and explicitly assessed, than with traditional active portfolios.

THE ULTIMATE OBJECTIVE

The ultimate objective of investment management, of course, is to establish an investment structure that will, in the aggregate and over time, provide a return that compensates for the risk incurred, where the risk incurred is consistent with the investor's risk tolerance. The objective may be the equity market's return at the market's risk level or the market return plus incremental returns commensurate with incremental risks incurred.

This may be accomplished by focusing on the core universe and a passive representation or by mixing universes (core and static subsets, for example) and approaches (e.g., passive with traditional active or engineered). Whatever the selection universe and investment approach chosen, success is more likely when investors start off knowing their risk-tolerance levels and their potential managers' skill levels. The goal is to take no more risk than is compensated by expected return, but to take as much risk as risk-aversion level and manager skill allow.

Success is also more likely when equity market architecture is taken into account. Without explicit ties between portfolios and the underlying market or market subsets (and thus between market subsets and the overall market), managers may be tempted to stray from their "fold" (core, value, or growth investing, say) in search of return. If value stocks are being punished, for example, an undisciplined value manager may be tempted to "poach" return from growth stock territory. An investor utilizing this manager cannot expect performance consistent with value stocks in general, nor can the investor combine this manager's "value" portfolio with a growth portfolio in the hopes of achieving an overall market return; the portfolio will instead be overweighted in growth stocks, and susceptible to the risk of growth stocks falling out of favor. The investor can mitigate the problem by balancing non-benchmark-constrained, traditional portfolios with engineered or passive portfolios that offer benchmark-accountability.

When investors set goals in terms of return only, with no regard to equity architecture, similar problems can arise. Consider an investor who hires active managers and instructs them to "make money," with no regard to market sector or investment approach. Manager holdings may overlap to an extent that the overall portfolio becomes overdiversified and individual manager efforts are diluted. The investor may end up paying active fees and active transaction costs for essentially passive results.

Equity architecture provides a basic blueprint for relating equity investment choices to their potential rewards and their risks. It can help investors construct portfolios that will meet their needs. First, however, the investor must determine what those needs are in terms of desire for return and tolerance for risk.

Then the investor can choose managers whose investment approaches and market focuses offer, overall, the greatest assurance of fulfilling those needs.

We believe that engineered management can provide the best match between client risk-return goals and investment results. An engineered approach that combines range with depth of inquiry can increase both the number and goodness of investment insights. As a result, engineered management offers better control of risk exposure than traditional active management and incremental returns relative to passive management, whether the selection universe is core equity, static style subsets, or dynamic style subsets.

Chapter 2

Investment Analysis: Profiting from a Complex Equity Market

Bruce I. Jacobs, Ph.D.
Principal
Jacobs Levy Equity Management

Kenneth N. Levy, CFA
Principal
Jacobs Levy Equity Management

[Handwritten marginal notes:]

Role of Info :

① ORdered
$$r_{it} = a_i + b_i r_{m,t}$$

② Random
b. $r_{it} = a_i + b_i r_{I,t-1} + e_{it}$
where $b_i = \phi$

a. $P_{it} = c_i + d_i P_{i,t-1} + e_{it}$
where $d_i = 1$

③ Complex
$$r_{it} = a_i + b_{i1} F_{1t} + \ldots b_{ik} F_{kt} + e_{it}$$

INTRODUCTION

Scientists classify systems into three types — ordered, random, and complex. Ordered systems, such as the structure of diamond crystals or the dynamics of pendulums, are definable and predictable by relatively simple rules and can be modeled using a relatively small number of variables. Random systems like the Brownian motion of gas molecules or white noise (static) are unordered; they are the product of a large number of variables. Their behavior cannot be modeled and is inherently unpredictable.

Complex systems like the weather and the workings of DNA fall somewhere between the domains of order and randomness. Their behavior can be at least partly comprehended and modeled, but only with great difficulty. The number of variables that must be modeled, and their interactions, are beyond the capacity of the human mind alone. Only with the aid of advanced computational science can the mysteries of complex systems be unraveled.[1]

The stock market is a complex system.[2] Stock prices are not completely random, as the efficient market hypothesis and random walk theory would have it.

[1] See, for example, Heinz Pagels, *The Dreams of Reason: The Computer and the Rise of the Sciences of Complexity* (New York, NY: Simon and Schuster, 1988).

[2] See, for example, Bruce I. Jacobs and Kenneth N. Levy, "The Complexity of the Stock Market," *Journal of Portfolio Management* (Fall 1989).

The authors thank Judith Kimball for her editorial assistance.

Some price movements can be predicted, and with some consistency. But nor is stock price behavior ordered. It cannot be successfully modeled by simple rules or screens such as low price/earnings ratios or even elegant theories such as the Capital Asset Pricing Model or Arbitrage Pricing Theory. Rather, stock price behavior is permeated by a complex web of interrelated return effects. A model of the market that is complex enough to disentangle these effects provides opportunities for modeling price behavior and predicting returns.

This chapter describes one such model, and its application to the stock selection, portfolio construction, and performance evaluation problems. We begin with the very basic question of how one should approach the equity market. Should one attempt to cover the broadest possible range of stocks, or can greater analytical insights be garnered by focusing on a particular subset of the market or a limited number of stocks? As we will see, each approach has its advantages and disadvantages. Combining the two, however, may offer the best promise of finding the key to market complexity and unlocking investment opportunity.

AN INTEGRATED APPROACH TO A SEGMENTED MARKET

While one might think that U.S. equity markets are fluid and fully integrated, in reality there exist barriers to the free flow of capital. Some of these barriers are self-imposed by investors. Others are imposed by regulatory and tax authorities or by client guidelines.

Some funds, for example, are prohibited by regulation or internal policy guidelines from buying certain types of stock — non-dividend-paying stock, or stock below a given capitalization level. Tax laws, too, may effectively lock investors into positions they would otherwise trade. Such barriers to the free flow of capital foster market segmentation.

Other barriers are self-imposed. Traditionally, for example, managers have focused (whether by design or default) on distinct approaches to stock selection. Value managers have concentrated on buying stocks selling at prices perceived to be low relative to the company's assets or earnings. Growth managers have sought stocks with above-average earnings growth not fully reflected in price. Small-capitalization managers have searched for opportunity in stocks that have been overlooked by most investors. The stocks that constitute the natural selection pools for these managers tend to group into distinct market segments.

Client preferences encourage this Balkanization of the market. Some investors, for example, prefer to buy value stocks, while others seek growth stocks; some invest in both, but hire separate managers for each segment. Both institutional and individual investors generally demonstrate a reluctance to upset the apple cart by changing allocations to previously selected "style" managers. Several periods of underperformance, however, may undermine this loyalty and motivate a flow of capital from one segment of the market to another (often just as the out-of-favor segment begins to benefit from a reversion of returns back up to their historical mean).

In the past few decades, a market segmented into style groupings has been formalized by the actions of investment consultants. Consultants have designed style indexes that define the constituent stocks of these segments and have defined managers in terms of their proclivity for one segment or another. As a manager's performance is measured against the given style index, managers who stray too far from index territory are taking on extra risk. Consequently, managers tend to stick close to their style "homes," reinforcing market segmentation.

An investment approach that focuses on individual market segments can have its advantages. Such an approach recognizes, for example, that the U.S. equity market is neither entirely homogeneous nor entirely heterogeneous. All stocks do not react alike to a given impetus, but nor does each stock exhibit its own, totally idiosyncratic price behavior. Rather, stocks within a given style, or sector, or industry tend to behave similarly to each other and somewhat differently from stocks outside their group.

An approach to stock selection that specializes in one market segment can optimize the application of talent and maximize the potential for outperformance. This is most likely true for traditional, fundamental analysis. The in-depth, labor-intensive research undertaken by traditional analysts can become positively ungainly without some focusing lens.

An investment approach that focuses on the individual segments of the market, however, presents some severe theoretical and practical problems. Such an approach may be especially disadvantaged when it ignores the many forces that work to integrate, rather than segment, the market.

Many managers, for example, do not specialize in a particular market segment but are free to choose the most attractive securities from a broad universe of stocks. Others, such as style rotators, may focus on a particular type of stock, given current economic conditions, but be poised to change their focus should conditions change. Such managers make for capital flows and price arbitrage across the boundaries of particular segments.

Furthermore, all stocks can be defined by the same fundamental parameters — by market capitalization, price/earnings ratio, dividend discount model ranking, and so on. All stocks can be found at some level on the continuum of values for each parameter. Thus growth and value stocks inhabit the opposite ends of the continuums of P/E and dividend yield, and small and large stocks the opposite ends of the continuums of firm capitalization and analyst coverage.

As the values of the parameters for any individual stock change, so too does the stock's position on the continuum. An out-of-favor growth stock may slip into value territory. A small-cap company may grow into the large-cap range.

Finally, while the values of these parameters vary across stocks belonging to different market segments — different styles, sectors, and industries — and while investors may favor certain values — low P/E, say, in preference to high P/E — arbitrage tends to counterbalance too pronounced a predilection on the part of investors for any one set of values. In equilibrium, all stocks must be owned. If too many investors want low P/E, low-P/E stocks will be bid up to higher P/E levels, and some investors will step in to sell them and buy other stocks deserving of higher P/Es. Arbitrage works toward market integration and a single pricing mechanism.

A market that is neither completely segmented nor completely integrated is a complex market. A complex market calls for an investment approach that is 180 degrees removed from the narrow, segment-oriented focus of traditional management. It requires a complex, unified approach that takes into account the behavior of stocks across the broadest possible selection universe, without losing sight of the significant differences in price behavior that distinguish particular market segments.

Such an approach offers three major advantages. First, it provides a coherent evaluation framework. Second, it can benefit from all the insights to be garnered from a wide and diverse range of securities. Third, because it has both breadth of coverage and depth of analysis, it is poised to take advantage of more profit opportunities than a more narrowly defined, segmented approach proffers.[3]

A COHERENT FRAMEWORK

To the extent that the market is integrated, an investment approach that models each industry or style segment as if it were a universe unto itself is not the best approach. Consider, for example, a firm that offers both core and value strategies. Suppose the firm runs a model on its total universe of, say, 3000 stocks. It then runs the same model or a different, segment-specific model on a 500-stock subset of large-cap value stocks.

If different models are used for each strategy, the results will differ. Even if the same model is estimated separately for each strategy, its results will differ because the model coefficients are bound to differ between the broader universe and the narrower segment. What if the core model predicts GM will outperform Ford, while the value model shows the reverse? Should the investor start the day with multiple estimates of one stock's alpha? This would violate what we call the "Law of One Alpha."[4]

Of course, the firm could ensure coherence by using separate models for each market segment — growth, value, small-cap — and linking the results via a single, overarching model that relates all the subsets. But the firm then runs into a second problem with segmented investment approaches: To the extent that the market is integrated, the pricing of securities in one segment may contain information relevant to pricing in other segments.

For example, within a generally well integrated national economy, labor market conditions in the U.S. differ region by region. An economist attempting to

---

[3] See, for example, Bruce I. Jacobs and Kenneth N. Levy, "Engineering Portfolios: A Unified Approach," *Journal of Investing* (Winter 1995).

[4] See Bruce I. Jacobs and Kenneth N. Levy, "The Law of One Alpha," *Journal of Portfolio Management* (Summer 1995).

model employment in the Northeast would probably consider economic expansion in the Southeast. Similarly, the investor who wants to model growth stocks should not ignore value stocks. The effects of inflation, say, on value stocks may have repercussions for growth stocks; after all, the two segments represent opposite ends of the same P/E continuum.

An investment approach that concentrates on a single market segment does not make use of all available information. A complex, unified approach considers all the stocks in the universe — value and growth, large and small. It thus benefits from all the information to be gleaned from a broad range of stock price behavior.

Of course, an increase in breadth of inquiry will not benefit the investor if it comes at the sacrifice of depth of inquiry. A complex approach does not ignore the significant differences across different types of stock, differences exploitable by specialized investing. What's more, in examining similarities and differences across market segments, it considers numerous variables that may be considered to be defining.

For value, say, a complex approach does not confine itself to a dividend discount model measure of value, but examines also earnings, cash flow, sales, and yield value, among other attributes. Growth measurements to be considered include historical, expected, and sustainable growth, as well as the momentum and stability of earnings. Share price, volatility, and analyst coverage are among the elements to be considered along with market capitalization as measures of size.[5]

These variables are often closely correlated with each other. Small-cap stocks, for example, tend to have low P/Es; low P/E is correlated with high yield; both low P/E and high yield are correlated with DDM estimates of value. Furthermore, they may be correlated with a stock's industry affiliation. A simple low-P/E screen, for example, will tend to select a large number of bank and utility stocks. Such correlations can distort naive attempts to relate returns to potentially relevant variables. A true picture of the variable-return relationship emerges only after "disentangling" the variables.

DISENTANGLING

The effects of different sources of stock return can overlap. In Exhibit 1, the lines represent connections documented by academic studies; they may appear like a ball of yarn after the cat got to it. To unravel the connections between variables and return, it is necessary to examine all the variables simultaneously.

---

[5] At a deeper level of complexity, one must also consider alternative ways of specifying such fundamental variables as earnings or cash flow. Over what period does one measure earnings, for example? If using analyst earnings expectations, which measure provides the best estimate of future real earnings? The consensus of all available estimates made over the past six months? Only the very latest earnings estimates? Are some analysts more accurate or more influential? What if a recent estimate is not available for a given company? See Bruce I. Jacobs, Kenneth N. Levy, and Mitchell C. Krask, "Earnings Estimates, Predictor Specification, and Measurement Error," *Journal of Investing* (Summer 1997), pp. 29-46.

Exhibit 1: Return Effects Form a Tangled Web

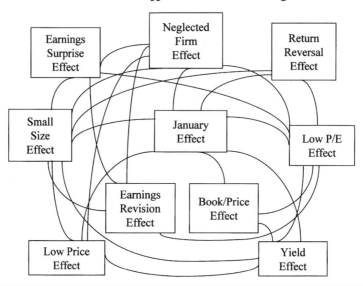

For instance, the low-P/E effect is widely recognized, as is the small-size effect. But stocks with low P/Es also tend to be of small size. Are P/E and size merely two ways of looking at the same effect? Or does each variable matter? Perhaps the excess returns to small-cap stocks are merely a January effect, reflecting the tendency of taxable investors to sell depressed stocks at year-end. Answering these questions requires disentangling return effects via multivariate regression.[6]

Common methods of measuring return effects (such as quintiling or univariate — single-variable — regression) are "naive" because they assume, naively, that prices are responding only to the single variable under consideration — low P/E, say. But a number of related variables may be affecting returns. As we have noted, small-cap stocks and banking and utility industry stocks tend to have low P/Es. A univariate regression of return on low P/E will capture, along with the effect of P/E, a great deal of "noise" related to firm size, industry affiliation and other variables.

Simultaneous analysis of all relevant variables via multivariate regression takes into account and adjusts for such interrelationships. The result is the return to each variable separately, controlling for all related variables. A multivariate analysis for low P/E, for example, will provide a measure of the excess return to a portfolio that is market-like in all respects except for having a lower-than-average P/E ratio. Disentangled returns are "pure" returns.

---

[6] See Bruce I. Jacobs and Kenneth N. Levy, "Disentangling Equity Return Regularities: New Insights and Investment Opportunities," *Financial Analysts Journal* (May/June 1988).

Exhibit 2: Naive and Pure Returns to High Book-to-Price Ratio

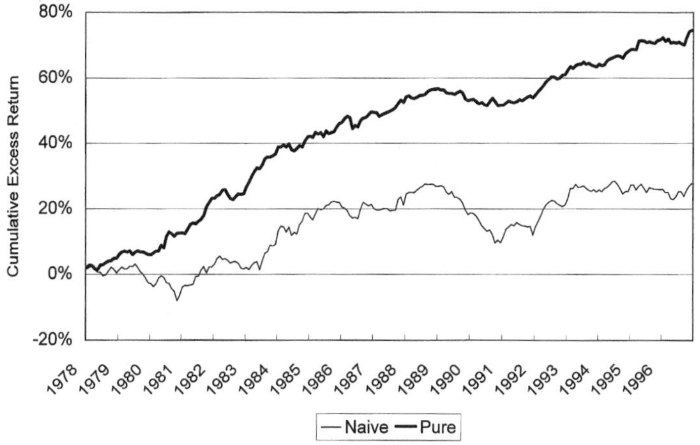

Noise Reduction

Exhibit 2 plots naive and pure cumulative excess (relative to a 3,000-stock universe) returns to high book-to-price ratio.[7] The naive returns show a great deal of volatility; the pure returns, by contrast, follow a much smoother path. There is a lot of noise in the naive returns. What causes it?

Notice the divergence between the naive and pure return series for the 12 months starting in March 1979. This date coincides with the crisis at Three Mile Island nuclear power plant. Utilities such as GPU, operator of the Three Mile Island power plant, tend to have high-B/Ps, and naive B/P measures will reflect the performance of these utilities along with the performance of other high-B/P stocks. Electric utility prices plummeted 24% after the Three Mile Island crisis. The naive B/P measure reflects this decline.

But industry-related events such as Three Mile Island have no necessary bearing on the book/price variable. An investor could, for example, hold a high-B/P portfolio that does not overweight utilities, and such a portfolio would not have experienced the decline reflected in the naive B/P measure in Exhibit 2. The naive returns to B/P reflect noise from the inclusion of a utility industry effect. A pure B/P measure is not contaminated by such irrelevant variables.

Disentangling distinguishes real effects from mere proxies and thereby distinguishes between real and spurious investment opportunities. As it separates high B/P and industry affiliation, for example, it can also separate the effects of firm size from the effects of related variables. Disentangling shows that returns to small firms in January are not abnormal; the apparent January seasonal merely proxies for

---

[7] In particular, naive and pure returns are provided by a portfolio having a book-to-price ratio that is one standard deviation above the universe mean book-to-price ratio. For pure returns, the portfolio is also constrained to have universe-average exposures to all the other variables in the model, including fundamental characteristics and industry affiliations.

year-end tax-loss selling.[8] Not all small firms will benefit from a January rebound; indiscriminately buying small firms at the turn of the year is not an optimal investment strategy. Ascertaining true causation leads to more profitable strategies.

Return Revelation

Disentangling can reveal hidden opportunities. Exhibit 3 plots the naively measured cumulative excess returns (relative to the 3,000-stock universe) to portfolios that rank lower than normal in market capitalization and price per share and higher than normal in terms of analyst neglect.[9] These results derive from monthly univariate regressions. The "small-cap" line thus represents the cumulative excess returns to a portfolio of stocks naively chosen on the basis of their size, with no attempt made to control for other variables.

All three return series move together. The similarity between the small-cap and neglect series is particularly striking. This is confirmed by the correlation coefficients in the first column of Exhibit 4. Furthermore, all series show a great deal of volatility within a broader up, down, up pattern.

Exhibit 3: Naive Returns Can Hide Opportunities: Three Size-Related Variables

Exhibit 4: Correlations between Monthly Returns to Size-Related Variables*

Variable	Naive	Pure
Small Cap/Low Price	0.82	−0.12
Small Cap/Neglect	0.87	−0.22
Neglect/Low Price	0.66	−0.11

* A coefficient of 0.14 is significant at the 5% level.

[8] See Bruce I. Jacobs and Kenneth N. Levy, "Calendar Anomalies: Abnormal Returns at Calendar Turning Points," *Financial Analysts Journal* (November/December 1988).

[9] Again, portfolios with values of these parameters that are, on average, one standard deviation away from the universe mean.

Exhibit 5: Pure Returns Can Reveal Opportunities: Three Size-Related Variables

Exhibit 5 shows the pure cumulative excess returns to each size-related attribute over the period. These disentangled returns adjust for correlations not only between the three size variables, but also between each size variable and industry affiliations and each variable and growth and value characteristics. Two findings are immediately apparent from Exhibit 5.

First, pure returns to the size variables do not appear to be nearly as closely correlated as the naive returns displayed in Exhibit 3. In fact, over the second half of the period, the three return series diverge substantially. This is confirmed by the correlation coefficients in the second column of Exhibit 4.

In particular, pure returns to small capitalization accumulate quite a gain over the period; they are up 30%, versus an only 20% gain for the naive returns to small cap. Purifying returns reveals a profit opportunity not apparent in the naive returns. Furthermore, pure returns to analyst neglect amount to a substantial loss over the period. Because disentangling controls for proxy effects, and thereby avoids redundancies, these pure return effects are additive. A portfolio could have aimed for superior returns by selecting small-cap stocks with a higher-than-average analyst following (i.e., a negative exposure to analyst neglect).

Second, the pure returns appear to be much less volatile than the naive returns. The naive returns in Exhibit 3 display much month-to-month volatility within their more general trends. By contrast, the pure series in Exhibit 5 are much smoother and more consistent. This is confirmed by the standard deviations given in Exhibit 6.

The pure returns in Exhibit 5 are smoother and more consistent than the naive return responses in Exhibit 3 because the pure returns capture more "signal" and less noise. And because they are smoother and more consistent than naive returns, pure returns are also more predictable.

Exhibit 6: Pure Returns are Less Volatile, More Predictable: Standard Deviations of Monthly Returns to Size-Related Variables*

Variable	Naive	Pure
Small Cap	0.87	0.60
Neglect	0.87	0.67
Low Price	1.03	0.58

* All differences between naive and pure return standard deviations are significant at the 1% level.

Exhibit 7: Market Sensitivities of Monthly Returns to Value-Related Variables

Variable	Naive	(t-stat.)	Pure	(t-stat.)
DDM	0.06	(5.4)	0.04	(5.6)
B/P	-0.10	(-6.2)	-0.01	(-0.8)
Yield	-0.08	(-7.4)	-0.03	(-3.5)

Predictability

Disentangling improves return predictability by providing a clearer picture of the relationship between stock price behavior, fundamental variables, and macroeconomic conditions. For example, investors often prefer value stocks in bearish market environments, because growth stocks are priced more on the basis of high expectations, which get dashed in more pessimistic eras. But the success of such a strategy will depend on the variables one has chosen to define value.

Exhibit 7 displays the results of regressing both naive and pure returns to various value-related variables on market (S&P 500) returns over the 1978-1996 period. The results indicate that DDM value is a poor indicator of a stock's ability to withstand a tide of receding market prices. The regression coefficient in the first column indicates that a portfolio with a one-standard-deviation exposure to DDM value will tend to outperform by 0.06% when the market rises by 1.00% and to underperform by a similar margin when the market falls by 1.00%. The coefficient for pure returns to DDM is similar. Whether their returns are measured in pure or naive form, stocks with high DDM values tend to behave procyclically.

High book-to-price ratio appears to be a better indicator of a defensive stock. It has a regression coefficient of -0.10 in naive form. In pure form, however, B/P is virtually uncorrelated with market movements; pure B/P signals neither an aggressive nor a defensive stock. B/P as naively measured apparently picks up the effects of truly defensive variables — such as high yield.

The value investor in search of a defensive posture in uncertain market climates should consider moving toward high yield. The regression coefficients for both naive and pure returns to high yield indicate significant negative market sensitivities. Stocks with high yields may be expected to lag in up markets but to hold up relatively well during general market declines.

Exhibit 8: Forecast Response of Small Size to Macroeconomic Shocks

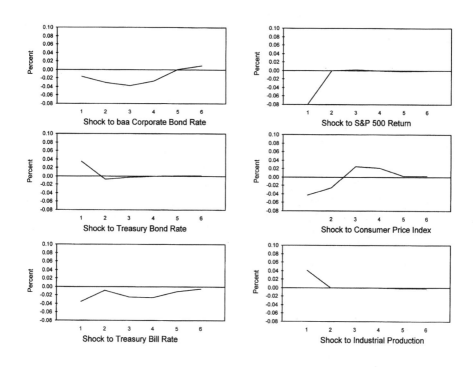

These results make broad intuitive sense. DDM is forward-looking, relying on estimates of future earnings. In bull markets, investors take a long-term outlook, so DDM explains security pricing behavior. In bear markets, however, investors become myopic; they prefer today's tangible income to tomorrow's promise. Current yield is rewarded.[10]

Pure returns respond in intuitively satisfying ways to macroeconomic events. Exhibit 8 illustrates, as an example, the estimated effects of changes in various macroeconomic variables on the pure returns to small size (as measured by market capitalization). Consistent with the capital constraints on small firms and their relatively greater sensitivity to the economy, pure returns to small size may be expected to be negative in the first four months following an unexpected increase in the BAA corporate rate and positive in the first month following an unexpected increase in industrial production.[11] Investors can exploit such predict-

---

[10] See also Bruce I. Jacobs and Kenneth N. Levy, "On the Value of 'Value'," *Financial Analysts Journal* (July/August 1988).

[11] See Bruce I. Jacobs and Kenneth N. Levy, "Forecasting the Size Effect," *Financial Analysts Journal* (May/June 1989).

able behavior by moving into and out of the small-cap market segment as economic conditions evolve.[12]

These examples serve to illustrate that the use of numerous, finely defined fundamental variables can provide a rich representation of the complexity of security pricing. The model can be even more finely tuned, however, by including variables that capture such subtleties as the effects of investor psychology, possible nonlinearities in variable-return relationships, and security transaction costs.

Additional Complexities

In considering possible variables for inclusion in a model of stock price behavior, the investor should recognize that pure stock returns are driven by a combination of economic fundamentals and investor psychology. That is, economic fundamentals such as interest rates, industrial production, and inflation can explain much, but by no means all, of the systematic variation in returns. Psychology, including investors' tendency to overreact, their desire to seek safety in numbers, and their selective memories, also plays a role in security pricing.

What's more, the modeler should realize that the effects of different variables, fundamental and otherwise, can differ across different types of stocks. The value sector, for example, includes more financial stocks than the growth sector. Investors may thus expect value stocks in general to be more sensitive than growth stocks to changes in interest rate spreads.

Psychologically based variables such as short-term overreaction and price correction also seem to have a stronger effect on value than on growth stocks. Earnings surprises and earnings estimate revisions, by contrast, appear to be more important for growth than for value stocks. Thus Intel shares can take a nose dive when earnings come in a penny under expectations, whereas Ford shares remain unmoved even by fairly substantial departures of actual earnings from expectations.

The relationship between stock returns and relevant variables may not be linear. The effects of positive earnings surprises, for instance, tend to be arbitraged away quickly; thus positive earnings surprises offer less opportunity for the investor. The effects of negative earnings surprises, however, appear to be more long-lasting. This nonlinearity may reflect the fact that sales of stock are limited to those investors who already own the stock (and to a relatively small number of short-sellers).[13]

Risk-variable relationships may also differ across different types of stock. In particular, small-cap stocks generally have more idiosyncratic risk than large-cap stocks. Diversification is thus more important for small-stock than for large-stock portfolios.

---

[12] See, for example, Bruce I. Jacobs and Kenneth N. Levy, "High-Definition Style Rotation," *Journal of Investing* (Fall 1996), pp. 14-23.

[13] See Bruce I. Jacobs and Kenneth N. Levy, "Long/Short Equity Investing," *Journal of Portfolio Management* (Fall 1993).

Return-variable relationships can also change over time. Recall the difference between DDM and yield value measures: high-DDM stocks tend to have high returns in bull markets and low returns in bear markets; high-yield stocks experience the reverse. For consistency of performance, return modeling must consider the effects of market dynamics — the changing nature of the overall market.

The investor may also want to decipher the informational signals generated by "informed agents." Corporate decisions to issue or buy back shares, split stock, or initiate or suspend dividends, for example, may contain valuable information about company prospects. So, too, may insiders' (legal) trading in their own firms' shares.

Finally, a complex model containing multiple variables is likely to turn up a number of promising return-variable relationships. But are these perceived profit opportunities translatable into real economic opportunities? Are some too ephemeral? Too small to survive frictions such as trading costs? Estimates of expected returns must be combined with estimates of the costs of trading to arrive at realistic returns net of trading costs.

CONSTRUCTING, TRADING, AND EVALUATING PORTFOLIOS

To maximize implementation of the model's insights, the portfolio construction process should consider exactly the same dimensions found relevant by the stock selection model. Failure to do so can lead to mismatches between model insights and portfolio exposures.

Consider a commercially available portfolio optimizer that recognizes only a subset of the variables in the valuation model. Risk reduction using such an optimizer will reduce the portfolio's exposures only along the dimensions the optimizer recognizes. As a result, the portfolio is likely to wind up more exposed to those variables recognized by the model — but not the optimizer — and less exposed to those variables common to both the model and the optimizer.

Imagine an investor who seeks low-P/E stocks that analysts are recommending for purchase, but who uses a commercial optimizer that incorporates a P/E factor but not analyst recommendations. The investor is likely to wind up with a portfolio that has a less than optimal level of exposure to low P/E and a greater than optimal level of exposure to analyst purchase recommendations. Optimization using all relevant variables ensures a portfolio whose risk and return opportunities are balanced in accordance with the model's insights. Furthermore, the use of more numerous variables allows portfolio risk to be more finely tuned.

Insofar as the investment process — both stock selection and portfolio construction — is model-driven, it is more adaptable to electronic trading venues. This should benefit the investor in several ways. First, electronic trading is generally less costly, with lower commissions, market impact, and opportunity costs.

Second, it allows real-time monitoring, which can further reduce trading costs. Third, an automated trading system can take account of more factors, including the urgency of a particular trade and market conditions, than individual traders can be expected to bear in mind.

Finally, the performance attribution process should be congruent with the dimensions of the selection model (and portfolio optimizer). Insofar as performance attribution identifies sources of return, a process that considers all the sources identified by the selection model will be more insightful than a commercial performance attribution system applied in a "one-size-fits-all" manner. Our investor who has sought exposure to low P/E and positive analyst recommendations, for example, will want to know how each of these factors has paid off and will be less interested in the returns to factors that are not a part of the stock selection process.

A performance evaluation process tailored to the model also functions as a monitor of the model's reliability. Has portfolio performance supported the model's insights? Should some be reexamined? Equally important, does the model's reliability hold up over time? A model that performs well in today's economic and market environments may not necessarily perform well in the future. A feedback loop between the evaluation and the research/modeling processes can help ensure that the model retains robustness over time.

PROFITING FROM COMPLEXITY

It has been said that: "For every complex problem, there is a simple solution, and it is almost always wrong."[14] For complex problems more often than not require complex solutions.

A complex approach to stock selection, portfolio construction, and performance evaluation is needed to capture the complexities of the stock market. Such an approach combines the breadth of coverage and the depth of analysis needed to maximize investment opportunity and potential reward.

Grinold and Kahn present a formula that identifies the relationships between the depth and breadth of investment insights and investment performance:

$$IR = IC \times \sqrt{BR}$$

tracking error

IR is the manager's information ratio, a measure of the success of the investment process. IR equals annualized excess return over annualized residual risk (e.g., 2% excess return with 4% tracking error provides 0.5 IR). IC, the information coefficient, or correlation between predicted and actual results, measures the goodness of the manager's insights, or the manager's skill. BR is the breadth of

---

[14] Attributed to H.L. Mencken.

the strategy, measurable as the number of independent insights upon which investment decisions are made.[15]

One can increase *IR* by increasing *IC* or *BR*. Increasing *IC* means coming up with some means of improving predictive accuracy. Increasing *BR* means coming up with more "investable" insights. A casino analogy may be apt (if anathema to prudent investors).

A gambler can seek to increase *IC* by card-counting in blackjack or by building a computer model to predict probable roulette outcomes. Similarly, some investors seek to outperform by concentrating their research efforts on a few stocks: by learning all there is to know about Microsoft, for example, one may be able to outperform all the other investors who follow this stock. But a strategy that makes a few concentrated stock bets is likely to produce consistent performance only if it is based on a very high level of skill, or if it benefits from extraordinary luck.

Alternatively, an investor can place a larger number of smaller stock bets and settle for more modest returns from a greater number of investment decisions. That is, rather than behaving like a gambler in a casino, the investor can behave like the casino. A casino has only a slight edge on any spin of the roulette wheel or roll of the dice, but many spins of many roulette wheels can result in a very consistent profit for the house. Over time, the odds will strongly favor the casino over the gambler.

A complex approach to the equity market, one that has both breadth of inquiry and depth of focus, can enhance the number and the goodness of investment insights. A complex approach to the equity market requires more time, effort, and ability, but it will be better positioned to capture the complexities of security pricing. The rewards are worth the effort.

Define:
Residual Risk
Tracking Error

---

[15] Richard C. Grinold and Ronald N. Kahn, *Active Portfolio Management* (Chicago, IL: Probus, 1995).

Chapter 3

Medium and Small Capitalization Indexing

George U. Sauter
Principal
Quantitative Equity Department
The Vanguard Group

INTRODUCTION

Every December the annual ritual of predicting performance for the upcoming year takes center stage. Despite consistent outperformance by index funds, money managers, investment strategists, and advisers repeatedly declare that index funds will perform poorly in the ensuing year. Disregard the advantages of indexing! The next year will be a stock picker's year.

The belief that "stock pickers" will prevail in the future is based more on hope, or rationalization, than it is on logic. In one sense, every year is a stock picker's year because there are always some stocks that greatly outperform the market, while others greatly underperform. There will always be outperforming equities for an astute, or lucky, stock picker to uncover. However, other stock pickers must own the underperforming stocks.

Collectively, there is no such thing as stock picking. Stocks are merely shifted from one investor to another. It is not possible for the entire investment community to purge its portfolios of the "dog" stocks. Somebody has to own them, and index funds only own them in proportion to their size, leaving active investors their fair share.

Actually, the message from the pundits is misstated. Active managers will not magically gain the skill to outperform unmanaged indexes that has proven so elusive heretofore. Instead, the true forecast is that the market will favor small capitalization stocks. Since active managers purchase large-, medium-, and small-capitalization stocks, they have a natural advantage relative to the large-cap-biased Standard & Poor's 500 when small caps outperform. However, this should not be confused with value added through superior stock picking. It merely reflects that in a small-cap market they purchase stocks from a broader universe that is performing better than the S&P 500.

37

INDEXING DEFINED

Indexing is nothing more than a computer-assisted investment strategy to gain low-cost exposure to either the broad market, or a reasonably diversified segment of the market. The original concept, derived in academia, applied to the entire U.S. stock market, not to the S&P 500 which is merely a popular measure of the market. Nevertheless, indexing's low-cost approach is equally appropriate for the market's large-capitalization or small-capitalization segments, for investment styles, such as value or growth, for international investing, and for other asset classes such as bonds, or REITs. Regardless of the benchmark, indexing provides three major advantages when compared with actively managed funds with similar objectives: superior long-term performance, performance that is predictable relative to the benchmark, and tax efficiency resulting from the buy-and-hold nature of the strategy.

Indexing Outperforms in the Long Run

There is a misconception that indexing works only in an efficient market. Certainly, if the stock market were perfectly efficient and all prices reflected all information that could possibly be known about a company, then systematically outperforming the market would be possible only by consistently guessing what events will occur that will impact a stock. Clearly, outperformance could be attained only by luck, and the only prudent investment strategy would be to purchase the entire stock market in the lowest-cost fashion (broad market indexing).

The debate over the efficiency of the market rages on, but even the most ardent proponents of efficient markets will concede the probable existence of some mispricings — perhaps minor ones. Regardless of the degree of market inefficiency, the advantages of indexing still apply, even in a market with gross inefficiencies. Collectively, all investors own the entire market, and, therefore, their aggregate performance, before costs, will match that of the market. In order for one investor to outperform, another must underperform since the average must be the market rate of return. Consequently, assuming a somewhat normal distribution of portfolio returns, as has occurred in the past, half of the investors will outperform the market at the expense of the other half that must underperform.

In the real world, though, there are significant costs of investing, including expense ratios of about 1.4% for the average active fund, and transaction costs of 0.5% to 1.0%. The marginal outperformers before costs become underperformers after costs. So a majority of investors must lag the market rate of return.

Of course, managing an index fund also has costs, but certainly these are less substantial, typically ranging from about 0.2% to 0.3% for a complete market fund including operating expense ratios and transaction costs. This approximate 2% cost savings of an index fund is a large proportion of the 10% return historically provided by the market and is the sole source of the performance advantage of indexing.

Importantly, this rationale does not require a belief in efficient markets. It merely relies on the understanding that outperformance is a zero sum game before costs and a loser's game after costs. Certainly, there will be some funds that outperform their appropriate index, but it is very difficult to determine if they have succeeded by luck or by skill. And to make the correct determination requires many years, usually longer than the tenure of the managers of most funds.

Indexing Excels in Inefficient, Illiquid Markets

Many investors concede that indexing is appropriate for gaining exposure to large-capitalization stocks, which are more efficiently priced. But, they contend, active managers will be able to add significant value in less efficient markets, such as small-capitalization domestic stocks and international stocks of both developed and emerging countries. These markets, while being less efficiently priced, are also the highest-cost markets, which is precisely the type of environment in which indexing succeeds. Mutual fund expense ratios are higher because of significantly greater custodial fees plus the higher costs of acquiring information about companies. Transaction costs are also significantly higher, reflecting less liquidity.

Admittedly, the Russell 2000 index, an index of very small companies, has not performed well against active small-cap funds during the last decade, which decidedly favored large-cap stocks. However, the Russell 2000 has a much smaller capitalization than the average small-cap fund. The average market capitalization of the Russell 2000 on March 31, 1997, was $630 million compared with $1.23 billion for the average small-cap fund. This small-cap bias has obviously been a handicap in this environment. Exhibit 1 shows the percentage of small-cap funds that were outperformed by the Russell 2000 in each year from 1987 through 1996. For instance, in 1990 the index outperformed only 13% of the small-cap funds, while in 1992 it outperformed an amazing 80%.

The Russell 2000 outperformed less than half of the active managers in each of the six years of the last decade in which the S&P 500 outperformed the Russell 2000. However, during three of the four years in which small-cap stocks did outperform large-cap stocks (1988 and 1991-1993), the Russell 2000 outperformed 64% or more of the actively managed small-cap funds. Furthermore, cumulatively over the four years dominated by small caps, the Russell 2000 outperformed 55% of the actively managed small-cap funds. Importantly, this ranking is understated because of severe survivorship bias. Many of the unsuccessfully managed active funds have gone out of business and are not included in the comparison, as if they never existed.

So the Russell 2000 works well in small-cap markets but it lags in large-cap markets because it is being compared with an inappropriate small-cap peer group that has a larger-cap bias.

The Russell 2500 index is an index of medium- and small-cap companies with a market cap of $1.39 billion, which is very close to the $1.23 billion of small-cap managers, providing a better apples-to-apples comparison. For the 10-year period 1987-1996, it has provided very consistent performance relative to small cap funds as shown in Exhibit 2.

Exhibit 1: Small-Cap Funds Outperformed by the Russell 2000: 1987-1996 (in %)

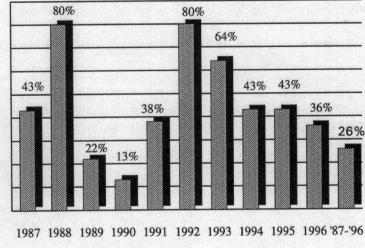

Performance	1987	1988	1989	1990	1991	1992	1993	1994	1995	1996
S&P 500	5.26	16.61	31.68	-3.12	30.48	7.64	10.08	1.32	37.57	22.96
Russell 2000	-8.77	24.89	16.24	-19.51	46.05	18.41	18.91	-1.82	28.44	16.49

Performance: S&P 500 15.29, Russell 2000 12.41

Source: Lipper Analytical and the Vanguard Group

Exhibit 2: Russell 2500 versus Small-Cap Managers: 1987-1996

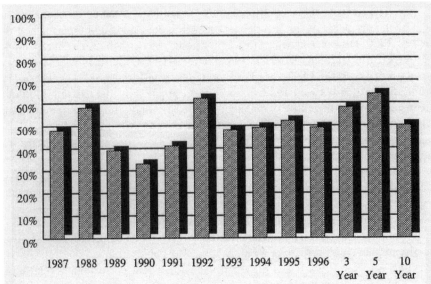

Exhibit 3: Performance of Popular Benchmarks

	Medium & Small Cap Extended Market		Medium Cap		Small Cap	
	Wilshire 4500 (%)	Russell 2500 (%)	Russell Midcap (%)	S&P MidCap 400 (%)	Russell 2000 (%)	S&P SmallCap 600 (%)
1987	−3.51	-4.68	0.23	−2.04	−8.77	−13.50
1988	20.54	22.73	19.80	20.87	24..89	19.49
1989	23.94	19.43	26.27	35.55	16.24	13.89
1990	−13.56	−14.88	−11.50	−5.12	−19.51	−23.69
1991	43.45	46.70	41.51	50.10	46.05	48.49
1992	11.87	16.1	16.34	11.91	18.41	21.04
1993	14.57	16.54	14.30	13.95	18.91	18.79
1994	−2.66	−1.06	−2.09	3.58	−1.82	−4.77
1995	33.48	31.70	34.45	30.995	28.44	29.96
1996	17.25	19.03	19.00	19.20	16.49	21.32
1987-1996	13.31	13.87	14.74	15.93	12.41	11.16

Even though the index outperformed the median small-cap fund in only three of the 10 years, over the entire period it has bested 50% of the funds. This rank suffers from an even greater survivorship bias than that of the Russell 2000 during the four small-cap years stated above because it covers a longer time period, over which more funds have gone out of business.

Contrary to the popular perception that actively managed small-cap funds will outperform index funds, the long-term outperformance of the Russell 2500, the success of the Russell 2000 in markets favoring small-cap stocks, and the tax efficiency of indexing make it a very attractive option for medium- and small-cap investing.

SELECTING A BENCHMARK

There are numerous benchmarks that measure the performance of medium- and small-capitalization stocks. Each index is established under a different set of criteria. However, two indexes that are measuring the performance of the same portion of the market will generally produce the same long-term rates of return with some year-to-year variation. The performances of several popular benchmarks are compared in Exhibit 3.

Inevitably, over a given time period, one index will outperform another with the same objective. Does that mean the outperforming index is superior and should be preferred? Probably not. Most likely there were certain factors over the particular time period that favored the one benchmark. Unless there is reason to believe that the marginal outperformance is systematic, the difference in performance should be considered noise. After all, since different indexes have slightly different holdings, they should not perform exactly the same. The outperformance by one index is meaningless. An investor should be very careful projecting the outperformance into the future.

Extended Market Indexes

Both the Wilshire 4500 and the Russell 2500 are extended market indexes. They are designed to measure the performance of the U.S. stock market not covered by the S&P 500. Both include only stocks of companies domiciled in the United States. The Wilshire 4500 consists of all such companies that trade regularly on the New York or American Stock Exchanges or the NASDAQ over-the-counter market, except for the companies contained in the S&P 500. There are approximately 6,800 stocks in the index. The Russell 2500 starts with only the 3,000 largest market capitalization stocks. From this list, the U.S. stocks in the S&P 500 are subtracted, leaving approximately 2,500. Additionally, the weight of each stock in the Russell 2500 is reduced by the amount of closely held and cross-held shares.

These slightly different rules for constructing the two indexes result in three reasons for differences in the constituents. First, the Wilshire 4500 contains some 4,300 more stocks than the Russell 2500. However, these stocks are extremely small, collectively accounting for about 9.5% of the Wilshire 4500. Second, some stocks in the Russell 2500 are accorded less weight in the index because of the share adjustments for cross-holdings. Finally, the Russell 2500 starts with the largest 3,000 U.S. stocks. These 3,000 stocks change over time. Some smaller stocks grow into the index, while others within the index decline in value and fall out of the bottom. This reconstitution is made once a year on June 30 and results in turnover of the index of 1% to 3%, depending on the year.

These differences have naturally led to slightly different performance. However, there is no reason to necessarily expect one to consistently outperform the other. It seems like a distinction without a meaningful difference.

Mid-Cap Benchmarks

Standard & Poor's has created the MidCap 400 Stock Index using a process similar to that used to create and maintain its S&P 500 Index. The index is determined by a committee. The committee weighs both objective and subjective considerations. The index is designed to reflect the performance of medium-capitalization stocks and has market capitalizations and industry weights that approximate the middle part of the market. Before inclusion in the index, stocks are screened for liquidity so the index can be tracked closely.

The MidCap 400 Index has the advantage of being replicable. It also has controlled turnover as there are no rigid rules that dictate a stock must enter or leave the index. The committee decides. However, the index may suffer from the very subjectivity of the committee. There are many stocks that might be considered medium cap that are not included in the benchmark. The index may also suffer from a liquidity bias — the illiquid stocks not included in the index might systematically outperform because the market may demand a higher rate of return for illiquidity.

The Russell Midcap Index consists of 800 stocks of U.S.-domiciled companies that range from the 201st largest to the 1,000th largest. Like the Russell 2500, this index is adjusted for cross-holdings and is reconstituted on June 30 of every year, resulting in turnover as some companies grow to be larger than the 201st ranking while others decline in value to no longer qualify for inclusion in the top 1000. This, of course, results in significant turnover, which diminishes the tax efficiency of the index. But it has the advantage of insuring that the index always reflects medium-capitalization companies. The Russell Midcap does have a larger average market capitalization than the S&P MidCap 400 because it contains the stocks ranked from 201st largest through 500th largest, most of which are in the S&P 500, not the S&P MidCap 400.

Small-Cap Indexes

The two most broadly recognized small-capitalization indexes are the Russell 2000 and the S&P SmallCap 600. The Russell 2000 is constructed similarly to the Russell Midcap and has the same advantages and disadvantages. The index consists of the 2,000 stocks ranked from the 1001st largest to the 3,000th largest. The index is adjusted for cross-holdings and is reconstituted on June 30. Consequently, it consistently maintains its exposure to small-capitalization companies at the cost of annual turnover ranging from approximately 15% to 25% of assets.

Like the S&P 500 and the S&P MidCap 400, the S&P 600 is constructed by a committee that objectively and subjectively decides what stocks are representative of the small-capitalization portion of the market. The index consists of components that are relatively liquid, considering that they are small-capitalization stocks. It also has controlled turnover.

The Russell 2000 has a smaller average market capitalization than the S&P SmallCap 600 because the Russell 2000 contains the 1,501st through 3,000th largest stocks, most of which are not included in the S&P SmallCap Index.

This list of medium- and small-capitalization indexes is certainly not comprehensive. The indexes described are generally the most popular and are considered to be well constructed and maintained. There are differences between the indexes, but there is no obvious reason to expect these differences to favor one index over the other over the long term. One index might have greater average liquidity that makes it tradable with fewer transaction costs. But, if there is an illiquidity premium, it will not participate in that return. Another index may have lower turnover, making it more tax-efficient. However, as time passes the index may no longer completely reflect its intended portion of the market without the turnover. There are tradeoffs with any index.

The selection of an index may be less important than staying with that index over time. Unless there is a very compelling reason to switch to another index with a similar objective, an investor is probably best served by following the original selection. The transaction costs and taxes on capital gains that would be incurred to make the switch would probably outweigh the benefits. Furthermore, the factors that may have caused another index to outperform over one period are transitory and will probably reverse at about the time the investor is most likely to change directions.

MANAGING A MID-CAP OR SMALL-CAP INDEX FUND

There are generally two portfolio management techniques that can be used to track a desired index — complete replication and sampling. Complete replication involves purchasing all of the stocks in the benchmark in the percentage that their market capitalization represents in the total market capitalization of the index. Assume the market capitalization of Company A is $2.5 billion, as determined by multiplying its current price by the number of shares outstanding. If the sum of the market capitalization of all of the stocks in the benchmark is $799 billion, then Company A has a weighting of 0.31% in the index. Accordingly, 0.31% of the assets of the index fund is invested in Company A. Every other stock is also purchased in proportion to its size within the index. This indexing technique should provide very tight tracking error relative to the index. Typically, it should lag by no more than the expense ratio, or cost of managing and administering the fund, plus the transaction costs of investing or disinvesting cash flows, and any frictional drag from not having every penny of the fund invested at all times.

The second technique employed to manage an index account is a sampling process. Since only a portion of the securities in the index are purchased, the fund will track its benchmark less precisely, exhibiting the same cost drag on performance from which a complete replication fund suffers, plus an additional tracking error due to the sampling procedure. Ideally, this additional component of tracking error should be random, enhancing returns over certain time periods while detracting from them over others.

While there are limitless ways to create and maintain a sampled portfolio, they may be broadly classified into two types — stratified sampling and optimization.

Stratified Sampling

Under the technique of stratified sampling, every stock in the index is classified by its industry and size decile, which are the two most significant factors that determine a stock's return. A matrix is then created with the index's industry on one axis and its size characteristics on the other. Next, the index weight of each stock is accumulated within the cell of the matrix into which the stock is classified. In other words, if there are three stocks in the auto industry that are also in the largest decile of market capitalization, then the sum of the weights of those three stocks will be reflected in the first market cap decile/auto industry cell. The weight is calculated for each cell in the matrix by considering each stock in the index and adding its weight to its corresponding matrix cell. The portfolio is then created by randomly selecting a sampling of the stocks from each cell and purchasing them so that their collective weight in the portfolio matches that of the cell within the benchmark matrix.

For example, suppose companies A, B, and C are the only three stocks in the first size decile of autos, with index weights of 0.60%, 0.40%, and 0.30%, respectively. Then the first decile of size/auto industry cell contains 1.30% of the weight of the index. Depending on the desired number of stocks to be held by the portfolio, a sample of two of the three stocks might be selected. The stocks should be selected randomly in order to avoid any selection bias by the portfolio manager.

If companies A and C are selected, then they should both be overweighted so that their cumulative weight equals 1.30% of the portfolio. Each stock should be overweighted by the same amount because the overweighting represents a bet on the specific risk of the stock and there is no unbiased reason to believe the specific risk of one stock is less than that of another. It is important to remember that the overweight factor is additive, not multiplicative. So Company A should be weighted 0.80% of the portfolio and Company C should have a weight of 0.50%, even though Company A is actually twice the size of Company C. The portfolio thus has a weight of 1.30% in the first size decile/auto industry cell.

This algorithm is applied to every cell within the matrix. Consequently, the portfolio will have the exact same exposure to the two most important return factors, industry and size. There will be some random tracking error resulting from the bets on the specific risk of the stocks contained in the fund. Of course, some of these risks will offset each other and, as the number of securities in the portfolio is increased, the size of the bets will diminish and the specific risk will be diversified away, producing tighter tracking.

Optimization

Since stratified sampling typically considers only two factors of return, a more sophisticated sampling technique known as optimization might produce tighter tracking. Optimization involves creating and solving a formula known as a utility function. The utility function has a theoretical justification for why it should minimize tracking error. A common utility function is the mathematical formula that minimizes the expected tracking error of the portfolio. This equation includes such mathematical characteristics of each stock as its estimated covariance with a host of return factors that are considered important determinants of stock market returns. Also, each stock's exposure to each of the return factors is included in the utility function. With all of this information, a utility function can be quite unwieldy. Fortunately, computers can solve the problem relatively simply by using routine iterative techniques.

If the estimates of each stock's covariance with, and exposure to, the return factors are accurate, then optimized portfolios should track their targeted indexes quite closely. However, any errors in these estimates are sought and maximized by the solution algorithm. So an optimization procedure will also result in tracking error. Since the model described above is specifically designed to minimize expected tracking error, the expected tracking error of the portfolio is easily calculated and reported.

However, there are estimation errors in the covariances of stocks with the return factors as well as misspecifications of the exposures to the return factors.

Due to these errors, the estimate of the overall tracking error will always be understated. The severity of the understatement is inversely related to the magnitude of the expected mistracking. For relatively large predicted tracking errors in the 2%-3% range, the understatement is not problematic.

For estimates of relatively tight tracking of 0.10%-0.30%, the actual tracking error is frequently twice the predicted level. Still, the ability to track a benchmark is usually better with an optimizer than with stratified sampling, particularly when a relatively few number of stocks are purchased. When many stocks are included in the portfolio, either approach is probably fine.

In order to improve the tracking of either the optimized or stratified sampling approach, the largest stocks in the index may be completely replicated. This will insure nearly perfect tracking of a significant portion of the index. The tracking error of the balance of the portfolio will be diluted by the close tracking of the replicated portion, resulting in a better tracking portfolio.

When to Replicate, When to Sample

The portfolio management techniques employed to track a mid-cap or small-cap index depend on several criteria, including the liquidity of the index, the size of the fund, the nature of the cash flows into the fund, and the benefits of producing tighter tracking. Large capitalization indexes such as the S&P 500 contain very liquid securities and are almost always completely replicated by commercially offered funds. In these funds, tracking error is closely scrutinized and almost every basis point must be explained. However, medium- and small-capitalization indexes contain some less liquid securities and strong consideration must be given to a sampling technique.

The most significant impediment to completely replicating an index is the liquidity of the individual stocks. Consequently, the appropriate technique for managing an index fund tracking a medium- or small-capitalization index depends on the specific characteristics of the target index. For instance, Standard & Poor's Corporation has a committee that determines the constituents of its 500, MidCap 400 and SmallCap 600 indexes. The committee has specifically designed the MidCap and SmallCap indexes to have sufficient liquidity so that they may be completely replicated. A fund that has $50 million to $100 million or more total net assets should probably be replicated.

Other indexes, such as the Russell 2000 and Wilshire 4500, are constructed using objective screening criteria without regard to liquidity. Both of these indexes are very broadly diversified, and both contain many stocks that are extremely illiquid. These stocks have extremely high transaction costs, sometimes approaching 10% of the purchase price.

In these cases, the costs of purchasing the very illiquid stocks frequently outweigh the benefits they provide to the portfolio. Employing a sampling approach to the management of funds tracking these benchmarks can be very prudent.

Other considerations, such as the size of the fund, may dictate the portfolio management approach. During the startup phase of an index fund, when total net assets are typically small, a sampling approach may be necessary. It is not cost-effective to replicate a new fund with $5 million. As the fund grows, though, the sampling process can be replaced by complete replication if appropriate.

Certain types of index funds or accounts may not have smooth cash flows, such as a separately managed account for a company's pension fund which may have large monthly or quarterly contributions. With sufficiently large cash flow, such an account may not be able to invest in some of the less liquid securities in a timely fashion. It may be advantageous to invest in a liquid, sampled subset of the index immediately to gain the desired market exposure. The other stocks in the fund, whose positions were not increased, can be "back filled" with more gradual cash flow from either smaller interim contributions or receipt of dividends. By slowly adding to positions of stocks that are thinly traded, transaction costs can be minimized while still gaining the desired exposure to all stocks.

Endowments or foundations with very long time horizons may be less sensitive to short-term tracking error than they are to the higher costs of complete replication of a very broadly diversified index. A number of large corporations manage index funds internally using a sampling process because purchasing large numbers of stocks can drive up the costs of both the front office and the back office. These expenses include such direct costs as adding traders to trade the less liquid securities and adding back-office employees to track corporate actions, settle trades, lend securities, and price securities. Indirect expenses from potentially higher transaction costs also impact the performance.

TRADING CONSIDERATIONS

Even the most liquid medium- and small-capitalization companies have significant transaction costs. Brokerage commissions, the most visible component of transaction costs, are actually the smallest component of these costs, ranging from 0.1% to 0.2%. Much more significant are the market impact and the difference between the bid/asked spread.

For a round trip, the cost of the bid/asked spread can range from 0.6% to 10%. So, buying a stock will cost half the round turn, or from 0.3% to 5%, with an average closer to 0.75%-1%. When purchasing a larger position, one may not be able to purchase the entire amount at the prevailing offer price. If the presence of the order impacts the market, this impact cost can swamp the other two components of transaction costs. In total, estimates of transaction costs for a one-way purchase of medium- and small-cap stocks range from 1% to 2%. The lower end of this range may be achieved when orders are small, such as with cash flow into a fund, while the upper end may apply when there are significant changes, or reconstitutions to an index. In any event, transaction costs will significantly impair the ability of the indexer to track the index.

Some funds charge a transaction fee on purchases or redemptions. The fee is paid to the fund, not the adviser, and reimburses the fund for the transaction costs it incurs when investing the cash flow. Since the new investment is being charged directly for the transaction costs, the fund will be able to track the index more closely. If there is no transaction fee, then all investors in the fund are subsidizing the transaction costs in the form of lower fund performance and tracking error. Whether or not a transaction fee is assessed, the adviser must attempt to minimize transaction costs.

There are a number of techniques used to minimize transaction costs. Of course, the stocks can be purchased through a broker in a traditional fashion, using either market or limit orders. Electronic trading networks offer an attractive alternative to trading over-the-counter stocks, while other electronic systems may be appropriate for listed securities. Stocks may also be crossed with another investor who naturally desires to trade the other side. This crossing opportunity can be with another fund managed by the adviser, with another manager that the adviser knows, with another manager identified by a broker, or through an electronic crossing network. Finally, futures contracts can be purchased to gain exposure to the market.

Electronic trading networks, such as Instinet, enable an institutional investor to trade over-the-counter stocks inside of the dealers' spread. The network allows the trader to find another natural trader on the other side of the market. The natural buyer and seller can then transact anonymously, usually at the middle of the bid/offer spread, avoiding the dealer's profit margin. However, liquidity can be an issue on such a system. Listed securities also trade on Instinet, but the majority of the trades are of unlisted securities.

Listed orders can be facilitated through other electronic systems, such as a Designated Order Turnaround (DOT) Box. These systems are provided to an indexer by their brokers. The "Super DOT" gives the trader electronic access to the floor of the exchange with a tremendous amount of flexibility that is not possible through a traditional brokerage relationship. The trader controls the order flow to the floor. A complete list of stocks can be instantaneously sent to the floor. The orders can be traded with limits or at market. If traded with limits, the limits can be set to adjust automatically as the market moves. Alternatively, a slice of the entire order may be executed and the remaining slices can follow in additional waves, allowing the market to "fill in" during the interval between waves.

An electronic crossing network, such as POSIT, aggregates orders until a specified execution time. All orders are undisclosed prior to execution, so a crossing network offers a hit-or-miss opportunity. Most orders are not executed, but the 20%-30% that do cross are traded with very low transaction costs — typically only the reasonable brokerage cost of POSIT, with no bid/asked spread and no market impact.

Futures contracts may be purchased to gain exposure to the market in a very low-cost fashion. However, most medium- and small-capitalization indexes do not have futures contracts that are designed to track them. Of the indexes that do have corresponding futures contracts, most of the contracts are not sufficiently liquid to trade effectively. The one noticeable exception is the S&P MidCap 400 futures contract.

There are many ways to trade. No one method is optimal for all types of trades. The trader has to consider all possible alternatives and select the method that is most appropriate given the number of trades and the size and liquidity of the trades. The capabilities of the index trading desk will be a very major determinant of the tracking error of the fund.

SUMMARY

Indexed investing has received considerable attention in the media and the investment community over the three years ended 1996, primarily because of the absolute and relative performance of the Standard & Poor's 500 Index, which outperformed 90% of broadly diversified equity funds, with a 71% total return. However, with the growth of indexing and its coverage in the popular press, a number of misconceptions about the advantages of indexing have developed.

While most investors will agree that indexing to the S&P 500 is a very cost-effective and prudent method of gaining exposure to large-capitalization stocks, few will concede the same relative advantages to indexing in the medium- and small-capitalization sectors of the market. However, when appropriate comparisons are made, indexing has performed quite well in the extended portion of the market. In fact, if an investor has a strong belief that small-capitalization stocks will outperform, then indexing to the Russell 2000 is quite attractive compared with actively managed small-cap funds.

There are numerous indexes designed to measure the medium and small end of the market. Each has slightly different nuances, resulting in both advantages and disadvantages. The most important consideration in choosing an index is deciding exactly which portion of the market is to be indexed — the entire extended market or either of its two components, the medium- and small-cap sectors. The decision of a specific, recognized index within the desired sector of the market is secondary. However, it is important to "stay the course," once selected.

Trading within this portion of the market is significantly more difficult than trading large-capitalization stocks. This is reflected in significantly higher transaction costs and an inability to trade large dollar amounts over short intervals. There are many tools that a small-cap trader must use to execute the strategy effectively. Since the only performance advantage indexing has is lower costs, the success of indexing ultimately relies on the low expense ratio of the fund and the trader's ability to minimize transaction costs.

Chapter 4

Enhanced Equity Indexing

John S. Loftus, CFA
Executive Vice President
Pacific Investment Managment Company

INTRODUCTION

Enhanced indexing is, in a sense, an oxymoron. The essential task of indexing is to match the return of a benchmark index. Does enhanced indexing, then, imply doing a better job than regular indexing does of matching the index? Providers of enhanced indexing services will be quick to say, "No. It means beating the index." But that's the job of active managers. Elaborating, the enhanced indexer would say, "True, but enhanced indexing seeks to consistently outperform a benchmark index by a moderate amount, while closely controlling both tracking error and the risk of significant underperformance."

Given this definition, where does enhanced indexing belong? Active management seeks to outperform. Indexing seeks to match the index. If enhanced indexing is to outperform, it must involve active management techniques. If it is to closely track the targeted index, it must share with indexing certain techniques designed to control risk.

"Risk-controlled active management" would seem an apt phrase, synonymous with enhanced indexing but resolving the apparent oxymoron. That enhanced indexing has become the more popular phrase may reflect marketing imperatives more than any desire for linguistic precision. Whether the phrase is here to stay, however, will almost certainly be driven by the results. If enhanced indexing delivers consistent excess returns with close tracking and few disappointments, it is hard to imagine investors not preferring it to traditional forms of indexing or active management.

How enhanced indexing accomplishes its laudable objective varies across a spectrum of techniques. This chapter surveys the major methods of enhanced equity indexing. To help the reader distinguish between traditional active management and an enhanced index strategy, I develop a returns-based framework to motivate the distinction. I then divide the enhanced indexing world into two principal categories: stock-based strategies and synthetic strategies. After discussing the primary approaches in each category, the chapter closes with a discussion of how an investor may achieve optimal results by combining a synthetic strategy with a stock-based approach.

THE NATURE OF ENHANCED INDEXING

As noted above, enhanced indexing draws from active management techniques in order to generate excess returns, while controlling risk in part through methods common to indexing. In seeking to provide the best of both worlds, enhanced indexing does not deliver a free lunch. Excess returns stem from risk exposures, but providers of enhanced indexing tend to share a heightened emphasis on risk control as compared with traditional active management.

As an important illustration, one of the principal manifestations of risk control in enhanced indexing is the modest level of excess return both sought and delivered by the strategies. Simplistically, the "best" active manager could be thought of as the one who delivers the highest excess returns. Risk or tracking error is generally only a secondary consideration in traditional active management. In contrast, the "best" enhanced indexer would be the manager who optimizes the tradeoff between excess return and close tracking of the index.

While not universally valid, this qualitative distinction between active management and enhanced indexing leads to a potentially helpful quantitative means of separating active management from enhanced indexing. By focusing on returns or expected returns, it is possible for an investor to separate the two types of managers more easily than by focusing on the methods employed to achieve excess returns, as these methods often blur with those of active managers.

Returns-Based Tools

A returns-based distinction between active management and enhanced indexing relies on three tools: alpha, tracking error, and information ratio. These are defined in turn.

Alpha

Alpha is defined as risk-adjusted excess return over the benchmark, from the model:

expected return = alpha + beta × (index return)

For enhanced indexing, the simplified expressions,

alpha = expected return − index return

or

alpha = expected excess return

stem from the assumption that beta will be very close to one. This assumption is consistent with the intended design of most enhanced indexing strategies. A further simplifying assumption (and certainly a more heroic one) will allow alpha to be defined in terms of a manager's historical performance,

alpha = historical excess return

The usual disclaimers apply, of course. Nevertheless, a focus on *ex post* returns allows some inferences to be drawn based on observable rather than forecast returns.

Tracking Error

Tracking error measures the dispersion of excess returns and, therefore, the consistency of a manager's excess performance. Tracking error is sometimes confused with alpha, as in, "...the manager's negative tracking error was due to the decision to underweight energy stocks, the top-performing sector last year." In fact, tracking error is always a positive number, defined as follows:

tracking error = annualized standard deviation of monthly excess returns

Note that a manager does not necessarily have tracking error simply because of outperformance or underperformance. By the above definition, a manager who outperformed (or underperformed) by exactly 20 basis points every single month would have zero tracking error, despite a positive (negative) alpha.

Information Ratio

If alpha is taken to be a manager's mean historical excess return, then tracking error measures the standard deviation of the alpha. If one makes the assumption that managers' excess returns are normally distributed, then knowing the mean and the standard deviation of those excess returns allows statistical inferences to be drawn. The most common inference is the measure of confidence that a manager's historical alpha is not zero. In other words, if the manager demonstrates a positive excess return over time, what is the probability that the excess return did not arise simply by chance?

Defining the information ratio as,

$$\text{information ratio} = \frac{\text{alpha}}{\text{tracking error}}$$

we see that the information ratio is closely related to the t-statistic used to measure the statistical significance of a manager's alpha[1]

$$t = \frac{\text{alpha} \times \sqrt{T}}{\sigma}$$

where T is the number of independent observations and σ is the standard deviation.

Relating the information ratio to the t-statistic allows one to answer the question, "How confident am I that a given manager's historical results indicate an alpha that was achieved by skill rather than luck?" In other words, what is the confidence that the measured historical alpha is, statistically speaking, different

---

[1] Richard Grinold and Ronald Kahn, *Active Portfolio Management* (Chicago: Probus Publishing Company, 1995).

than zero. Let's assume we have measured a manager's annualized alpha and tracking error over a 5-year period and computed the information ratio. Exhibit 1 shows the degree of confidence (using a two-tail test) that historical alphas are non-zero for various information ratios. To be 95% confident that a manager's 5-year historical alpha was obtained by skill rather than luck, an information ratio of 1.25 is required.

Note that it would be inappropriate to say that the probability of future excess returns is given by the information ratio. Of course, hiring an active manager or an enhanced indexer implies a prediction that alpha will be positive. Otherwise, the correct choice would be a straight index fund. Having a high confidence that favorable historical performance was due to skill rather than luck would seem to be an appropriate precondition to making such a prediction, however.

A TAXONOMY OF EQUITY MANAGEMENT APPROACHES

Having defined the concepts of alpha, tracking error, and information ratio, I now propose a means of categorizing various equity management approaches using these measures. The following taxonomy is intended as a general guide for distinguishing between indexing, active management, and enhanced indexing. There are doubtless many equity managers whose results represent exceptions to these rules of thumb, but the rules are typical of the average results in each category, particularly with respect to large-capitalization portfolios for which the most appropriate benchmark, the S&P 500, has been the target of the lion's share of indexed assets.

Indexing

Indexing has an expected alpha of zero, and most successful managers of large index funds have exhibited historical tracking error of 0.2% (20 basis points) or lower. Thus, the information ratio of an index fund manager is essentially zero. In terms of the confidence measure discussed above, an information ratio of zero is not puzzling. Investors in index funds are not seeking positive alpha, so the lack of statistical confidence in a positive alpha (as implied by an information ratio of zero) is not troubling.

Exhibit 1: Confidence that Alphas are Non-Zero

Information Ratio	Confidence that alpha $\neq 0$ (%)
0.25	39.4
0.33	49.8
0.50	67.3
0.75	83.1
1.00	91.1
1.25	95.1

Exhibit 2: Measures of Management Categories

	Indexing	Active Management	Enhanced Indexing
Expected Alpha	0%	2.0% or higher	0.5% to 2.0%
Tracking Error	0% to 0.2%	4% or higher	0.5% to 2.0%
Information Ratio	0	0.5 or lower	0.5 to 2.0

Exhibit 3: Factoring in the Length of Track Record

Information Ratio	Years to Achieve 95% Confidence in Significance of Alpha
0.25	64.0
0.33	38.0
0.50	18.0
0.75	9.5
1.00	6.5
1.25	5.0

Active Management

Classically, active managers have an expected annualized alpha of 2% (200 basis points) or higher. However, as the traditional focus within the active management community has been oriented more toward production of excess returns than toward controlling tracking error, it is common to find tracking error in excess of 4%. As a result, information ratios for active management have averaged 0.5 or less.

Enhanced Indexing

Enhanced indexing focuses on generating modest levels of alpha, generally 0.5% to 2.0% annualized. Enhanced index managers also strive for low tracking error. Most strategies marketed as enhanced indexing have exhibited historical tracking error of between 0.5% and 2.0% as well. Thus, the information ratios for offerings in the enhanced index category are often in the range of 0.5 to 2.0. Exhibit 2 summarizes these measures.

Recalling the statistical confidence analysis above, it is interesting to look at the typical information ratios of active management and enhanced indexing to perform a somewhat different analysis. Let's ask the question, "for a given information ratio, how many years long must the track record be to indicate at the 95% confidence level that the true alpha is not zero?" Exhibit 3 presents the results. Plan sponsors/consultants may wish to ask themselves how many managers they have hired/recommended based on five years of data whose information ratios require a significantly longer measurement horizon to attribute statistical significance to the alpha.

Of course, statistical significance of a manager's alpha is not the sole relevant criterion in a hiring decision. Economic significance of the alpha matters as well. Consider the manager who, using a very complex active-management or enhanced-indexing process, produces 10 basis points of alpha with 10 basis points of tracking error. This alpha is statistically significant at the 95% level after only 6.5 years of results. Relative to indexing, however, the plan sponsor may not find 10 basis points (gross of fees) of alpha to be worth the effort to understand and monitor the more complex process.

Alternatively, consider the very active manager who has produced 500 basis points of alpha in five years but with 1,500 basis points of tracking error. The manager's process is easy to understand and monitor. While one can only be about 50% confident that the true alpha of the process is nonzero, some plan sponsors might be willing to trade off lower statistical confidence for the chance of obtaining dramatic outperformance over the long run. Hopefully, however, the plan sponsor can endure the possibility of dramatic underperformance over shorter time horizons, as is implied by such high tracking error.

Information ratios then, while useful, are but one tool in assisting in a decision between indexing, active management, and enhanced indexing. The best choice for a given investor will be based on individual circumstances. An investor driven by a desire to reduce management fees and eliminate all uncertainty as to benchmark tracking will no doubt prefer traditional indexing. An investor focused primarily on maximizing return, who has confidence in his or her ability to identify successful managers, would most likely prefer traditional active management, although they should seek out long track records and the highest possible information ratios nevertheless. Enhanced indexing can represent a comfortable middle ground between these two emphases, bringing the potential for moderate but meaningful alpha with a greater degree of confidence and consistency.

Not surprisingly, investment management fees for enhanced indexing strategies tend to lie in between those of traditional active management and indexing. Perhaps driven by confidence in their own ability to generate consistent alpha, enhanced index managers commonly offer their services with performance-based fee options.

TYPES OF ENHANCED INDEXING STRATEGIES

Thus far, I've explained that enhanced indexing attempts to deliver moderate and consistent alpha with relatively low tracking error. In a qualitative sense, enhanced indexing differs from active management processes primarily in having moderate objectives for alpha and a significant emphasis on risk control. Successful enhanced indexing strategies produce relatively high information ratios that can greatly increase confidence in the statistical significance of the alpha and/or lower the required measurement period to gain such confidence.

The types of strategies marketed as enhanced index approaches can be divided into two broad groups: stock-based strategies and synthetic strategies. I'll characterize each group in turn, focusing on the sources of alpha, the different risk exposures taken to achieve the alpha, and the techniques involved in controlling tracking error.

Stock-Based Strategies

Stock-based enhanced indexing strategies are typically broadly diversified portfolios that rely on some form of stock selection process in an attempt to generate a moderate, consistent alpha. In common with traditional active management, for the strategy to be successful the manager must have some means of identifying stocks within the index that will either outperform or underperform the index. There will also generally be a risk control regimen that limits the degree of individual stock underweighting/overweighting as well as the degree of portfolio exposure to factor risks and industry/sector concentrations. A variety of approaches are pursued. These are discussed below.

Tilts

Probably the first stock-based strategies that could be characterized as enhanced indexing involved so-called *tilting techniques.* Starting with a pure index fund, a manager would obtain modest overweights in a direction favored by the client. Value, growth, and yield are among the more common tilts. Obviously, the expectation of alpha comes from the belief that value stocks, growth stocks, or high dividend-paying stocks outperform over time. (Note that yield tilts may be offered to or used by those with a motivation other than attempting to increase alpha.)

A plan sponsor opting for a value tilt strategy versus a traditional active manager with a clear value style believes in the outperformance of value stocks but either doesn't want to make a big bet in that direction or wants to minimize dependence on an active manager's stock selection process. The simplest value tilt would establish some price/earnings ratio threshold, overweight all stocks in the index below the threshold and underweight those above it. Risk control would depend on diversification (owning all stocks in the index to some degree) and limits on the underweights and overweights.

With the development in recent years of specific value and growth style benchmarks, style tilts have become less relevant as enhanced indexing strategies. Rather, the tilts have given way to passive style indexing as a way for plan sponsors to implement their style biases.

Portfolio Construction-Based Techniques

Another stock-based strategy that might qualify as an enhanced index would still own most or all of the stocks in the index but would combine them in a way that differs from the construction of the index itself. The simplest example might be equal weighting all stocks in a capitalization weighted index. Risk control again comes primarily from diversification although, depending on the index itself, a modified equal weighting strategy might be required to maintain tracking error below an acceptable threshold. As is the case with style tilts, equal weighted indices have been developed, and pure equal weighted index products have developed alongside, rendering this strategy more of a passive choice than an enhanced index approach.

Quantitative Strategies

A third form of stock-based enhanced indexing would attempt to use quantitative stock selection models in an effort to sort stocks into likely outperformers and underperformers, then weight the stocks accordingly. One or a combination of quantitative screens may be employed, including earnings growth, earnings surprise, earnings momentum, price momentum, foreign exposure, liquidity, etc, in addition to value/growth, yield, and capitalization. Risk controls would include diversification and limits on measured factor exposures in the portfolio, sector and industry weights, and other techniques.

Fundamental Strategies

A fourth stock-based method involves a manager forming opinions about the companies most likely to outperform or underperform based on fundamental research, then overweighting and underweighting stocks accordingly. Fundamental research, as opposed to quantitative techniques, focuses on the strengths of a company's underlying business (market share, proprietary technology, competitive position, trends in demand, quality of earnings, balance sheet strength, etc). Risk controls in addition to diversification might include limits on sector and industry weights, and possibly limits on exposures to quantitative factors as well.

Mathematical Strategies

As distinct from quantitative strategies, mathematical strategies focus on identifying patterns in the price of a stock, such as its trend persistence, volatility, mean reversion, etc., and basing overweighting and underweighting decisions on such mathematical properties. Some or all of the risk control techniques already listed can be applied to reduce tracking error.

Issues with Stock-Based Strategies

The success of any stock-based strategy is predicated on the belief that some form of active stock selection can add value. Proponents of the efficient market hypothesis may reject any such notion and prefer indexing. Yet the debate over the efficiency of the stock market continues. Some believe that small-cap stocks are less efficiently priced than large-cap stocks, raising the odds of success for stock-based enhanced index strategies against smaller capitalization indices. Whatever one's views are regarding market efficiency, in both large cap and small cap domains, the emphasis on risk control in these strategies can potentially improve confidence in success and lower the risk of dramatic underperformance.

Other important issues to consider in evaluating a stock-based strategy include:

- *Turnover/Transactions Costs* Too much of either can potentially swamp the alpha of an otherwise effective process.
- *Exploitation or Obsolescence* A successful model or an identified anomaly tends to attract both invested assets and imitators. Alphas can shrink through time as the model or anomaly becomes increasingly exploited.
- *Model Risk* Quantitative and mathematical models derived from analysis of historical factors, returns, and prices are always subject to the risk that the world can change.

Despite these concerns, a well-specified and managed stock-based strategy can fulfill the potential for alpha that enhanced indexing offers and can improve the consistency of results relative to traditional active management.

Synthetic Strategies

Synthetic enhanced indexing strategies make no attempt to select stocks within the index being tracked. Rather, they effectively obtain ownership of all the stocks in the index by means of futures, options, or stock index swaps. Some synthetic strategies rotate between these vehicles and a stock index itself, seeking to add value but at all times owning the index through the cheapest vehicle. Other synthetic strategies stay fully invested in a particular synthetic vehicle, focusing on managing the underlying cash reserves to generate a higher rate of return.

Within the field of synthetic strategies, there are three primary groups:

- Index arbitrage-related strategies
- Index futures plus enhanced cash management
- Volatility-based strategies

In the first two instances, the role of the futures or other synthetic investment vehicle is limited to completely capturing the price return of the underlying index. As such, the index futures become the primary risk control element in the strategy, completely eliminating any tracking error or risk of underperforming the index due to adverse results in stock selection. In the case of volatility-based strategies, stock index futures, options, or swaps can take on an additional role of altering overall market exposure in response to or anticipation of changes in overall stock market volatility and how that volatility is priced. I now describe the three synthetic categories in more detail.

Index Arbitrage-Related Strategies

Stock index arbitrage was perhaps the first enhanced index strategy employed. With the introduction of S&P 500 index futures in 1984, traders had an opportunity to observe two essentially equivalent assets, a basket containing the 500 stocks on the one hand and the futures on the other, trading simultaneously in different markets. Enhancements in the ability to trade all 500 physical stocks in the index in automated fashion created virtually riskless arbitrage opportunities. Any time the futures were trading at a price significantly different from their fair value (defined more fully below), a simultaneous order to buy/sell futures and sell/buy the 500 stocks generated a profit. During the first several years of S&P futures trading, index funds could employ this strategy and risklessly enhance their return by as much as 100 basis points annually.

Over time, the stock index arbitrage opportunity has become fully exploited. In S&P 500 stocks, the annualized excess returns available from arbitrage have shrunk to perhaps 20 basis points or less, and the ability to earn this excess return has gravitated for the most part to those able to execute the trades most efficiently, the primary dealers on Wall Street. As this trend has occurred, money managers offering index arbitrage as an enhanced index strategy have employed vehicles other than futures (including stock index swaps and index options structured as long call/short put combinations) in search of additional arbitrage opportunities. The trend towards increased pricing efficiency of these synthetic vehicles compared to fair value has continued, limiting the magnitude of alpha available from arbitrage-related strategies.

Index Futures Plus Enhanced Cash Management

An alternative to stock index arbitrage is to own futures (or swaps or long-call/short-put options combinations) as a permanent means of obtaining exposure to the underlying index. The use of futures, for example, as a more or less permanent means of obtaining equity exposure capitalizes on the prevalence of stock index arbitrage as the marginal price setting mechanism in the futures market.

The theory behind the approach is relatively straightforward. Because the price of the S&P futures contract is determined by arbitrage, for which the holding period is short and uncertain, a longer-term investor can expect to buy futures at fair value and invest his or her cash reserves at a higher rate of return which reflects his longer time horizon. So long as the risk exposures in the investment of the cash reserves are appropriately constrained, the potential alpha generated by the strategy can be obtained with relatively low tracking error.

To explain further, stock index futures and stocks are essentially equivalent ways of owning the S&P 500 index. One can pay cash today and own the 500 stocks that make up the S&P index. Alternately, one can own an equivalent value of futures on the S&P 500. A feature of the futures strategy is that an investor only has to post a small margin deposit (generally around 4% of the total contract value) in order to own the futures contract. To avoid leveraging the portfolio, the remaining 96% of the cash not needed for initial margin can be invested in short-duration securities which provide additional reserves to cover potential margin flows stemming from a decline in the value of the S&P futures.

The goal in the enhanced index strategy is to obtain a rate of return on the reserve assets which exceeds the implied interest rate in the S&P futures contract. To understand the concept of an implied interest rate, note that the investor in stocks receives dividends, while the investor in futures forgoes dividends but can earn interest on cash reserves. Thus, the fair value of futures (*FV*) is (simplistically):

$$FV = \text{stock index price} - \text{dividend return} + \text{implied interest rate}$$

As noted above, stock index arbitrage occurs whenever the actual price of futures deviates significantly from fair value, where the implied interest rate in the fair value calculation is the arbitrager's cost of capital. With the bulk of index arbitrage carried out by Wall Street dealers, their cost of capital (for which a reasonable proxy is short-term LIBOR) becomes the implied interest rate in the price of the futures contract. Thus, an investor who buys stock index futures at fair value and can invest reserves at a rate exceeding LIBOR should expect to outperform the underlying stock index with this strategy.

The strategies involved in generating above-LIBOR returns on the reserve assets are numerous, ranging from traditional fixed income techniques to other arbitrage trades and long/short strategies. Traditional fixed income strategies can exploit the term premium emanating from the prevailing upward slope of the short end of the yield curve as a structural advantage available to the investor with a longer time horizon.

The investor may also expect to earn a yield premium by attempting to use less liquid market sectors for that portion of the reserve portfolio which serves as a quasi-permanent layer of reserves after allowing for an appropriate liquidity pool to fund margin flows associated with a stock market decline. Risk control in the case of the more traditional fixed income techniques centers on limiting the duration or interest rate exposure as well as credit quality of the fixed income assets to a level consistent with low tracking error over time. Appropriate diversification of assets across issuers, security types, and fixed income market sectors is also important to risk control.

In the case of cash enhancement involving arbitrage trades and long/short strategies, an investor searches for pricing inefficiencies between, say, convertible bonds and the underlying stock, takes an offsetting position between the two, hedges out the economic risk differences, and awaits the anticipated convergence in price between the convertible and the stock. Long/short portfolios attempt to identify overpriced and underpriced securities in numerous markets and collectively outperform a risk-free rate with low total volatility. In these types of strategies it is important to limit potential tracking error by diversifying across a range of opportunities and employing stop loss limits in the event that the asset prices diverge rather than converge.

The common feature of futures plus enhanced cash strategies is that they offer the opportunity to "transfer" alpha from asset management arenas outside those represented by the indices being enhanced. This allows an investor who sees the assets in the index being enhanced as being efficiently priced to take advantage of perceived pricing inefficiencies or structural opportunities that may exist outside the index. If these enhancement opportunities show low total return volatility and low correlation to the index being enhanced, the alpha can be obtained at low total tracking error, resulting in a high information ratio.

Volatility-Based Strategies

Volatility-based strategies involve "owning" the market index through futures or options in a manner similar to the other synthetic strategies. However, an alpha is sought by making small alterations to the total market exposure based on realized or implied volatility in the underlying index.

These strategies may be based on various observations about stock price volatility that can be exploited in the context of a long holding period. For example, if a manager observes a tendency of stock prices to revert toward the mean after unusually volatile moves in one direction or the other, the manager may reduce market exposure to less than 100% after a volatile market rise, or increase market exposure above 100% after a violent market decline, then normalize the exposure back to 100% after prices exhibit the anticipated mean reversion.

Other volatility-based strategies entail the purchase or writing of put or call options against a fully invested portfolio to exploit perceived mispricing of the market volatility implied in options prices as opposed to actual or forecast market volatility. In both types of strategies, risk control centers on explicit limits on the extent to which market exposure will deviate from 100% at any given time, plus the implementation of stop loss strategies should the market make an unexpected move in the adverse direction. The potential alpha being captured by these strategies stems from a view that the market systematically prices volatility based on a horizon shorter than the investor's actual holding period for stocks. If so, the long-term investor may generally expect to profit by selling options to capture the higher implied volatility over time.

The key difference between volatility-based synthetic strategies and index arbitrage or futures plus enhanced cash is that the potential enhancement in volatility-based strategies comes from movements in the price of the underlying index. The enhancement from index arbitrage and futures plus enhanced cash strategies is independent of the movement of the market index.

Issues with Synthetic Strategies

The success of synthetic strategies is based on the view that individual stocks within the index are efficiently priced, but that pricing inefficiencies and structural factors exist outside the individual stocks. If these inefficiencies can be found and exploited, they can be "tacked on" to a market index such as the S&P 500 through the use of synthetic investment vehicles such as futures, options, or swaps. However, there are practical issues to be addressed in the use of such synthetic vehicles:

• Futures may not at all times be priced at fair value, and some futures markets close their trading day at different times than the stocks in the underlying index. For example, the S&P 500 stocks close at 4:00 P.M. Eastern time, whereas the futures exchange continues trading until 4:15 P.M. While ultimately any tracking error which results from deviations from fair value and non-simultaneous pricing tends to wash out over time,[2] the impact can be significant over short measurement periods.

- Futures must be "rolled" from one expiration month to the next in order to maintain market exposure over time. Any deviation between the actual price spread at which the roll occurs and the fair value of the spread will add to or subtract from performance.
- A manager wishing to avoid the risk of rolling futures quarterly at a price above fair value can employ a longer dated stock index swap. While this technique locks in the stock price exposure for a longer time period, swaps are generally less liquid and require management of a credit exposure to an individual swap counterparty. The larger futures exchanges are generally thought to involve counterparty exposure which is *de minimis.*

Despite the issues associated with synthetic vehicles, enhanced index strategies using such vehicles have proven effective in capturing index price exposure, eliminating the underperformance risk of individual stock selection, and opening up opportunities to add alpha to an index with low tracking error.

IMPLEMENTING AN ENHANCED INDEX PROGRAM

The preceding section analyzed the differences between stock-based and synthetic-enhanced indexing strategies. The major difference between the two is the reliance on versus the avoidance of stock selection as the means of enhancement. Plan sponsors and consultants who have employed or analyzed enhanced index strategies have frequently shown some preference for either stock-based approaches or synthetic approaches. Those who believe that the individual stocks are not efficiently priced or who find stock selection processes more readily understandable may prefer the stock-based approaches. Those who see individual stocks as efficiently priced but believe alpha can be found elsewhere are likely to favor the synthetic approaches.

This chapter closes with the view that a strong preference for one type of strategy versus another can be counterproductive. Indeed, there is value in the differences between the two major types of strategies. Because the sources of potential alpha in stock-based and synthetic strategies are so different, intuitively one may expect them to be uncorrelated. If so, then combining the two types of strategies in an enhanced index program will bring diversification benefits and provide superior results compared with using only one strategy or the other.

In what sense might a combination of a stock-based strategy and a synthetic strategy be superior? Consider the impact of the correlation of monthly

---

[2] The deviations from fair value exhibit a strong pattern of negative serial correlation, which is a statistician's fancy name for "noise."

excess returns between two distinct strategies that have similar alphas. If the excess returns are highly positively correlated, little diversification benefit results from a combination of the strategies. Total alpha and tracking error are about the same for the combination as they are for the individual pieces. If excess returns of two strategies were perfectly negatively correlated, then combining the strategies would bring about the ideal result of zero tracking error with the average of the two alphas. The information ratio would go to infinity! Unfortunately, the probability of finding two such strategies with perfect negative correlation of excess returns is quite low. If this result were easily attainable, one could hedge out the equity exposure and leverage the resulting alpha into a money machine.

Excess returns with near zero correlation, however, should be attainable from combining a stock-based and a synthetic manager. A combination of these two managers would preserve their average alphas, but the tracking error of the combination would be lower than that of the individual pieces, resulting in a higher information ratio for the combination. Again, intuition leads one to expect that the excess returns from, say a fundamental analysis stock-based strategy might have little correlation with those of a synthetic strategy whose alpha comes from fixed-income security selection.

Suppose, for example, that two such enhanced index managers generated monthly performance as indicated in the following exhibits. The managers produced consistent alphas and relatively low tracking errors individually, but their monthly excess returns had very low correlation. Exhibits 4 and 5 illustrate how monthly results from the two different enhanced index strategies with low correlation of excess returns interact in a combined portfolio.[3]

First, note from Exhibit 4 how the strategies exhibit a low, stable correlation of their excess returns. Next, in Exhibit 5, note the rolling 5-year alpha of the stock-based strategy, the synthetic strategy, and that of a 50-50 combination of the two. The alpha of the 50-50 combination is approximately the average of the two individual alphas. Now, in Exhibit 6, look at the tracking error of the two strategies separately and in combination. Note that the tracking error of the combination is not the average of the tracking errors of the individual strategies, but is instead significantly lower than that of either individual strategy. This is the benefit of diversification which stems from the low correlation of the alphas. As a result, the observed information ratio of a 50-50 combination of the strategies is higher than that for either strategy individually, as seen in Exhibit 7.

The analysis demonstrates how it might be possible to create powerful combinations of enhanced index strategies by combining different styles. If one starts with two strategies that have economically significant alphas, then combines them in such a way that the level of alpha is preserved but the information ratio increases, then the resulting gain in statistical significance should cause the combination to be preferred over either of the individual strategies.

---

[3] The monthly results presented in these exhibits bear a strong resemblance to actual quarterly results of two well-known enhanced index managers.

Exhibit 4: Rolling 5-Year Correlation of Excess Returns Between Synthetic Strategy and Stock-Based Strategy

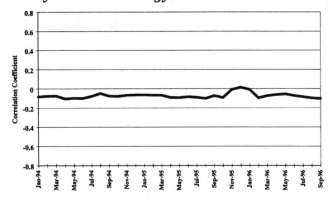

Exhibit 5: Rolling 5-Year Alpha

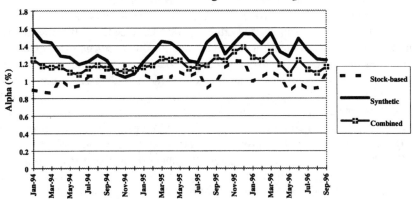

Exhibit 6: Rolling 5-Year Tracking Error

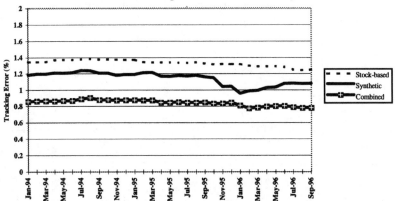

Exhibit 7: Rolling 5-Year Information Ratio

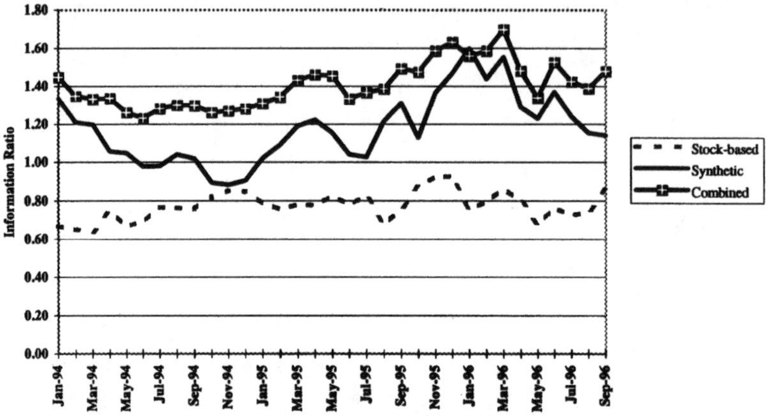

The analysis illustrates a point that even staunch proponents of active management may wish to consider. For years plan sponsors have been combining various active management styles (value, growth, large cap, small cap) effectively searching for the diversification of alphas (and absolute returns to an extent) that style mixes purportedly achieve. Against this backdrop, the same sponsors have had to cope with style drift as managers seek value outside their respective disciplines. As a result, plan sponsors may feel that the types of results illustrated in the exhibits above have proven elusive.

A well specified and executed enhanced index strategy may bring to the table more than just a higher information ratio than the average traditional active manager has achieved. In principle, at least, enhanced indexing should also attain a more stable adherence to a style or methodology as a result of the required emphasis on risk control. If true, it could be that, although enhanced indexing surely involves a degree of active management, as a discipline it may be better suited to obtaining efficient combinations of managers than has been the case with traditional active management. Enhanced indexing, while it may be an oxymoron for some, may be optimal for others.

Chapter 5

The Active versus Passive Debate: Perspectives of an Active Quant

Robert C. Jones, CFA
Managing Director
Goldman Sachs Asset Management

INTRODUCTION

Active or passive? Passive or active? The debate rages on. Proponents of indexing cite theory and mountains of evidence: the average active manager has simply not outperformed the S&P 500 on a consistent basis. Still the vast majority of equity assets are managed actively: investors seem to believe that they, or at least their chosen agents, can earn risk-adjusted excess returns. This chapter examines both sides of the issue. We use behavioral analysis and empirical evidence to argue that the theoretical basis for indexing is weak, yet the performance of active managers is weaker still. We end up with something of a paradox: investor behavior argues against *both* market efficiency *and* active management. Our solution to this dilemma is to follow an objective, disciplined and risk-controlled approach to active management.

We begin by presenting the case for passive investing, which is based on both financial theory and the historical performance of active managers. We then lay out the case against efficient markets (and, by implication, passive investing), using theoretical, behavioral and empirical arguments. We also discuss the failure of active managers to add value, and try to reconcile this failure with the case against market efficiency. This leads to some natural implications for ways to improve the active management process in the face of known behavioral tendencies and market inefficiencies. The chapter ends with a summary and some concluding remarks.

This chapter benefited from insightful comments from (and discussions with) Cliff Asness, Peter Bernstein, Kent Clark, Bob Krail, John Liew, and Diane Misra, among others. I would also like to thank Kent Clark, Jacques Friedman, Vinti Khanna, and Jason Segal for supplying much of the statistical analysis contained herein.

THE CASE FOR INDEXING

The case for indexing is based on both theory and empirical evidence. First we will discuss theory.

The Theoretical Case

The theoretical case for indexing boils down to this: Because markets are efficient, prices immediately, fully and correctly reflect all commonly-known information. Thus, the only way for active managers to add value is to use inside information, which is illegal. Since active managers can't beat the market, yet they charge fees and incur transactions costs, investors are better served by passive management (i.e., indexing). Below we outline the formal theory behind indexing in a bit more detail.

Assume the following: (1) investors are perfectly rationale (i.e., they develop expectations using Bayesian strategies), utility-maximizing agents with a shared set of homogeneous expectations; and (2) markets are "frictionless," meaning primarily that taxes and trading costs are inconsequential. In such a world, prices and expected returns will remain stable until new value-relevant information reaches the market, at which point investors will immediately alter their expectations to reflect this information, and prices will adjust accordingly. Thus, prices will only change in response to new, *unexpected* information. Since the arrival of unexpected information is essentially random, prices will follow a random walk, and returns will be normally distributed (i.e., the entire return distribution can be described by its mean and its standard deviation).

More than 40 years ago, Harry Markowitz[1] described how rational investors should create portfolios, given a set of return expectations, volatilities, and cross correlations. Markowitz showed that we can calculate an expected return and volatility measure for every possible portfolio, given the expected returns, volatilities, and cross correlations of the component stocks. His genius was in seeing that a stock's risk should be evaluated not in isolation, but in terms of its contribution to the risk of a diversified portfolio. From this, he derived the concept of an efficient frontier, which is depicted graphically in Exhibit 1. The efficient frontier is the set of portfolios that has the highest expected return at each level of risk — or, conversely, the lowest risk at each level of expected return. If investors are rational utility maximizers, and utility is defined in terms of risk and return, then all investors will hold portfolios along the efficient frontier depicted in Exhibit 1.

In the 1960s, Sharpe[2] and Lintner,[3] extended the original work of Markowitz and developed the Capital Asset Pricing Model (CAPM). If we assume

---

[1] Harry Markowitz, "Portfolio Selection," *Journal of Finance* (March 1952), pp. 77-91.

[2] William F. Sharpe, "Capital Asset Prices: A Theory of Market Equilibrium Under Conditions of Risk," *Journal of Finance* (September 1964), pp. 425-442.

[3] John Lintner, "The Valuation of Risk Assets and the Selection of Risky Investments in Stock Portfolios and Capital Bedgets," *Review of Economics and Statistics* (February 1965), pp. 13-37.

a risk-free asset (R_f), and costless borrowing and lending, then some combination of R_f and the tangency efficient portfolio (or TEP,[4] see Exhibit 2) will offer a better risk/reward trade-off, at every level of risk, than other points on the Markowitz efficient frontier. The straight line from R_f through TEP will therefore define a new efficient frontier, and all rational investors will hold some portfolio on that line (i.e., some combination of R_f and TEP). Since there is only one risky portfolio (namely, TEP) that is held by all rational investors, that portfolio must be "the market." Therefore, all rational investors will hold some combination of R_f and the market. This, in a nutshell, is the theoretical case for indexing.

Exhibit 1: The Markowitz Efficient Frontier

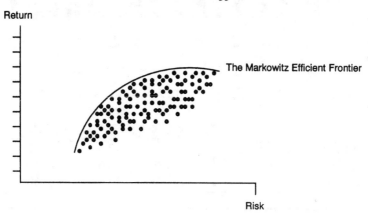

Exhibit 2: The CAPM Efficient Frontier

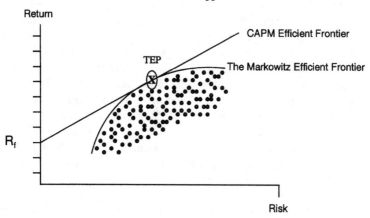

[4] The TEP concept was originally presented in James Tobin, "Liquidity Preference as Behavior Towards Risk," *Review of Economic Studies* (February 1958), pp. 65-86.

Exhibit 3: Median Large-Cap Fund versus the S&P 500 Index

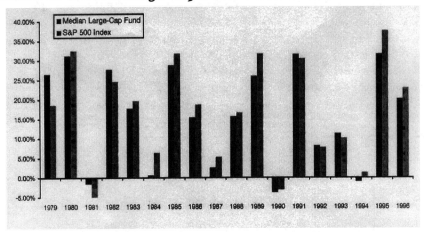

Exhibit 4: Actively Managed Mutual Funds versus the S&P 500 Index

	1979-1984	1985-1990	1991-1996	1979-1996
Percent of Funds that Outperformed	54.7%	12.3%	31.3%	30.9%
Median Fund Return	16.0%	13.6%	16.4%	15.4%
S&P 500 Return	15.4%	16.4%	17.6%	16.4%

The Empirical Evidence

Active managers themselves provide perhaps the most persuasive case for passive investing. Dozens of studies[5] have examined the performance of mutual funds and other professionally-managed assets, and virtually all of them have concluded that, on average, active managers underperform passive benchmarks. Exhibit 3 shows annual returns, from 1979 through 1996, for the median fund in the Lipper large-cap fund universe[6] and for the S&P 500 Index. The median active fund underperformed the passive index in 12 out of 18 years. Exhibit 4 show the percentage of funds that outperformed the S&P 500 over various time periods. Note that these returns are net of fees and expenses, but before taxes. Comparing after-tax returns would make the case for indexing even more compelling.[7] The bottom line is that, over most periods, the majority of mutual fund investors would have been better off investing in an S&P 500 Index fund.

---

[5] For a particularly thorough example, see Burton G. Malkiel, "Returns from Investing in Equity Mutual Funds, 1971 to 1991," *Journal of Finance* (June 1995), pp. 549-572.

[6] These include all funds in the Lipper "Growth" and "Growth and Income" categories.

[7] Since index funds follow a buy-and-hold strategy, realized capital gains are minimal compared to those of actively managed funds.

THE CASE AGAINST INDEXING

The case against indexing is based on (1) theoretical arguments; (2) empirical arguments; and, (3) behavioral arguments. We'll begin with theory.

Theoretical Arguments

The efficient market hypothesis (EMH) is based on a set of simplifying and unrealistic assumptions. Below we discuss how relaxing two of these assumption would impact the case for passive investing.

Assumptions

No Taxes or Trading Costs Assumption In the real world, taxes and trading costs are significant and variable, both through time and across investors. If one group of investors (e.g., pension funds) pays no taxes, while another group of investors (e.g., individuals) pays high taxes, they will have very different optimal portfolios. Individuals will avoid high-yielding stocks, and will delay realizing capital gains. Because of tax consequences, they may not trade even if new information produces a reasonably large change in (pretax) expected returns. Similarly, if one group of investors (e.g., dealers) has lower transactions costs, while another group (e.g., investors) has higher costs, they will respond differently to a small change in value-relevant information. If the change in expected return exceeds the dealers' trading costs, but is less than the investors' trading costs, then the former will trade while the latter will not. Note that all of the above observations will be true even if all four groups (i.e., pension funds, individuals, dealers, and investors) share the same expectations for nominal pre-tax risks and returns. Because of their varying circumstances, they will hold different optimal portfolios even if they share the same expectations. Thus, there is no single "market" portfolio that is optimal for all investors.

Of course passive investing may still be appropriate, even if there is no single optimal portfolio. Perhaps there is enough similarity among members of different groups, that each group could have its own optimal index, and all members of the group could passively hold the "group-optimal" portfolio. Ignoring the fact that no one has developed a set of indices targeted at different investor groups,[8] we believe that, in most cases, individual circumstances are so different that such a solution is impractical. The most obvious exception is tax-exempt pension funds, which is also the investor group that has been most receptive to passive investing.[9]

Homogenous Expectations Assumption In the EMH world, risk is defined by the uncertainty of events. But while events may be uncertain, *probabilities* are assumed to be known and agreed on by all investors. Thus, all investors share the same expectations for risk and return. In such a world, almost by tautology, prices

---

[8] We will return later to the inability of the EMH to describe how investors actually invest and behave.

[9] Of course, behaviorists would argue that pension funds embrace indexing to avoid the pain of "regret" that comes form picking a manager who underperforms the index.

will quickly and accurately reflect investors' shared expectations. But what if investors don't agree on the basic probabilities? What if investors who share the same information, but different models of how the world works, arrive at very different probabilities for the same outcome?

In the real world, heterogeneity rules. For example, although they share essentially the same information, different economic schools have radically different assessments for the likelihood that inflation will increase over the coming year. Keynesians see strong growth and low unemployment as signs that inflation is likely to increase. Monetarists and supply-siders see increasing production and stable money supply (i.e., more goods chased by the same number of dollars) as signs that inflation will remain stable or decline. Similarly, despite years of debate and numerous empirical studies (i.e., shared information), financial economists still can't agree on whether the market is efficient or not. Who is right? Nobody. All theories are imperfect models of reality that are wrong in ways that are both unknown and unknowable. The more important question is: who is "less wrong?" Those will be the investors whose forecasts will prove most accurate and profitable.

Even in a world of heterogeneous expectations, however, the "consensus" view can, on average, be more correct (or less wrong) than the various views of most investors. In such a world, passive investing (or accepting the consensus) may still be the best solution for *most* investors. But this does not mean that passive investing is optimal for *all* investors. Investors with a comparative advantage — e.g., better technology, better information, better analytic capabilities, and/or a better model of how the world works — should be able to outperform a passive benchmark. Of course, these investors need to be pretty darned sure that their information, technology, analysis, and/or models are actually better. If not, they will underperform the benchmark. This is the risk in active management.

Efficient Markets: A Catch-22?[10]

Our final theoretical argument against passive investing concerns the "catch-22 of market efficiency." In a perfectly efficient market, prices always equal fair values. There will be no profit opportunities from estimating fair values, and hence no incentive to gather and evaluate information. But if no one bothers to gather and evaluate information, how will prices come to reflect fair values? Trading will cease and markets will collapse. Therefore, there must be sufficient profit opportunities (i.e., market inefficiencies), net of trading costs, to encourage market participants to gather information and estimate fair values. Efficiency, then, is a relative characteristic of markets: markets can be more efficient or less efficient, but perfect efficiency is an unattainable and undesirable goal.

In quasi-efficient markets, the return to gathering and evaluating information can be thought of as an economic rent that is proportional to the risks and marginal costs involved. But who pays the rent? If all investors are passive and share

---

[10] The gist of this argument was originally presented in Sanford Grossman and Joseph Stiglitz, "On the Impossibility of Informationally Efficient Markets," *American Economic Review* (1980), pp. 393-408.

homogenous expectations, then the information gatherers will have no one to trade with, and markets will again collapse. Thus, for markets to exist at all, we need a sufficiently large group of active managers, with enough variation in expectations and information, to ensure continued trading activity. Now who pays the rent? Active managers whose information gathering and processing skills are below average.[11] Of course, if these managers realized their skills were sub-par, they would become passive investors. Thus, for unskilled managers to remain in the game, either: (1) they must be naive enough to think that their sub-par results are actually above average; or, more likely, (2) there is enough random noise in the system that many unskilled managers earn above-average returns purely by chance, but they attribute their good fortune to skill. Either condition violates the assumption of investor rationality — which we will discuss in more detail in a later section.

Empirical Arguments

Many researchers have offered empirical results that seem to contradict market efficiency, damaging the case for passive investing. We think the most persuasive and influential results are related to: (1) the failure of CAPM beta to explain returns; (2) the "excess" volatility in market prices; and, (3) a variety of "anomalies" whereby publicly-available information can apparently be used to generate risk-adjusted excess returns.

Beta and Returns

From the Black, Jensen and Scholes[12] study in 1972 through the oft-cited Fama and French[13] study in 1992, researchers have consistently been unable to demonstrate a significant positive relationship between CAPM beta and realized stock returns. Since sensitivity to market movements (or beta) is the sole determinant of expected stock returns in the CAPM world, this failure means either (1) the market is inefficient, in the sense that expected returns consistently differ from realized returns; or (2) the market is efficient, but investors don't base their expectations on the CAPM (or, perhaps, that their "true" beta estimates are not equal to the historical beta estimates used in these studies). Since both explanations are consistent with the evidence, we can't reach a final conclusion. This so-called "joint hypothesis" problem pervades all tests of asset-pricing models and market efficiency. Because all market efficiency tests assume an implicit asset-pricing model, we can *never* determine if an apparent inefficiency is real, or the result of a mis-specified model. Still, at the very least, the failure of CAPM beta to explain returns implies that no *single* index is optimal for all investors.

---

[11] Since prices will reflect the opinions of both skilled and unskilled managers, passive investors will also pay *some* of the rent, but less than that paid by unskilled managers.

[12] See Fischer Black, Michael C. Jenson, and Myron Scholes, "The Capital Asset Pricing Model: Some Empirical Tests," in M. Jenson (ed.), *Studies in the Theory of Capital Markets* (1972).

[13] Eugene F. Fama and Kenneth R. French, "The Cross-Section of Expected Stock Returns," *Journal of Finance* (June 1992), pp. 427-466.

Excess Volatility

If prices "fully reflect all available information," then they will only respond to new information. Furthermore, price volatility should be roughly similar to the volatility in underlying fundamentals (i.e., interest rates and cash flows). Many studies have compared stock price volatility to the volatility of pricing fundamentals.[14] Most conclude that prices are just too volatile to be justified by the less volatile changes in interest rates and cash flows. Other studies have attempted to tie major price moves to the arrival of new information, usually concluding that many large price swings occur in an information vacuum. Essentially, price moves are just too large, and too capricious, to be consistent with a market where prices fully reflect all available information. Instead, it seems that prices often change simply because investors reassess their interpretation of existing information. Such behavior, although inconsistent with perfect market efficiency, is perfectly consistent with the notion of a quasi-efficient market, where investors have heterogeneous, quasi-rational expectations, and earn economic rents from information gathering and analysis.

Anomalies

The anomaly literature consists of dozens (or even hundreds) of studies showing how investors can apparently earn positive risk-adjusted returns using publicly-available information. An anomaly is a regular and predictable return pattern that is widely known, yet continues to exist. Examples include: the "January effect;" the "turn-of-the-month effect;" the "size effect;" the "low-P/E effect;" "post earnings announcement drift;" and a host of others. Although the joint hypothesis problem makes it impossible to refute market efficiency based solely on anomalies — EMH proponents will argue that these variables are surrogates for unknown risk factors, or that the excess returns disappear after trading costs — we believe it is a bit of a stretch to derive a risk story that can explain all these varied relationships. As we will explain in the next section, however, most anomalies are perfectly consistent with the known cognitive errors that influence human decisions.

Exhibit 5 shows the results of some of our tests on global anomalies. In each test, we regressed monthly stock returns against beginning-of-month factor values (properly lagged, where necessary) and calculated the average monthly regression coefficient and t-statistic for the series.[15] We ran these tests on two separate groups: (1) stocks in the Russell 1000 Index (large-cap domestic stocks); and (2) stocks in the MSCI-EAFE Index (large-cap stocks from 20 developed markets). All excess returns and factor values were standardized relative to the

---

[14] For example, see Robert Shiller, "Do Stock Prices Move Too Much To Be Justified By Subsequent Changes in Dividends," *American Economic Review* (1981), pp. 421-436.

[15] These are called "Fama-MacBeth regressions" and are described in Eugene F. Fama and James D. MacBeth, "Risk, Return, and Equilibrium: Empirical Tests," *Journal of Political Economy* (May-June 1973), pp. 607-636.

local-market mean (i.e., the coefficients measure stock-selection ability, not country-selection ability). Finally, we also report the number of countries (out of 21 considered) where the local-market regression produces the same sign as the global regression, and the number of countries where the local results are statistically significant.[16]

Because of data limitations, our non-U.S. results only go back to 1989, but they are remarkably similar to the longer-term U.S. results that begin in 1979. In both tests, the coefficients have the same sign and similar levels of statistical significance. Furthermore, the regressions produce the same signs in most countries. The fact that the results are not statistically significant in many countries is primarily due to the lack of observations in those countries — both in time and (for most markets) number of companies. When we test whether the local regression coefficient is significantly different from the global coefficient, we get results that are consistent with the power of the test — i.e., 17 of the 210 comparisons[17] (8.1%) are statistically significant at the 95% confidence level, with only 10 comparisons (4.8%) in the "wrong" tail. Our conclusion is that these anomalies are significant and pervasive, on both the local and global level.

Exhibit 5: Global Anomalies

	U.S. Results (1979-1996)		Int'l. Results (1989-1996)		Number of Countries	
	Coeff.	t-Stat	Coeff.	t-Stat	Same Sign	Significant
Value Factors						
Book/market	0.24	2.96	0.18	3.04	17	4
Earnings/price	0.40	5.46	0.16	2.95	15	4
Sales/price	0.28	4.25	0.10	1.75	12	3
Cash flow/price	0.38	5.28	0.14	3.38	17	4
Momentum Factors						
Estimate revisions	0.56	13.22	0.27	4.99	19	12
Revisions ratio	0.55	14.72	0.29	6.80	20	8
Price momentum	0.61	7.17	0.21	2.44	19	13
Risk Factors						
CAPM beta	−0.17	−1.83	−0.09	−0.88	14	3
Residual risk	−0.42	−4.05	−0.22	−2.38	17	5
Estimate uncertainty	−0.33	−6.39	−0.16	−2.33	18	9

[16] Further details on these tests are available on request.

[17] Comparisons to the global mean are made for 21 countries (including the United States) across 10 variables.

EMH supporters might argue that, because these relationships are so universal, they are probably proxies for unidentified risk factors rather than true market anomalies. If so, they need to identify the risks. We categorized these anomalies/risk factors according to their underlying investment themes: (1) value; (2) momentum; and (3) low-risk. Some would argue that the excess return to value investing is really compensation for accepting distress risk,[18] but they fail to demonstrate that a diversified portfolio of value stocks has above-average risk of actual distress (e.g., bankruptcy, default or dividend omission). The momentum effect is even more difficult to explain using unidentified risks. But perhaps the most perplexing results for EMH-adherents are those for the risk variables. How is it rational for investors to price stocks in such a way that those with the *least* amount of uncertainty have the *highest* expected returns? In the next section we will show how all three results have a perfectly logical and consistent behavioral explanation.

Behavioral Arguments

People aren't perfectly rational. Behavioral psychologists have demonstrated that people frequently make systematic errors in judgment and probability assessment.[19] These departures from perfect rationality are quite common, and can be both large and economically relevant. Although there are a whole litany of systematic cognitive errors — which go by such terms "selective perception," "illusory correlation," "wishful thinking," "availability," "illusion of control," and "hindsight bias" — one of the most pervasive and damaging is "overconfidence." Psychologists have found that people are far more confident in their abilities and predictions than they have any right to be. Studies show that when people are asked to place a 95% confidence band around their predictions, the band includes the actual observation roughly 50% of the time. Similarly, surveys show that most people consider themselves to be better-than-average automobile drivers, and more than 90% of American males describe themselves as having above-average athletic ability. We suspect that most, if not all, active managers believe that they can generate above-average investment returns.

We also believe that overconfidence alone can explain all of the anomalies discussed in the previous section,[20] although other cognitive errors also play a part. If investors make overconfident predictions based on limited information, then they will either overreact and underreact to new information based on whether it supports or contradicts their prior beliefs. That is, if investors are bull-

---

[18] See Eugene F. Fama and Kenneth R. French, "Multifactor Explanations of Asset Pricing Anomalies," *Journal of Finance* (March 1996), pp. 55-84.

[19] For a more complete discussion, see Daniel Kahneman, Paul Slovic, and Amos Tversky, *Judgment Under Uncertainty: Heuristics and Biases* (New York, NY: Cambridge University Press, 1982).

[20] For a developed theory of how overconfidence affects market return patterns, see Kent Daniel, David Hirshleifer, and Avanidhar Subrahmanyam, "A Theory of Overconfidence, Self-Attribution, and Security Market Under- and Over-reactions," University of Michigan Working Paper #9605-26-R (February 1997).

ish on a company's prospects, and new information arrives that seems to support that outlook, they will overreact to the information, become increasingly bullish and overconfident, and push prices to excessive levels. The opposite holds when investors are bearish. This overreaction to confirming information largely explains the value effect. Conversely, if new information challenges the original bullish outlook, it will usually be discounted or "explained away." Investors will underreact to the information, become only marginally less bullish and overconfident, and fail to adjust prices appropriately. This underreaction to conflicting information — along with the related phenomenon of continuing overreaction — largely explains the momentum effect.

But what about the low-risk effect? If there is no prevailing consensus (that is, uncertainty reigns), then there will be both over-confident pessimists and over-confident optimists. In the idealized academic world, the two competing groups will cancel each other out and prices will reflect fair values. In the real world, however, optimists will usually set prices. Why? Because short selling is rare,[21] leaving only pessimistic owners to sell. Furthermore, because of "regret aversion," few owners are likely to be pessimists — i.e., they won't want to admit that their original purchase decision was wrong. Thus, on balance, over-confident optimists will set prices for risky stocks, which means they will usually be over-valued.[22] Therefore, the low-risk effect should be related to the value effect, since they both rely on investor overreaction. Our analysis confirms this: in the United States, the average correlation between the monthly returns to value anomalies and low-risk anomalies has been 0.55.

The final behavioral argument against efficient markets and passive investing is the most obvious: no one actually behaves the way theory says they should. For example: most investors don't use optimizers to build risk-return efficient portfolios; they don't hold some combination of risk-free securities and the optimal risky portfolio; they don't measure a security's risk in terms of its contribution to the risk of a diversified portfolio;[23] and, most important, *they don't forego active management.* If investors don't behave as if the market is efficient, then they must not believe it is. If the market really is efficient, but investors don't believe it, then this itself implies inefficiencies (i.e., irrational behavior). Conversely, if investors are right, then the market must not be efficient. We are back to the catch-22 of efficient markets: if the market really is efficient, then investors

---

[21] Short selling is probably rare because: (1) it is too complicated for most investors; (2) fiduciaries view it as "imprudent" due to the potential for unlimited loss; and/or (3) Americans are naturally optimistic (i.e., shorting is "un-American").

[22] Similarly, lottery tickets are overpriced because of overconfident optimists (i.e., the rest of us can't short lottery tickets).

[23] For example, most investors view individual low price-to-book (or value) stocks as being quite risky, without realizing that a diversified portfolio of value stocks is actually less volatile than a similar portfolio of growth stocks — i.e., even after 45 years, most investors still haven't accepted Markowitz's basic lesson that the only risks that matter are those which can't be diversified away.

must behave as if it is (i.e., become passive); but if investors quit gathering and evaluating information, markets prices will no longer fully reflect available information.

THE VERDICT

This is not a criminal trial in which we must decide the ultimate fate of the EMH. Rather, it is more like a civil trial where we must decide whether the EMH paradigm is now clouding our understanding of the way markets work. Thus, our decision criterion should be the "preponderance of evidence" rather than "beyond a reasonable doubt." We believe that theoretical inconsistencies, empirical evidence, behavioral analysis, and the catch-22 of efficient markets, all point to a world where active management must (and does) exist and *can* add value. In fact, there really is no such thing as purely passive management, since selecting a benchmark is itself an active decision.[24] We believe the important question is not whether the markets are efficient or not, or whether active management can add value, but rather, how do investors form expectations, and how do those expectations impact market prices. Behavioral psychologists have shown that investors, like all people, make systematic errors when forming expectations and making probability assessments.[25] Of course, it is *possible* that a collection of irrational and overconfident investors can still come together to create an efficient market — it just seems a bit unlikely. (The burden should be on EMH proponents to explain exactly how this would occur.) Thus, we believe that active managers who can minimize their behavioral biases, and develop more realistic expectations and probability assessments, can and will add value.

WHY DO ACTIVE MANAGERS UNDERPERFORM?

Active management *can* add value, but on balance it hasn''t. The evidence presented earlier indicates that, over the past 18 years, most active large-cap domestic mutual funds underperformed the S&P 500 Index. Why have most active managers lagged the market? We believe the culprits are: (1) poor investment decisions; (2) poor risk control; and (3) high fees and expense.

---

[24] Even for a nominally "passive" investor, choosing among the S&P 500, the Wilshire 5000, and the MSCI-World Indices (GDP-weighted or cap-weighted) will have a significant impact on terminal wealth.

[25] For a concrete example of how errors in expectations cause return regularities (anomalies), see Rafeal La Porta, "Expectations and the Cross-Section of Stock Returns," *Journal of Finance* (December 1996), pp. 1715-1741. La Porta demonstrates that security analysts' growth expectations are too extreme, and that these extreme forecasts largely explain the value effect. La Porta also shows that a contrarian strategy of buying the slowest expected growers and shorting the fastest expected growers produces 20% annualized hedged returns (before trading costs).

Poor Investment Decisions

Like all people, most active managers are overconfident, form irrational expectations, and make unrealistic probability assessments. They equate good companies with good investments; they overreact to confirming information, pushing valuation levels to extremes; they underreact to information that doesn't fit their prior beliefs; and so forth. Accordingly, most investors would be better off investing in a buy-and-hold passive vehicle than in active funds managed by faulty decision makers — i.e., when it comes to investing, it is better to make no decisions than to make bad ones. Thus, we are left with something of a paradox: behavioral arguments both support and reject active management. We believe that a solution to this dilemma can be found in an objective, disciplined and quantitative approach to active management — which we will discuss in more detail later.

Poor Risk Control

Exhibits 3 and 4 compared the average large-cap mutual fund to the S&P 500 Index. But is this a fair comparison? The average mutual fund may have different risk parameters that make a simple direct comparison inappropriate. We analyzed the performance of the average mutual fund using a three-factor model similar to the one proposed by Fama and French.[26] The dependent variable (ACTIVE) is the average of the return on the Lipper Growth and the Lipper Growth and Income Indices, less the return on the S&P 500.[27] The independent variables are: (1) MARKET, which equals the difference between the S&P 500 return and the 90-day Treasury rate; (2) VALUE, which equals the difference between the return on the Russell 3000 Value Index and the Russell 3000 Growth Index; and (3) SIZE, which equals the difference between the return on the Russell 1000 Index (large-cap stocks) and the Russell 2000 Index (small-cap stocks). The regression was run over 219 months from January 1979 through March 1997, with the results shown in equation (1) (t-statistics in parentheses):

$$\text{ACTIVE} = -0.007 - 0.083 \times \text{MARKET} - 0.071 \times \text{VALUE} - 0.244 \times \text{SIZE} \quad (1)$$
$$(-0.192)\ (-8.771) (-3.628) (-17.380)$$

Thus, relative to the S&P 500, the average large-cap mutual fund makes statistically significant bets against the market, against value, and against size. Together, these bets explain 63% of the variation in the average mutual fund's active returns (i.e., the adjusted r-squared of the regression is 0.63). Furthermore, after controlling for risk (i.e., net of these bets), the average active return is indistinguishable from zero (−0.7 basis points). Thus, since the Lipper Index returns

---

[26] See Eugene F. Fama and Kenneth R. French, "Multifactor Explanations of Asset Pricing Anomalies," *Journal of Finance* (March 1996), pp. 55-84.

[27] Using the Lipper Indices eliminates survivorship bias, since they are defined as the average return on the largest 30 funds in each category at that time. Tests using the median fund (not shown) produced very similar results.

are net of fees and expenses, the average mutual funds covers its costs on a risk-adjusted basis.

Although this is a more intellectually-satisfying conclusion, we hardly think it provides a ringing endorsement for actively-managed funds. Why? Because we believe that all three "bets" reflect poor risk control, rather than well-conceived and intentional decisions. Of the three "bets," only that against SIZE has any sort of empirical or theoretical justification — and that is tenuous at best.[28] Over any extended period, stocks should and usually do outperform cash, so it would be silly for active *equity* managers to consistently bet against the MARKET. Instead, we believe this "bet" reflects the tendency of active mutual-fund managers to hold cash for reasons unrelated to risk management or market timing — e.g., to meet redemptions, fund future purchases, or avoid accidental leverage (outspending available cash). Similarly, we believe the bet against SIZE results from the common practice of holding equally-weighted positions — thereby giving proportionately more weight to smaller stocks relative to a cap-weighted index — rather than a conscious decision to exploit the small-cap effect. Finally, the bet against VALUE is empirically misguided, but is easily explained by overreaction and the other cognitive errors discussed earlier.

High Fees and Expenses

All mutual fund returns, including those in the Lipper Indices, are net of fees and expenses. Thus, high fees and expenses could also account for the average manager's underperformance. The average large-cap mutual fund has an expense ratio of approximately 100 basis points. To this we add 45 basis points, reflecting the average fund's annual turnover (roughly 90%) and the average round-trip trading costs on large-cap stocks (estimated at 50 basis points). Therefore, we estimate that the average mutual fund needs to outperform the S&P 500 Index by roughly 145 basis points before fees and expenses just to break even. In the last section we saw that the average mutual fund had a risk-adjusted net excess return of −8.4 basis points per year (−0.7 times 12) after statistically eliminating "bets" against the market, value, and size. This means that, before fees and expenses, the average active manager must have some real stock selection skill, amounting to approximately 135-140 basis points per year. Hence, the $64,000 question: How can investors access these skills without also being trapped by the pitfalls of active management?

QUANTITATIVE SOLUTIONS

This section describes how active managers can use quantitative techniques to maximize the value of their insights and minimize potential underperformance.

---

[28] We believe the so-called "size effect" has little theoretical basis, is extremely inconsistent through time, and is generally overrated.

Specifically we will discuss (1) risk control; (2) process discipline; and, (3) portable alpha strategies.[29] Essentially our advice is to "be the House" — e.g., only invest when the odds are in your favor, and makes lots of small, diversified bets.

Risk Control

Perhaps the easiest way for active managers to improve their relative comparisons to the S&P 500 (or any relevant benchmark) is to eliminate any misguided and/or unintentional bets. Exhibit 6 is from a study by RogersCasey[30] that compares the relative performance of different types of institutional managers in their PIPER database. Managers are first placed into one of three style categories: (1) large-cap value; (2) large-cap growth; and (3) risk-controlled (or "enhanced index"). The study then compares the 5-year (June 1991 through June 1996) average excess returns (versus the S&P 500) and t-statistics for managers at various percentile breakpoints within their style categories. Note that at the higher percentiles, value and growth managers outperformed risk-controlled managers, but the volatility of their excess returns were higher as well. Thus, except for the very best growth managers, t-tests find it hard to reject the hypothesis that these excess returns are due to luck, and that the true excess returns are zero. Conversely, risk-controlled managers have lower excess returns at the higher percentiles, but also much lower volatility. The t-tests indicate that these risk-controlled managers very probably have true excess returns that exceed zero. In fact, even at the median it would be reasonable to conclude that risk-controlled managers can add value (the one-tailed p-value is 95.4%).

Exhibit 6: Comparisons of Active Management Styles (June 1991 - June 1996)

Percentile	Large-Cap Growth		Large-Cap Value		Risk-Controlled	
	Excess Return	t-Statistic	Excess Return	t-Statistic	Excess Return	t-Statistic
95th	5.8%	2.01	3.5%	1.30	1.7%	3.78
75th	3.9%	0.74	0.9%	0.49	1.4%	3.02
50th	0.4%	0.16	−0.2%	−0.11	0.8%	1.72
25th	−1.2%	−0.51	−1.6%	−0.98	0.3%	0.27
5th	−3.4%	−1.36	−4.0%	−2.55	−0.3%	−0.13

Source: Drew D. DeMakis, "Active Management Effectiveness," RogersCasey, October, 1996.

---

[29] For an excellent tutorial on how to improve the active management with quantitative techniques, see Richard C. Grinold and Ronald N. Kahn, *Active Portfolio Management* (Chicago, IL: Richard D. Irwin Inc., 1995).

[30] Drew D. DeMakis, "Active Management Effectiveness," RogersCasey, October, 1996.

How exactly should active managers control risk? We suggest following the advise offered by Harry Markowitz back in 1952: use optimization technology to find the portfolio with the least amount of risk for a given level of expected return. Expected returns should reflect the investor's private insights, but should be statistically defensible (see the next section). Risks and covariances should be based on a relevant risk model that seems intellectually appealing (e.g., a historical covariance matrix, a factor model, or an industry- and style-based model). Risk can be defined as either total risk (volatility), downside risk, active risk (tracking error), or some other measure that best reflects the portfolio's objectives. In order to avoid over-trading to achieve small improvements in expected return, the optimization algorithm should explicitly include trading costs in its objective function.

Finally, when first using optimization technology, it is important to "play around" with the various inputs until the optimizer produces a portfolio that fits the manager's style and intuition. Some educational assistance is usually needed to help most active managers understand why optimizers pick some stocks over others, but once they understand the process, it is easier to accept the result. Conversely, understanding the process also helps managers learn how to massage the input parameters to reach a more acceptable portfolio. Even if the ultimate portfolio is not too different from what it would have been without an optimizer, this exercise will at least help managers understand the tradeoffs involved.

Process Discipline

If return regularities (anomalies) are caused by irrational investor behavior, over-confidence, and poor probability assessments, then a second "fix" for active managers is to minimize these cognitive errors by following a well-conceived and disciplined investment process. Managers should design stock-selection systems that reflect their investment philosophies, *and then test those systems on historical data to determine their statistical probability of success.* If a preferred system has no statistical correlation with stock returns, the manager should consider whether s/he has unfounded confidence in the system. We believe the best systems will be those that explicitly attempt to exploit the return regularities that arise from the cognitive shortcomings of other investors. In particular, managers should look for stocks that sell at reasonable valuations, have strong momentum, and below-average risk.

Similarly, if the manager's process is based on private forecasts, the manager needs to consider whether these forecasts are realistic. Overconfidence in extreme forecasts is the bane of active management. All active managers should maintain a history of their prior forecasts to determine their statistical accuracy, and to derive appropriate confidence intervals for future forecasts. This can prove to be a valuable lesson in humility that can minimize overconfidence in future decisions — and the resultant underperformance that often comes with it.

Finally, once a manager has designed a strategy that seems sound and has some statistical validity, s/he should stick with it even when things seem uncomfortable. Situations that seem risky in isolation often disappear in a diversified portfolio. If the manager still decides to override the system, it is particularly important to maintain a record of that decision and its ultimate resolution. Again, this exercise in humility can only improve the investment process: If statistics show that the history of overrides produces random results or worse, this will help managers avoid the temptation in the future.

Portable Alpha Strategies

Most of the dismal comparisons for active managers are for large-cap domestic managers versus the S&P 500 Index. Active managers have a much better record in the small-cap and international markets. For example, although only 23% of Lipper growth funds beat the S&P 500 for the 10-year period ending in May 1997, 79% of international funds beat the MSCI-EAFE Index (unhedged), and 77% of small-cap funds outperformed the Russell 2000 Index. Given the impossibility of perfectly efficient markets (i.e., the catch-22 discussed earlier), efficiency is a *relative* term rather than an absolute one. In fact, we can define a relatively efficient market as one where few active managers outperform, and where it requires a significant competitive advantage (skill) to add value. Conversely, a relatively inefficient market is one where more active managers add value, and less skill is required. A viable active strategy, then, is to seek alpha in less-efficient markets (using a risk-controlled and disciplined process) and use derivatives to get exposure to more-efficient ones.

For example, if a pension fund wants to get $100 million exposure to the highly-efficient large-cap domestic market, it could hire a superior small-cap manager, then short $100 million of Russell 2000 futures while simultaneously going long $100 million of S&P 500 futures. Assuming the futures are fairly priced, the net return on this position would be the S&P 500 return plus the small-cap manager's alpha relative to the Russell 2000. Similarly, the fund could hire a market-neutral (or long/short) manager and gain exposure to the large-cap market with S&P 500 futures. Here the fund would earn the S&P 500 return plus the return spread between the market-neutral manager's long and short portfolios. If futures don't exist (for example, if the active manager has an EAFE benchmark), the pension could transfer market exposures using the OTC swap market (i.e., swap EAFE returns for S&P 500 returns). Although a swap strategy will cost more than a futures strategy (reflecting the swap dealer's higher hedging costs in the cash market), the higher alpha should more than compensate for the higher cost. Thus, with portable alpha strategies, investors can separate the manager-selection decision from the market-selection decision — allowing them to pursue alpha in less-efficient markets, while maintaining their strategic exposure to more-efficient ones.

What About the Rest of Us?

Alpha transfer strategies work fine for large pension funds, but what about mutual fund investors? They are unlikely to be able to engage in the sophisticated types of futures and swaps transactions that such strategies require. Are retail investors doomed to a life without alpha? For mutual fund investors in the relatively efficient large-cap domestic market, an index fund may be the best solution — especially after considering the tax consequences of active management.[31] The alternative is to look for funds that: (1) stay fully invested; (2) don't make any bad bets against value or size;[32] (3) have modest fees and expenses; and, (4) follow a sound, disciplined, and *repeatable* investment process.

Unfortunately, the popular mutual fund rating services usually evaluate funds based on a combination of total return and return volatility, making it difficult to uncover effective managers. Our tests indicate that if investors use equation (1) to evaluate managers, they can get a better sense for both the fund's risks and its future ability to add value. That is, the coefficients on MARKET, VALUE, and SIZE will help define the manager's investment style so that investors can determine if they want the implied exposures. In addition, the alpha (or intercept) in equation (1) can tell investors whether the manager has added value above and beyond the fund's normal style exposures. Furthermore, as compared to looking only at prior excess returns, alpha is more predictive of future performance. For example, when we rank funds by their alphas from 1987 to 1991, and by their alphas from 1992 to 1996, the correlation between the two rankings is 0.16 (t-statistic = 2.72); the equivalent correlation using excess returns is −0.02 (−0.27). We think traditional pension fund consultants could provide a valuable service to retail investors by performing this type of risk-adjusted analysis on mutual funds.[33]

CONCLUSION

The efficient market hypothesis (EMH) and the capital asset pricing model (CAPM) fail miserably as descriptive theories, but guess what? They're pretty good proscriptive theories. They may do a lousy job of describing how investors and markets actually behave, but they are pretty good paradigms for how investors *should* behave. Most investors don't evaluate a security's risk in terms of its contribution to the risk of a diversified portfolio, but they *should*. They don't forego active management when they have no competitive advantage, but they *should*. They don't adjust their risk-reward posture by borrowing or lending against the optimal risky portfolio, but they *should*. They don't build portfolios

---

[31] A little-discussed tax disadvantage of index funds is their large unrealized gains. New (taxable) investors in an index fund will have to pay taxes on those gains, even though they didn't experience them, if the fund is ever forced to liquidate shares — as might happen, for instance, if there are net liquidations during a market correction.

[32] Investors who want to bet against the market, size, or value can do so directly using the appropriate vehicle.

[33] A good rating service would also evaluate the fund's current portfolio to detect style drift, and would also try to determine if the manager follows a sound, disciplined and repeatable investment process. Fortunately, consultants are already adept at such analysis from their work with institutional portfolios.

using optimizers that balance expected returns against portfolio risk, but they *should*. And finally, they don't form expectations using rational Bayesian decision rules, but they definitely *should*. (Unfortunately, they *shouldn't* have to pay taxes and transactions costs, but they most certainly do.)

Nonetheless, even though most investors *should* behave as proscribed by the EMH and the CAPM, we're glad they don't. If it weren't for the foibles and follies of active managers, the market would be even harder to beat than it already is. If it weren't for investor overconfidence and other cognitive errors, return regularities would disappear, and disciplined quantitative techniques would lose their competitive advantage. In short, if all investors were perfectly rational and shared homogenous expectations (and there were no taxes or transactions costs), the world would be a terribly boring place indeed: markets would be perfectly efficient; trading would cease; and most of the financial community would be unemployed. Although this might please many on Main Street, those of us on Wall Street should pray each day that the world continues to need active managers.

Chapter 6

Factor-Based Approach to Equity Portfolio Management

Frank J. Fabozzi, Ph.D., CFA
Adjunct Professor of Finance
School of Management
Yale University

INTRODUCTION

The theory of asset pricing in terms of factors is well developed in the academic literature and is explained in every textbook on investment management. In this chapter, we will show how factor models can be used to construct equity portfolios and control portfolio risk

TYPES OF FACTOR MODELS

There are three types of factor models being used today to manage equity portfolios: statistical factor models, macroeconomic factor models, and fundamental factor models.[1] We describe these three factor models below.

Statistical Factor Models

In a *statistical factor model,* historical and cross-sectional data on stock returns are tossed into a statistical model. The statistical model used is *principal components analysis* which is a special case of a statistical technique called *factor analysis.* The goal of the statistical model is to best explain the observed stock returns with "factors" that are linear return combinations and uncorrelated with each other.

For example, suppose that monthly returns for 1,500 companies for ten years are computed. The goal of principal components analysis is to produce "factors" that best explain the observed stock returns. Let's suppose that there are six "factors" that do this. These "factors" are statistical artifacts. The objective in a

---

[1] Gregory Connor, "The Three Types of Factor Models: A Comparison of Their Explanatory Power," *Financial Analysts Journal* (May-June 1995), pp. 42-57.

I wish to thank Bruce Jacobs and Kenneth Levy of Jacobs Levy for their helpful comments on an earlier draft of this chapter.

statistical factor model then becomes to determine the economic meaning of each of these statistically derived factors.

Because of the problem of interpretation, it is difficult to use the factors from a statistical factor model for valuation and risk control. Instead, practitioners prefer the two other models described below, which allow them to prespecify meaningful factors, and thus produce a more intuitive model.

Macroeconomic Factor Models

In a *macroeconomic factor model*, the inputs to the model are historical stock returns and observable macroeconomic variables. That is, the raw descriptors are macroeconomic variables. The goal is to determine which macroeconomic variables are pervasive in explaining historical stock returns. Those variables that are pervasive in explaining the returns are then the factors and included in the model. The responsiveness of a stock to these factors is estimated using historical time series data.

Two examples of proprietary macroeconomic factor models are the Burmeister, Ibbotson, Roll, and Ross (BIRR) model[2] and the Salomon Brothers model.[3] Salomon Brothers refers to its model as the "Risk Attribute Model" or RAM. A RAM is built for the United States and other countries

In the BIRR model, there are five macroeconomic factors that reflect unanticipated changes in the following macroeconomic variables:

- Investor confidence (confidence risk)
- Interest rates (time horizon risk)
- Inflation (inflation risk)
- Real business activity (business cycle risk)
- A market index (market timing risk)

Exhibit 1 explains each of these macroeconomic factor risks

In the U.S. version of the Salomon Brothers RAM model, the following six macroeconomic factors have been found to best describe the financial environment and are therefore the factors used:

- change in expected long-run economic growth
- short-run business cycle risk
- long-term bond yield changes
- short-term Treasury bill changes
- inflation shock
- dollar changes versus trading partner currencies

---

[2] Edwin Burmeister, Roger Ibbotson, Richard Roll, and Stephen A. Ross, "Using Macroeconomic Factors to Control Portfolio Risk," unpublished paper. The information used in this chapter regarding the BIRR model is obtained from various pages of the BIRR website (*www.birr.com*).

[3] This model is described in Eric H. Sorensen, Joseph J. Mezrich, and Chee Thum, *The Salomon Brothers U.S. Risk Attribute Model*, *Salomon Brothers*, Quantitative Strategy, October 1989, and Joseph J. Mezrich, Mark O'Donnell, and Vele Samak, *U.S. RAM Model: Model Update*, Salomon Brothers, Equity Portfolio Analysis, April 8, 1997.

Exhibit 1: Macroeconomic Factor Risks in the BIRR Factor Model

Confidence Risk

Confidence Risk exposure reflects a stock's sensitivity to unexpected changes in investor confidence. Investors always demand a higher return for making relatively riskier investments. When their confidence is high, they are willing to accept a smaller reward than when their confidence is low. Most assets have a positive exposure to Confidence Risk. An unexpected increase in investor confidence will put more investors in the market for these stocks, increasing their price and producing a positive return for those who already held them. Similarly, a drop in investor confidence leads to a drop in the value of these investments. Some stocks have a negative exposure to the Confidence Risk factor, however, suggesting that investors tend to treat them as "safe haven" when their confidence is shaken.

Time Horizon Risk

Time Horizon Risk exposure reflects a stock's sensitivity to unexpected changes in investors' willingness to invest for the long term. An increase in time horizon tends to benefit growth stocks, while a decrease tends to benefit income stocks. Exposures can be positive or negative, but growth stocks as a rule have a higher (more positive) exposure than income stocks.

Inflation Risk

Inflation Risk exposure reflects a stock's sensitivity to unexpected changes in the inflation rate. Unexpected increases in the inflation rate put a downward pressure on stock prices, so most stocks have a negative exposure to Inflation Risk. Consumer demand for luxuries declines when real income is eroded by inflation. Thus, retailer, eating places, hotels, resorts, and other "luxuries" are harmed by inflation, and their stocks therefore tend to be more sensitive to inflation surprises and, as a result, have a more negative exposure to Inflation Risk. Conversely, providers of necessary goods and services (agricultural products, tire and rubber goods, etc.) are relatively less harmed by inflation surprises, and their stocks have a smaller (less negative) exposure. A few stocks attract investors in times of inflation surprise and have a positive Inflation Risk exposure.

Market Timing Risk

Market Timing Risk exposure reflects a stock's sensitivity to moves in the stock market as a whole that cannot be attributed to the other factors. Sensitivity to this factor provides information similar to that of the CAPM Beta about how a stock tends to respond to changes in the broad market. It differs in that the Market Timing factor reflects only those surprises that are not explained by the other four factors.

Business Cycle Risk

Business Cycle Risk exposure reflects a stock's sensitivity to unexpected changes in the growth rate of business activity. Stocks of companies such as retail stores that do well in times of economic growth have a higher exposure to Business Cycle Risk than those that are less affected by the business cycle, such as utilities or government contractors. Stocks can have a negative exposure to this factor if investors tend to shift their funds toward those stocks when news about the growth rate for the economy is not good.

Source: Reproduced from pages of the BIRR website (*www.birr.com*).

Exhibit 2: Macroeconomic Factors in the Salomon Brothers U.S. Risk Attribute Model

Economic Growth[a]
Monthly change in industrial production as measured concurrently with stock returns.

Business Cycle[b]
The change in the spread between the yield on 20-year investment-grade corporate bonds and 20-year Treasury bonds is used as a proxy for the shorter-term cyclical behavior of the economy. Changes in the spread capture the risk of default resulting from the interaction of earnings cyclicality and existing debt structure.

Long-Term Interest Rates[b]
The change in interest rates is measured by the change in the 10-year Treasury yield. Changes in this yield alters the relative attractiveness of financial assets and therefore induces a change in the portfolio mix.

Short-Term Interest Rates[b]
The change in short-term interest rates is measured by changes in the 1-month Treasury bill rate.

Inflation Shock[a]
Inflation is measured by the Consumer Price Index. The inflation shock component is found by subtracting expected inflation from realized inflation. Expected inflation is measured using a proprietary econometric model.

U.S. Dollar[b]
The impact of currency fluctuations on the market is measured by changes in the basket of currencies. Specifically, a 15-country, trade-weighted basket of currencies is used.

a. Adapted from Joseph J. Mezrich, Mark O'Donnell, and Vele Samak, *U.S. RAM Model: Model Update*, Salomon Brothers, Equity Portfolio Analysis, April 8, 1997, p. 1.
b. Adapted from the discussion on page 4 of Eric H. Sorensen, Joseph J. Mezrich, and Chee Thum, *The Salomon Brothers U.S. Risk Attribute Model*, Salomon Brothers, Quantitative Strategy, October 1989.

In addition, there is another factor called "residual market beta" which is included to capture macroeconomic factors after controlling for the other six macroeconomic factors. Exhibit 2 provides a brief description of each macroeconomic factor.

We'll use the RAM model to explain the procedure for estimating the parameters of the model. For each stock in the universe used by Salomon Brothers (about 3,500) a multiple regression is estimated. The dependent variable is the stock's monthly return. The independent variables are the six macroeconomic factors, the residual market factor, and other market factors. The size and statistical significance of the regression coefficients of each of the macroeconomic factors is examined. Then for all stocks in the universe the regression coefficient for each of the macroeconomic factors is standardized. The purpose of standardizing the estimated regression coefficients is that it makes a comparison of the relative sensitivity of a stock to each macroeconomic factor easier.

The standardization methodology is as follows. For a given macroeconomic factor, the average value and standard deviation of the estimated regression coefficient from all the stocks in the universe are computed. The standardized regression coefficient for a stock with respect to a given macroeconomic factor is then found by calculating the difference between the estimated regression coefficient and the average value and then dividing this value by the standard deviation. The standardized regression coefficient is restricted to a value between −5 and +5.

A stock's standardized regression coefficient for a given macroeconomic factor is then the measure of the sensitivity of that stock to that risk factor. The standardized regression coefficient is therefore the factor sensitivity. If a stock has a factor sensitivity for a specific macroeconomic factor of zero, this means that it has average response to that macroeconomic factor. The more the factor sensitivity deviates from zero, the more responsive the stock is to that risk factor. For example, consider the economic growth factor. A positive value for this macroeconomic factor means that if all other factors are unchanged, a company is likely to outperform market returns if the economy improves. A negative value for the economic growth factor means that if all other factors are unchanged, a company is likely to underperform market returns if the economy improves.

The sensitivity for the factors are estimated so that they are statistically independent. This means that there will be no double counting the influence of a factor.

Fundamental Factor Models

Fundamental factor models use company and industry attributes and market data as raw descriptors. Examples are price/earnings ratios, book/price ratios, estimated economic growth, and trading activity. The inputs into a fundamental factor model are stock returns and the raw descriptors about a company. Those fundamental variables about a company that are pervasive in explaining stock returns are then the raw descriptors retained in the model. Using cross-sectional analysis the sensitivity of a stock's return to a raw descriptor is estimated.

As determined by Jacobs and Levy,[4] many of these descriptors are highly correlated. Adding highly correlated factors to a model neither enhances returns nor lowers risk. Factors that by themselves seem to be important may be unimportant when combined with other factors; factors that by themselves seem not to be important may be important when combined with other factors. A manager must be able to untangle these relationships.

Two commercially available fundamental factor models are the BARRA and the Wilshire models. The BARRA E2 model begins with raw descriptors.[5] It then combines raw descriptors to obtain risk indexes to capture related company attributes. For example, raw descriptors such as debt-to-asset ratio, debt-to-equity ratio, and fixed-rate coverage are measures that capture a company's financial leverage. These measures would be combined to obtain a risk index for financial leverage.

---

[4] Bruce I. Jacobs and Kenneth N. Levy, "Disentangling Equity Return Regularities: New Insights and Investment Opportunities," *Financial Analyst Journal* (May-June 1988), pp. 18-43.

[5] The BARRA E2 model is BARRA's second generation U.S. equity model. In 1997, BARRA released its third generation U.S. equity model (BARRA E3). The discussion in this chapter and the information provided in Exhibits 3 and 4 are based on the BARRA E2 model. The E3 model closely resembles the E2 model in structure, but with improved industry and risk index definitions.

The BARRA E2 fundamental factor model has 13 risk indexes and 55 industry groups. For 12 of the risk indexes and the 55 industry groups, the model is estimated for BARRA's HICAP universe (1,000 of the largest-capitalization companies plus selected slightly smaller companies to fill underrepresented industry groups) using statistical techniques. The universe has varied from 1,170 to 1,300 companies.

Exhibit 3 reproduces the information about the 13 risk indexes as published by BARRA. Also shown in the exhibit are the raw descriptors used to construct each risk index. For example, the earnings-to-price ratio is a combination of the following raw descriptors: current earnings-to-price ratio, earnings-to-price ratio for the past five years, and IBES earnings-to-price ratio projection. Before each raw descriptor in Exhibit 3 is a plus or minus sign. The sign indicates how the raw descriptor influences a risk index. The 55 industry classifications are shown in Exhibit 4.

Exhibit 3: BARRA E2 Model Risk Index Definitions *

1. Variability In Markets (VIM)

This risk index is a predictor of the volatility of a stock based on its behavior and the behavior of its options in the capital markets. Unlike beta, which measures only the response of a stock to the market, Variability in Markets measures a stock's overall volatility, including its response to the market. A high beta stock will necessarily have a high Variability in Markets exposure. However, a high exposure will not necessarily imply a high beta; the stock may be responding to factors other than changes in the market.

This index uses measures such as the cumulative trading range and daily stock price standard deviation to identify stocks with highly variable prices. BARRA uses different formulas for three categories of stocks.

    a. Optioned stocks — all stocks having listed options.
    b. Listed stocks — all stocks in the HICAP universe that are listed on an exchange but do not have listed options.
    c. Thin stocks — all stocks that are traded over the counter or are outside the HICAP universe, except those with listed options.

Optioned stocks are distinct for several reasons. First, the option price provides an implicit forecast of the total standard deviation of the stock itself. Second, optioned stocks tend to be those with greatest investor interest and with the most effective trading volume. Stock trading volume descriptors understate the effective volume because they omit option volume.

Thin stocks, about ten percent of the basic sample, are broken out because they tend to trade differently from other stocks. Over-the-counter stocks and other thinly traded securities show price behavior inconsistent with efficient and timely prices. Thin stocks are less synchronized with market movements, and exhibit frequent periods in which no meaningful price changes occur as well as occasional outlying price changes that are promptly reversed. These influences cause some indicators of stock price variability to be biased.

In calculating this index, BARRA standardizes the formulas for the three stock categories relative to one another to provide one index for the total population.

    A. Optioned Stock Descriptors
        + Cumulative Range, 12 months
        + Beta * Sigma
        + Option Standard Deviation
        + Daily Standard Deviation

Exhibit 3 (Continued)

B. Listed Stock Descriptors
+ Beta * Sigma
+ Cumulative Range, 12 months
+ Daily Standard Deviation
+ Trading Volume to Variance
− Log of Common Stock Price
+ Serial Dependence
− Annual Share Turnover
C. Thin Stock Descriptors
+ Beta * Sigma
+ Cumulative Range, 12 months
+ Annual Share Turnover
− Log of Common Stock Price
− Serial Dependence

2. Success (SCS)

The Success index identifies recently successful stocks using price behavior in the market (measured by historical alpha and relative strength) and, to a lesser degree, earnings growth information. The relative strength of a stock is significant in explaining its volatility.

+ Relative Strength
+ Historical Alpha
+ Recent Earnings Change
+ IBES Earnings Growth
− Dividend Cuts, 5 years
+ Growth in Earnings per Share

3. Size (SIZ)

The Size index values total assets and market capitalization to differentiate large stocks from small stocks. This index has been a major determinant of performance over the years as well as an important source of risk.

+ Log of Capitalization
+ Log of Total Assets
+ Indicator of Earnings History

4. Trading Activity (TRA)

Trading activity measures the relative activity of a firm's shares in the market, or the "institutional popularity" of a company. The most important descriptors are the share turnover variables. In addition, this index includes the ratio of trading volume to price variability, the logarithm of price, and the number of analysts following the stock, as reported in the IBES database. The stocks with more rapid share turnover, lower price, and signs of greater trading activity are generally the higher risk stocks.

+ Annual Share Turnover
+ Quarterly Share Turnover
+ Share Turnover, 5 years
+ Log of Common Stock Price
+ IBES Number of Analysts
+ Trading Volume to Variance

Exhibit 3 (Continued)

5. Growth (GRO)

The Growth index is primarily a predictor of a company's future growth but also reflects its historical growth. BARRA estimates earnings growth for the next five years using regression techniques on a comprehensive collection of descriptors, all of which are distinct elements of the growth concept. The Growth index includes descriptors of payout, asset growth and historical growth in earnings, the level of earnings to price, and variability in capital structure.

- − Payout, 5 years
- − Earnings to Price Ratio, 5 years
- + Earnings Growth
- + Capital Structure Change
- − Normalized Earnings to Price Ratio
- + Recent Earnings Change
- − Dividend Yield, 5 years
- + IBES Earnings Change
- − Yield Forecast
- + Indicator of Zero Yield
- − Earnings to Price Ratio
- − IBES Earnings to Price Ratio
- + Growth in Total Assets

6. Earnings to Price Ratio (EPR)

The Earnings to Price Ratio measures the relationship between company earnings and market valuation. To compute the Earnings to Price Ratio, BARRA combines measures of past, current, and estimated future earnings.

- + Current Earnings to Price Ratio
- + Earnings to Price Ratio, 5 years
- + IBES Earnings to Price Ratio Projection

7. Book to Price Ratio (BPR)

This index is simply the book value of common equity divided by the market capitalization of a firm.

8. Earnings Variability (EVR)

The Earnings Variability index measures a company's historical earnings variability and cash flow fluctuations. In addition to variance in earnings over five years, it includes the relative variability of earnings forecasts taken from the IBES database, and the industry concentration of a firm's activities.

- + Variance in Earnings
- + IBES Standard Deviation to Price Ratio
- + Earnings Covariability
- + Concentration
- + Variance of Cash Flow
- + Extraordinary Items

9. Financial Leverage (FLV)

The Financial Leverage index captures the financial structure of a firm as well as its sensitivity to interest rates using the debt to assets ratio, the leverage at book value, and the probability of fixed charges not being covered. Bond market sensitivity is included only for financial companies.

Exhibit 3 (Continued)

- Bond Market Sensitivity
+ Debt to Assets Ratio
+ Leverage at Book (Debt to Equity)
+ Uncovered Fixed Charges

10. Foreign Income (FOR)
This index reflects the fraction of operating income earned outside the United States. It is a measure of sensitivity to currency exchange rate changes.

11. Labor Intensity (LBI)
This index estimates the importance of labor, relative to capital, in the operations of a firm. It is based on ratios of labor expense to assets, fixed plant and equipment to equity, and depreciated plant value to total plant cost. A higher exposure to Labor Intensity indicates a larger ratio of labor expense to capital costs and can be a gauge of sensitivity to cost-push inflation.

+ Labor Share
- Inflation-adjusted Plant to Equity Ratio
- Net Plant to Gross Plant

12. Yield (YLD)
The Yield index is simply a relative measure of the company's annual dividend yield.

13. LOCAP
The LOCAP characteristic indicates those companies that are not in the HICAP universe. It permits the factors in the model to be applied across a broader universe of assets than that used to estimate the model. The LOCAP factor is, in part, an extension of the Size index, allowing the returns of approximately 4500 smaller companies to deviate from an exact linear relationship with the Size index.

*In 1997, BARRA released its E3 model which closely resembles the E2 model but with improved risk index definitions.
Source: *United States Equity Model Handbook* (Berkeley, CA: BARRA, 1996), pp. 19-23.

Exhibit 4: BARRA E2 Model Industry Classifications*

The industry classifications in the U.S. Model are:			
1. Aluminum	15. Liquor	29. Photographic, Optical	43. Retail (All Other)
2. Iron & Steel	16. Tobacco	30. Consumer Durables	44. Telephone, Telegraph
3. Precious Metals	17. Construction	31. Motor Vehicles	45. Electric Utilities
4. Misc. Mining, Metals	18. Chemicals	32. Leisure, Luxury	46. Gas Utilities
5. Coal & Uranium	19. Tires & Rubber	33. Health Care (Non-drug)	47. Banks
6. International Oil	20. Containers	34. Drugs, Medicine	48. Thrift Institutions
7. Dom. Petroleum Reserves	21. Producer Goods	35. Publishing	49. Miscellaneous Finance
8. For. Petroleum Reserves	22. Pollution Control	36. Media	50. Life Insurance
9. Oil Refining, Distribution	23. Electronics	37. Hotels, Restaurants	51. Other Insurance
10. Oil Service	24. Aerospace	38. Trucking, Freight	52. Real Property
11. Forest Products	25. Business Machines	39. Railroads, Transit	53. Mortgage Financing
12. Paper	26. Soaps, Housewares	40. Air Transport	54. Services
13. Agriculture, Food	27. Cosmetics	41. Transport by Water	55. Miscellaneous
14. Beverages	28. Apparel, Textiles	42. Retail (Food)	

* In 1997, BARRA released its E3 model which has improved industry classifications.
Source: *United States Equity Model Handbook* (Berkeley, CA: BARRA, 1996), pp. 32.

Exhibit 5: Fundamental Factors and Market Sensitive Factor Definitions for Wilshire Atlas Factor Model

1.Earnings/price ratio	Sum of the most recent four quarters' earnings per share divided by the closing price.
2. Book value/price ratio	Book value divided by common equity shares outstanding.
3. Market capitalization	The natural logarithm of the product of a security's price multiplied by the number of shares outstanding.
4. Net earnings revision	Analysts momentum measure: Net earnings revision, based on I/B/E/S data, measures analysts' optimism of earnings. Net earnings revision is the percentage of analysts who are feeling more optimistic about earnings in the next period. The higher the net earnings revision number, the more optimistic analysts are about an increase in that company's earnings.
5. Reversal	Price momentum measure: Reversal captures the mean reversion tendencies of stocks. It is a measure of the difference between a security's actual return in the last period and the expected return with respect to its beta. If a stock has a positive reversal this means that it had a higher than expected return in the last period given its beta. Thus, this security is expected to have a lower than expected return in the next period so that the returns for this security will conform to the norm expectations over the long run.
6. Earnings torpedo	Earnings momentum measure: Earnings torpedo, based on I/B/E/S data, is a measure of the estimated growth in earnings for a security relative to historical earnings. Earnings torpedo is based on the ratio of next years estimated earnings per share versus its historical earnings per share. The securities in the universe are then ranked by the estimate and given an earnings torpedo score. A security with a high earnings torpedo score is considered to be vulnerable to a large drop in price if earnings do not meet the higher earnings estimates forecasted by analysts in the next period.
7. Historical beta	Classic measure of security volatility. Measured for each security by regressing the past 60 months worth of excess returns against the S&P500. A minimum of 38 months are required for the data to be valid.

Source: Adapted from *U.S. Equity Risk Model* (Santa Monica, CA: Wilshire Associates, July 1997 draft).

As with the macroeconomic factor model, the raw descriptors are standardized or normalized. The risk indices are in turn standardized. The sensitivity of each company to each risk index is standardized.

The Wilshire Atlas model uses six fundamental factors, one market factor sensitivity, and 39 industry factors to explain stock returns. The six fundamental factors and the market factor sensitivity are listed in Exhibit 5, along with their definitions.

The BARRA and Wilshire factor models are commercially available. Now we'll look at a proprietary model developed by a firm for its own use in managing client equity portfolios — Goldman Sachs Asset Management (GSAM). This firm is the investment management subsidiary of Goldman Sachs & Co., a broker/dealer firm. There are nine descriptors used in the GSAM factor model. These descriptors which are the factors in the model are described in Exhibit 6. The factors fall into three categories: (1) value measures, (2) growth and momentum measures, and (3) risk measures.

Exhibit 6: Factor Definitions for the Goldman Sachs Asset Management Factor Model

Factor	Definition
Book/Price	Common equity per share divided by price
Retained EPS/Price	Year-ahead consensus EPS forecast less indicated annual dividend divided by price. One-year forecast EPS is a weighted average of the forecasts for the current and next fiscal years.
EBITD/Enterprise Value	Earnings before interest, taxes and depreciation divided by total capital. Total capital is equity at market plus long-term debt at book.
Estimate Revisions	The number of estimates raised in the past three months, less the number lowered, divided by the total number of estimates.
Price Momentum	Total return over the last 12 months, less the return for the latest month (to adjust for short-term reversals).
Sustainable Growth	The consensus long-term growth forecast.
Beta	The regression coefficient from a 60-month regression of the stock's excess returns (above the T-bill rate) against the market's excess returns.
Residual Risk	The "unexplained" variation from the above regression; the standard error of the regression.
Disappointment Risk	The risk that actual earnings will not meet projections. Stocks with high expected one-year earnings growth have high disappointment potential; stocks with low expectations have less disappointment risk.

Source: Table 4 in *Select Equity Investment Strategy*, Goldman Sachs Asset Management, February 1997, p. 4.

THE OUTPUT AND INPUTS OF A FACTOR MODEL

Now that we have identified the types of factor models, let's look at the output of the model and the inputs to the model after the estimation has taken place. The output of a factor model is found by first multiplying a factor sensitivity by the assumed value for the factor measure (assumed risk factor).[6] This gives the contribution to the model's output from a given risk factor exposure. Summing up over all risk factors gives the output. For a K-factor model this is expressed mathematically as follows:

$$\text{Output} = \text{Beta}_1 \times (\text{Factor}_1 \text{ measure}) + \text{Beta}_2 \times (\text{Factor}_2 \text{ measure}) + \ldots$$
$$+ \text{Beta}_K \times (\text{Factor}_K \text{ measure})$$

Let's look first at the Beta's. These are the factor sensitivities and are estimated statistically. As explained earlier, they are commonly standardized or normalized.

The output varies by model. For example, in the BIRR macroeconomic factor model, the output is the *expected excess return* given the estimated factor sensitivities and the assumed values for the factor measures. The expected excess return is the expected return above the risk-free rate. In contrast, in the Salomon

---

[6] For an example of quantitative estimation of returns to the size factor using economic variables, see Bruce I. Jacobs and Kenneth N. Levy, "Forecasting the Size Effect," *Financial Analysts Journal* (May-June 1989), pp.61-78.

Brothers RAM factor model, the output is a score that is used to rank the outcome given the estimated factor sensitivities and assumed values for the factor measures.

The factor measures vary by model. In the BIRR macroeconomic factor model, for example, a factor measure is the estimated market price of the risk factor expressed in percent per year. For the Salomon Brothers RAM factor model, a factor measure is the normalized value for the factor.

Let's use the two macroeconomic models described earlier to show how the output is obtained. First, the BIRR model. The estimated risk exposure profile for Reebok International Limited and the assumed values for the risk factors (expressed in percent per year) are shown below:

Risk factor	Estimated factor sensitivity	Estimated market price of risk (%)
Confidence risk	0.73	2.59
Time horizon risk	0.77	-0.66
Inflation risk	-0.48	-4.32
Business cycle risk	4.59	1.49
Market timing risk	1.50	3.61

The expected excess return is then found as follows:

$$\text{Expected excess return for Reebok} = 0.73\,(2.59) + 0.77\,(-0.66) + (-0.48)\,(-4.32) + 4.59\,(1.49) + 1.50\,(3.61) = 15.71\%$$

To obtain the expected return, the risk-free rate must be added. For example, if the risk-free rate is 5%, then the expected return is 20.71% (15.71% plus 5%).

In the Salomon Brothers RAM model, the set of forecasts for the factor measures are called *scenario factors*. Based on scenario factors, the sensitivity of a stock to each factor can be calculated. Adding up the sensitivity of a stock to each factor gives a stock's *scenario score*. Recall that in this factor model there are six macroeconomic factors (described in Exhibit 2) and the residual beta. Each factor is expressed in normalized or standardized form. For Pepsico (in October 1989) the factor betas and a factor scenario for a weakening economy are given below:[7]

Risk factor	Estimated factor sensitivity	Factor scenario (Weakening economy)
Economic growth	-1.8	-1.0
Business cycle	-0.9	-0.5
Long rate	0.0	0.5
Short rate	0.1	0.3
Inflation rate	-0.3	0.1
U.S. dollar	0.1	0.3
Residual beta	-1.1	-0.5

---

[7] Sorensen, Mezrich, and Thum, "The Salomon Brothers U.S. Stock Risk Attribute Model," p. 6.

The scenario score for Pepsico is then:

Pepsico scenario score = $-1.8(-1.0) + (-0.9)(-0.5) + 0(0.5) + 0.1(0.3)$
$+ (-0.3)(0.1) + 0.1(0.3) + (-1.1)(-0.5) = 1.7$

This scenario score is then compared to the scenario score of other stocks in the universe of purchase or short-sale candidates of a portfolio manager.

PORTFOLIO CONSTRUCTION WITH FACTOR MODELS

Now let's see how factor models are used in portfolio construction. Specifically, based on expectations about the future outcomes of the factors, an active equity manager can construct a portfolio to add value relative to some benchmark should those outcomes be realized.

Portfolio Expected Excess Returns and Risk Exposure Profiles

In factor models in which the output is an expected excess return for a stock, the expected excess return for a portfolio can be easily computed. This is the weighted average of the expected excess return for each stock in the portfolio. The weights are the percentage of a stock value in the portfolio relative to the market value of the portfolio. Similarly, a portfolio's sensitivity to a given factor risk is a weighted average of the factor sensitivity of the stocks in the portfolio. The set of factor sensitivities is then the portfolio's risk exposure profile. Consequently, the expected excess return and the risk exposure profile can be obtained from the stocks comprising the portfolio.

Since a stock market index is nothing more than a portfolio that includes the universe of stocks making up the index, an expected excess return and risk exposure profile can be determined for an index. This allows a manager to compare the expected excess return and the risk profile of a stock and/or a portfolio to that of a stock market index whose performance the portfolio manager is measured against. For example, in the BIRR model, the risk exposure profile for the S&P 500 is shown below, as well as that of Reebok for comparative purposes:

Risk factor	Estimated factor sensitivity for	
	S&P 500	Reebok
Confidence risk	0.27	0.73
Time horizon risk	0.56	0.77
Inflation risk	-0.37	-0.48
Business cycle risk	1.71	4.59
Market timing risk	1.00	1.50

By comparing the risk exposure profile of Reebok to the S&P 500, a portfolio manager can see the relative risk exposure. Using the same assumed values for the risk factors as used earlier for Reebok, the expected excess return for the S&P 500 is 8.09% compared to 15.71% for Reebok.

Exhibit 7: Portfolio Holdings for Manager X

BARRA Microcomputer Products:		Interactive PORCH					Page	1
Portfolio: SAMPLE		Market: S&P500				Pricing Date:	07-31-90	

IDENT	NAME	SHARES	PRICE	%WGT	BETA	%YLD	IND
1 FDX	FEDERAL EXPRESS CORP	80700	41.625	3.00	1.15	0.00	AIR
2 NEM	NEWMONT MNG CORP	67500	49.500	2.98	0.76	1.21	GOLD
3 I	FIRST INTST BANCORP	167700	33.000	4.94	1.32	9.09	BANKS
4 HWP	HEWLETT PACKARD CO	126900	43.125	4.89	1.15	0.97	BUS MN
5 IBM	INTERNATIONAL BUS MACH	141400	111.500	14.08	1.01	4.34	BUS MN
6 F	FORD MTR CO DEL	273100	41.500	10.12	0.98	7.17	MOT VH
7 HCSG	HEALTHCARE SVCS GRP IN	93000	24.250	2.01	1.29	0.28	SERVCS
8 TXN	TEXAS INSTRS INC	81500	32.000	2.33	1.41	2.25	ELCTRN
9 S	SEARS ROEBUCK & CO	342900	33.625	10.30	1.09	5.94	RET OT
10 AXP	AMERICAN EXPRESS CO	291900	29.125	7.59	1.20	3.15	FINANC
11 JNJ	JOHNSON & JOHNSON	205800	70.625	12.98	1.02	1.92	HEALTH
12 EK	EASTMAN KODAK CO	324800	38.125	11.06	1.10	5.24	PHOTOG
13 WMX	WASTE MGMT INC	185900	41.375	6.87	1.24	0.86	POLL C
14 PCI	PARAMOUNT COMMUNICATIO	118900	39.500	4.20	1.14	1.77	PUBLSH
15 TAN	TANDY CORP	79800	36.750	2.62	1.26	1.63	RET OT

Source: The information in this exhibit is adapted from Figure VI-1 of *United States Equity Model Handbook* (Berkeley, CA: BARRA, 1996), p. 40.

In factor models such as the Salomon Brothers RAM model where the output is a *scenario score*, the risk exposure profile of a portfolio and market index is calculated in the same manner as when the model's output is the expected excess return. However, in scenario score models the portfolio's and market index's output is a ranking.

The power of a factor model regardless of the type of output is that given the risk factors and the factor sensitivities, a portfolio's risk exposure profile can be quantified and controlled. The examples below show how this can be done with a fundamental factor model. This allows managers to avoid making unintended bets.

Assessing the Exposure of a Portfolio

A fundamental factor model can be used to assess whether the current portfolio is consistent with a manager's strengths. In this application of factor models and the one that follows, we will use the BARRA factor model.[8] Exhibit 7 is a list of the holdings of manager X as of July 31, 1990.[9] There are 15 stocks held with a total market value of $111.9 million.

Exhibit 8 assesses the risk exposure of manager X's portfolio relative to the risk exposure of the S&P 500. The boxes in the second column of the exhibit indicate the significant differences in the exposure of manager X's portfolio relative to the S&P 500. There are two risk indices boxed — success and foreign

---

[8] The illustrations are adapted from Chapter VI of *United States Equity Model Handbook* (Berkeley, CA: BARRA, 1996).

[9] This was an actual portfolio of a BARRA client.

income — and two industry groupings boxed — business machines and miscella-neous finance. Exhibit 3 describes the risk indices. The -0.45 exposure to the suc-cess risk index reveals that manager X's portfolio exhibits low relative strength as measured by stock price and earnings momentum — a style characteristic. Conse-quently, the success risk index indicates an exposure to style. Thus, we can see that manager X is making a style bet. The 0.62 exposure to the foreign income risk index tells manager X that the companies in the portfolio tend to earn a sig-nificant portion of their operating income abroad. Consequently, manager X is making an international bet. In terms of industry exposure, manager X is extremely more aggressive in his or her holdings of business machine stocks and miscellaneous finance stocks.

Notice in this example how the manager is able to identify where the bets are made. Manager X has made a style bet, an international bet, and a bet on two industries. If the manager did not intend to make these bets, the portfolio can be rebalanced to eliminate any unintended bets.

Tilting a Portfolio

Now let's look at how an active manager can construct a portfolio to make inten-tional bets. Suppose that manager Y seeks to construct a portfolio that generates superior returns relative to the S&P 500 by tilting it toward high-success stocks. At the same time, the manager does not want to increase tracking error risk sig-nificantly. An obvious approach may seem to be to identify all the stocks in the universe that have a higher than average success risk index. The problem with this approach is that it introduces unintentional bets with respect to the other risk indices.

Instead, an optimization method combined with a factor model can be used to construct the desired portfolio. The input to this process is the tilt expo-sure sought, the benchmark stock market index, and the number of stocks to be included in the portfolio. The BARRA optimization model also requires a specifi-cation of the excess return sought. In our illustration, the tilt exposure sought is high success stocks, the benchmark is the S&P 500, and the number of stocks to be included in the portfolio is 50. While we do not report the holdings of the opti-mal portfolio here, Exhibit 9 provides an analysis of that portfolio by comparing the risk exposure of the 50-stock optimal portfolio to that of the S&P 500.

Fundamental Factor Models and Equity Style Management

In Chapter 4, we covered equity style management. Notice that the factors used in fundamental factor models such as the BARRA factor model (Exhibit 3), Wilshire factor model (Exhibit 5), and the GSAM factor model (Exhibit 6) are the same characteristics used in style management. Since the factors can be used to add value and control risk, this suggests that factor models can be used in style man-agement for the same purposes.

Exhibit 8: Analysis of Manager X Portfolio's Exposure Relative to the S&P 500

Comparison Summary Report   Date: 07-31-90

Portfolio	SAMPLE	
Comparison Port.	SAP500	
Market	SAP500	

Number of Assets	15
Port. Value	111,940,087.50
Predicted Yield	3.78
Alpha	0.00
Utility	-0.36
Tracking Error	7.25

FACTORS	SAMPLE	SAP500	DIFF	MCTE
VARIABILITY IN MARKETS	0.02	-0.06	0.09	0.010
SUCCESS	-0.45	0.01	-0.47	-0.021
SIZE	0.54	0.29	0.26	0.004
TRADING ACTIVITY	0.22	0.00	0.22	-0.002
GROWTH	-0.12	-0.05	-0.07	0.016
EARNINGS/PRICE	0.08	0.01	0.08	0.007
BOOK/PRICE	0.18	-0.02	0.20	0.001
EARNINGS VARIATION	0.00	-0.05	0.05	0.003
FINANCIAL LEVERAGE	0.28	0.03	0.25	-0.001
FOREIGN INCOME	0.62	0.12	0.51	-0.001
LABOR INTENSITY	0.30	0.01	0.29	-0.003
YIELD	0.16	0.02	0.14	0.007
LOCAP	0.02	0.00	0.02	-0.005
ALUMINUM	0.00	0.60	-0.60	0.099
IRON AND STEEL	0.00	0.30	-0.30	0.081
PRECIOUS METALS	1.25	0.42	0.83	0.071
MISC. MINING, METALS	0.54	0.61	-0.07	0.073
COAL AND URANIUM	0.00	0.40	-0.40	0.013
INTERNATIONAL OIL	0.00	4.49	-4.49	-0.033
DOM PETROLEUM RESERVES	0.51	3.46	-2.96	-0.047
FOR PETROLEUM RESERVES	0.69	2.25	-1.56	-0.037
OIL REFINING, DISTRIBUTN	0.00	1.29	-1.29	-0.011
OIL SERVICE	0.00	1.02	-1.02	-0.017
FOREST PRODUCTS	0.00	0.30	-0.30	0.120
PAPER	0.00	2.06	-2.06	0.082
AGRICULTURE, FOOD	0.00	4.99	-4.99	0.047
BEVERAGES	0.00	1.41	-1.41	0.066
LIQUOR	0.00	1.05	-1.05	0.050
TOBACCO	0.00	1.38	-1.38	0.067
CONSTRUCTION	0.00	0.88	-0.88	0.098
CHEMICALS	1.99	3.44	-1.45	0.083
TIRE & RUBBER	0.00	0.10	-0.10	0.101
CONTAINERS	0.00	0.17	-0.17	0.069
PRODUCERS GOODS	0.02	4.49	-4.47	0.086
POLLUTION CONTROL	6.87	1.13	5.75	0.124
ELECTRONICS	2.21	2.39	-0.18	0.126
AEROSPACE	0.00	2.47	-2.47	0.089
BUSINESS MACHINES	19.07	4.80	14.26	0.130
SOAPS, HOUSEWARE	0.00	1.99	-1.99	0.084
COSMETICS	4.54	0.94	3.60	0.096
APPAREL, TEXTILES	0.00	0.77	-0.77	0.080
PHOTOGRAPHIC, OPTICAL	6.75	0.55	6.20	0.114
CONSUMER DURABLES	0.00	0.99	-0.99	0.104
MOTOR VEHICLES	8.91	2.42	6.49	0.114
LEISURE, LUXURY	0.00	0.18	-0.18	0.096
HEALTH CARE (NON-DRUG)	5.06	1.85	3.21	0.070
DRUGS, MEDICINE	5.70	6.81	-1.12	0.066
PUBLISHING	2.10	1.48	0.62	0.090
MEDIA	2.10	1.67	0.43	0.079
HOTELS, RESTAURANTS	0.00	1.75	-1.75	0.094
TRUCKING, FREIGHT	0.00	0.13	-0.13	0.098
RAILROADS, TRANSIT	0.00	0.92	-0.92	0.046
AIR TRANSPORT	3.00	0.59	2.41	0.139
TRANSPORT BY WATER	0.00	0.03	-0.03	0.039
RETAIL (FOOD)	0.00	0.85	-0.85	0.062
RETAIL (ALL OTHER)	6.12	5.19	0.93	0.098
TELEPHONE, TELEGRAPH	0.00	8.26	-8.26	0.036
ELECTRIC UTILITIES	0.00	4.37	-4.37	0.024
GAS UTILITIES	0.00	1.17	-1.17	0.019
BANKS	6.49	2.93	3.56	0.063
THRIFT INSTITUTIONS	0.00	0.28	-0.28	0.073
MISC. FINANCE	10.87	2.20	8.67	0.094
LIFE INSURANCE	0.00	0.92	-0.92	0.061
OTHER INSURANCE	2.37	2.24	0.13	0.059
REAL PROPERTY	0.82	0.19	0.63	0.107
MORTGAGE FINANCING	0.00	0.00	-0.00	0.068
SERVICES	2.01	1.89	0.12	0.070
MISCELLANEOUS	0.00	0.56	-0.56	0.053

Source: The information in this exhibit is adapted from Figure VI-3 of *United States Equity Model Handbook* (Berkeley, CA: BARRA, 1996), p. 42.

Exhibit 9: Analysis of a 50-Stock Portfolio Constructed to be Tilted Toward High Success Stocks

Comparison Summary Report		Date: 07-31-90	
Portfolio	SUCCESS		
Comparison Port.	SAP500		
Market	SAP500		
Number of Assets	50		
Port. Value	99,999,723.50		
Predicted Yield	3.04		
Alpha	0.31		
Utility	0.18		
Tracking Error	4.19		

FACTORS	U850	SAP500	DIFF
VARIABILITY IN MARKETS	0.10	-0.06	0.16
SUCCESS	0.77	0.01	0.76
SIZE	0.24	0.29	-0.05
TRADING ACTIVITY	-0.06	0.00	-0.07
GROWTH	0.10	-0.05	0.15
EARNINGS/PRICE	-0.00	0.01	-0.01
BOOK/PRICE	-0.16	-0.02	-0.14
EARNINGS VARIATION	0.00	-0.05	0.05
FINANCIAL LEVERAGE	-0.16	0.03	-0.19
FOREIGN INCOME	-0.10	0.12	-0.21
LABOR INTENSITY	-0.04	0.01	-0.05
YIELD	-0.11	0.02	-0.13
LOCAP	0.00	0.00	-0.00
ALUMINUM	1.98	0.60	1.38
IRON AND STEEL	0.00	0.30	-0.30
PRECIOUS METALS	0.50	0.42	0.07
MISC. MINING, METALS	0.47	0.61	-0.14
COAL AND URANIUM	0.42	0.40	0.02
INTERNATIONAL OIL	4.36	4.49	-0.13
DOM PETROLEUM RESERVES	2.45	3.46	-1.01
FOR PETROLEUM RESERVES	3.19	2.25	0.94
OIL REFINING, DISTRIBUTN	1.44	1.29	0.15
OIL SERVICE	1.79	1.02	0.77
FOREST PRODUCTS	0.03	0.30	-0.27
PAPER	1.07	2.06	-0.99
AGRICULTURE, FOOD	5.29	4.99	0.30
BEVERAGES	0.00	1.41	-1.41
LIQUOR	0.37	1.05	-0.68
TOBACCO	3.13	1.38	1.75
CONSTRUCTION	2.27	0.88	1.39
CHEMICALS	3.39	3.44	-0.05
TIRE & RUBBER	0.00	0.10	-0.10
CONTAINERS	0.00	0.17	-0.17
PRODUCERS GOODS	4.36	4.49	-0.14
POLLUTION CONTROL	2.38	1.13	1.25
ELECTRONICS	4.24	2.39	1.84
AEROSPACE	3.11	2.47	0.64
BUSINESS MACHINES	1.39	4.80	-3.42
SOAPS, HOUSEWARE	4.79	1.99	2.80
COSMETICS	0.29	0.94	-0.66
APPAREL, TEXTILES	0.98	0.77	0.21
PHOTOGRAPHIC, OPTICAL	0.00	0.55	-0.55
CONSUMER DURABLES	0.73	0.99	-0.27
MOTOR VEHICLES	4.35	2.42	1.94
LEISURE, LUXURY	0.00	0.18	-0.18
HEALTH CARE (NON-DRUG)	2.10	1.85	0.25
DRUGS, MEDICINE	4.60	6.81	-2.21
PUBLISHING	0.00	1.48	-1.48
MEDIA	0.16	1.67	-1.51
HOTELS, RESTAURANTS	0.59	1.75	-1.16
TRUCKING, FREIGHT	0.00	0.13	-0.13
RAILROADS, TRANSIT	0.00	0.92	-0.92
AIR TRANSPORT	0.00	0.59	-0.59
TRANSPORT BY WATER	0.00	0.03	-0.03
RETAIL (FOOD)	4.78	0.85	3.93
RETAIL (ALL OTHER)	9.80	5.19	4.62
TELEPHONE, TELEGRAPH	0.00	8.26	-8.26
ELECTRIC UTILITIES	12.31	4.37	7.95
GAS UTILITIES	1.03	1.17	-0.14
BANKS	0.00	2.93	-2.93
THRIFT INSTITUTIONS	0.00	0.28	-0.28
MISC. FINANCE	2.10	2.20	-0.10
LIFE INSURANCE	1.67	0.92	0.75
OTHER INSURANCE	1.55	2.24	-0.69
REAL PROPERTY	0.23	0.19	0.04
MORTGAGE FINANCING	0.00	0.00	-0.00
SERVICES	0.19	1.89	-1.70
MISCELLANEOUS	0.15	0.56	-0.42

Source: The information in this exhibit is adapted from Figure VI-7 of *United States Equity Model Handbook* (Berkeley, CA: BARRA, 1996), p. 47.

Exhibit 10: Summary of Perfect Foresight Tests Two
Strategies Using Factor Models: 12-Month Rolling Value
Added (%) from January 1987 to July 1995

Country	Long Stock Strategy			Market Neutral Strategy		
	High	Low	Average	High	Low	Average
United States	82%	39%	55%	195%	75%	138%
United Kingdom	131	52	82	326	50	155
Japan	106	56	74	236	66	121
Canada	91	63	77	—	—	—

Source: Table 15 from David J. Leinweber, Robert D. Arnott, and Christopher G. Luck, "The Many Sides of Equity Style," Chapter 11 in T. Daniel Coggin, Frank J. Fabozzi, and Robert D. Arnott (eds.), *The Handbook of Equity Style Management* (New Hope, PA: Frank J. Fabozzi Associates, 1997).

RETURN PERFORMANCE POTENTIAL OF FACTOR MODELS

It is interesting to see how well a portfolio constructed using a factor model would have performed with perfect foresight. For example, suppose we are examining monthly returns. We look at the actual factor return for the month and use that as our expectation at the beginning of the month. Given the forecasts an optimization model can be used to design the optimal portfolio.

Leinweber, Arnott, and Luck performed this experiment for several countries using the BARRA factor model for those countries — United States, United Kingdom, Japan, and Canada — for the period January 1987 to July 1995.[10] Transaction costs for rebalancing a portfolio each month were incorporated. A 12-month rolling value added return was calculated. A value added return is the return above a broad-based stock index for the country.

Two strategies were followed. One was simply a long position in the stocks. The second was a market neutral long-short strategy.[11] Exhibit 10 reports the results of the perfect foresight tests. With perfect foresight, the BARRA factor model would have added significant value for each country stock portfolio. For example, in the United States even in the worst 12-month rolling period the factor-based model added 39% for the long stock strategy and 75% for the market neutral long-short strategy.

Eric Sorensen, Joseph Mezrich, and Chee Thum performed two backtests of the Salomon Brothers RAM (a macroeconomic factor model) to assess the model. The tests were basically event studies.[12] In the first backtest, these

---

[10] David J. Leinweber, Robert D. Arnott, and Christopher G. Luck, "The Many Sides of Equity Style," Chapter 11 in T. Daniel Coggin, Frank J. Fabozzi, and Robert D. Arnott (eds.), *The Handbook of Equity Style Management* (New Hope, PA: Frank J. Fabozzi, 1997).

[11] See Bruce I. Jacobs and Kenneth N. Levy, "The Long and Short on Long-Short," *Journal of Investing* (Spring 1997), pp. 73-86.

[12] Sorensen, Mezrich, and Thum, *The Salomon Brothers U.S. Risk Attribute Model.*

researchers looked at daily returns following an unexpected announcement regarding an inflation measure. Specifically, on July 14, 1989 the Producer Price Index that was announced was sharply less than anticipated. As a result, the yield on Treasury bills with one month to maturity fell on that day from 8.6% to 8.4%. An optimized portfolio that had a high sensitivity to inflation was constructed. The inflation sensitive tilted portfolio outperformed the S&P 500 by 46 basis points from the day prior to the event (July 13, 1989) through the day after the event (July 15, 1989). This result supports the position that the factor model was an important tool for constructing a portfolio based on expectations.

The second backtest was based on a longer period of time. The event in this case was the movement of the U.S. dollar during the spring of 1989. Specifically, there was an unexpected strengthening (i.e., appreciation) of the U.S. dollar relative to the German mark from May 12 to June 2, 1989. An optimized portfolio was constructed that was tilted towards stocks that benefited from a stronger U.S. dollar. The RAM-based portfolio tilted with this bias outperformed the S&P 500 by 62 basis points.

DIVIDEND DISCOUNT MODELS VERSUS FACTOR MODELS

Another approach used to value common stock is a dividend discount model (DDM). Based on certain assumptions, a DDM gives the expected return for a stock. As explained in this chapter, a factor model also gives the expected return for a stock. Thus both a factor model and a DDM are valuation models. The DDM can be either a stand-alone model or one of several inputs to a factor model.

A study by Bruce Jacobs and Kenneth Levy suggests that simple factor models can outperform a traditional dividend discount model.[13] Specifically, when they compared the contribution of a simple factor model with a traditional dividend discount model they found that less than one-half of 1% of the quarterly average actual returns is explained by the DDM. In contrast, about 43% of the average actual returns is explained by a factor model which includes the DDM and other factors. Thus, in their study the factor model outperformed the DDM hands down.

SUMMARY

There are three types of factor models: statistical factor models, macroeconomic factor models, and fundamental factor models. Statistical factor models use a statistical technique called principal components analysis to identify which raw descriptors best explain stock returns. The resulting factors are statistical artifacts

---

[13] Jacobs and Levy, "On the Value of 'Value'," *Financial Analysts Journal* (July/August 1988).

and are therefore difficult to interpret. Consequently, a statistical factor model is rarely used in practice. The more common factor models are the macroeconomic factor model and the fundamental factor model.

In a factor model, the sensitivity of a stock to a factor is estimated. The risk exposure profile of a stock is identified by a set of factor sensitivities. The risk exposure profile of a portfolio is the weighted average of the risk exposure profile of the stocks in the portfolio. Similarly, the risk exposure profile of a market index can be obtained.

The output of a factor model can be either the expected excess return or a scenario score. The expected excess return of a stock is found by multiplying each factor sensitivity by the assumed value for the risk factor and summing over all risk factors. The expected return is the expected excess return plus the risk-free rate. The expected excess return for a portfolio and a market index is just the weighted average of the expected excess return of the stocks comprising the portfolio or the market index.

The power of a factor model is that given the risk factors and the factor sensitivities, a portfolio's risk exposure profile can be quantified and controlled. Applications of factor models include the ability to assess whether or not the current portfolio is consistent with a manager's strengths and to construct a portfolio with a specific tilt without making unintentional bets. Since many factors in a fundamental model are the same characteristics used in style management, factor models can be used in controlling risk in a style management strategy.

Both dividend discount models and factor models can be used to value common stock. The output of a dividend discount model can be used as a factor in a factor model. One study suggests that factor models have significantly outperformed dividend discount models.

Chapter 7

Dividend Discount Models

William J. Hurley, Ph.D.
Associate Professor of Business Administration
Department of Business Administration
The Royal Military College of Canada

Frank J. Fabozzi, Ph.D., CFA
Adjunct Professor of Finance
School of Management
Yale University

INTRODUCTION

Several models have been used to identify whether a stock is mispriced. These models fall into two general categories: factor-based models and dividend discount models. Factor-based models are the subject Chapter 6. In this chapter we provide a survey of dividend discount models.

Typically, the dividend discount models used by analysts are *deterministic* in that they make specific assumptions about what future dividends will be. Recently, a new approach to dividend discount modeling has been proposed.[1] This approach models the future dividend stream as *uncertain* or *stochastic*. Since the future dividend stream is uncertain, so too is the resulting valuation. The product of this approach to dividend discount modeling is a probability distribution for the stock's discounted value. An analyst can use this probability distribution to assess whether a stock is sufficiently undervalued or overvalued to justify a buy or sell recommendation. These models that treat the future dividend as uncertain are termed *stochastic models*.

To appreciate the importance of stochastic dividend discount models compared to deterministic dividend discount models, consider an analyst who uses a deterministic model and estimates a stock's value to be $42. Suppose further that the stock is trading at $35. The analyst concludes that the stock is undervalued and recommends purchase. But what confidence does the analyst have that

---

[1] See William J. Hurley and Lewis. D. Johnson, "A Realistic Dividend Valuation Model," *Financial Analysts Journal* (July-August 1994), pp. 50-54; William J. Hurley and Lewis D. Johnson, "Stochastic Two-Phase Dividend Discount Models," *Journal of Portfolio Management* (Summer 1997), pp. 91-98 and, William J. Hurley and Lewis D. Johnson, "Confidence Intervals for Stochastic Dividend Discount Models," forthcoming in *Journal of Portfolio Management* (1998).

his recommendation is a good one? He knows that the actual future dividend stream is unlikely to follow the exact pattern assumed by the deterministic model employed. One way around this problem is to assume that future dividends are uncertain. Given that the analyst is able to specify the nature of this uncertainty, a stochastic dividend discount model produces a probability distribution of discounted values. The distribution, for example, might have a mean (average) value of $42. Given a current market price of $35 and the probability distribution generated, the analyst will be able to assess the probability that there is some chance that the true discounted value exceeds $35. For example, the analyst might conclude that the probability that the stock's value is greater than $35 is 90%. In this case the analyst is confident that a buy recommendation is warranted. As we will see, if an analyst is prepared to make subjective assumptions about the uncertain nature of future dividends, he is then able to translate these beliefs into probabilistic assessments on the relationship between model value and the market price.

Valuation using a dividend discount model (DDM) represents a bottom-up investment management style. In theory, the DDM is unbiased and thus rationally reflects the consensus of market participants for the value of a stock. However, proponents of the DDM argue that market "inefficiencies" such as superior information and market psychology do exist and can be translated by the DDM to reveal overvaluation and undervaluation. The DDM can be used in combination with fundamental security analysis and/or factor models in trying to obtain a fair value for the stock.

DETERMINISTIC DIVIDEND DISCOUNT MODELS

The basis for the *dividend discount model* is simply the application of present value analysis, which asserts that the fair price of an asset is the present value of the expected cash flows.[2] In the case of common stock, the cash flows are the expected dividend payouts. The basic model is:

$$P = \frac{D_1}{(1 + r_1)} + \frac{D_2}{(1 + r_2)^2} + \dots \tag{1}$$

where

P = the fair value or theoretical value of the stock
D_t = the expected dividend for period t
r_t = the appropriate discount or capitalization rate for period t

We call equation (1) the *general model*. This model has an infinite number of parameters, so various assumptions must be made to make the valuation calculation tractable.

---

[2] John B. Williams, *The Theory of Investment Value* (Cambridge, MA: Harvard University Press, 1938).

The Finite Life General Model

One common approach is to estimate dividends for a finite time period (say N periods), and then assume some terminal value, P_N, intended to capture the future value of all subsequent dividends. The general model then becomes:

$$P = \frac{D_1}{(1+r_1)} + \frac{D_2}{(1+r_2)^2} + \dots + \frac{D_N}{(1+r_N)^N} + \frac{P_N}{(1+r_N)^N} \qquad (2)$$

where

$\quad P_N$ = the expected sale price (or terminal price) at the horizon (period N)
$\quad N$ = the number of periods in the horizon
$\quad r_t$ = the appropriate discount or capitalization rate for period t

Equation (2) is called the *finite-life general model*. The benefit of this model is that the dividend stream to be estimated is finite and within a reasonable forecast horizon (say, a business cycle). However, the model begs the question of how one estimates the terminal value, and still requires estimation of period-specific discount rates.

The first level of abstraction is to assume that the discount rate will be the same for all future periods. This is a fairly innocuous assumption, analogous to those associated with the term structure of interest rates. That is, we know that the year-by-year rate on a 10-year bond is not the same in each period (except for the case of a flat term structure), yet we use the 10-year yield, as a geometrically weighted average of the yearly rates, to describe the yield on that bond. In the same way, we can think of the constant discount rate, r, as being a (very) long-term weighted average of individual period discount rates. Any bias induced by this assumption is liable to be minimal in comparison with the estimation errors inherent in predicting individual period discount rates far into the future. Hence we posit the constant discount rate version of the finite-life model:

$$P = \frac{D_1}{(1+r)} + \frac{D_2}{(1+r)^2} + \dots + \frac{D_N}{(1+r)^N} + \frac{P_N}{(1+r)^N} \qquad (3)$$

For example, suppose that the following data are determined by an analyst for stock XYZ:

$\quad D_1$ = \$2.00 D_2 = \$2.20 D_3 = \$2.30 D_4 = \$2.55 D_5 = \$2.65
$\quad P_5$ = \$26 N = 5 r = 0.10

Given the assumption of a constant discount rate, the fair price of stock XYZ based on the constant discount rate version of the finite-life model given by equation (3) is:

$$P = \frac{\$2.00}{(1.10)} + \frac{\$2.20}{(1.10)^2} + \frac{\$2.30}{(1.10)^3} + \frac{\$2.55}{(1.10)^4} + \frac{\$2.65}{(1.10)^5} + \frac{\$26.00}{(1.10)^5} = \$24.895$$

The constant discount rate version of the finite-life model requires three forecasts as inputs to calculate the fair value of a stock:

1. the expected terminal price (P_N)
2. the dividends up to period N $(D_1$ to $D_N)$
3. the discount rate (r)

Thus the relevant question is, How accurately can these inputs be forecasted?

The terminal price is the most difficult of the three forecasts. According to theory, P_N is the present value of all future dividends after N; that is, D_{N+1}, D_{N+2}, ... , $D_{infinity}$. Also, the discount rate (r) must be estimated. In practice, forecasts are made of either dividends (D_N) or earnings (E_N) first, and then the price P_N is estimated by assigning an "appropriate" requirement for yield, price-earnings ratio, or capitalization rate. Note that the present value of the expected terminal price $P_N/(1 + r)^N$ in equation (3) becomes very small if N is very large. In practice, the value for r is typically generated from the capital asset pricing model (CAPM). Recall that CAPM provides the expected return for a company based on its systematic risk (beta).

Given the fair price derived from a dividend discount model, the assessment of the stock proceeds along the following lines. If the market price is below the fair price derived from the model, then the stock is *undervalued* or *cheap*. The opposite holds for a stock whose market price is greater than the model-derived price. In this case, the stock is said to be *overvalued* or *expensive*. A stock trading equal to or close to its fair price is said to be *fairly valued*.

The DDM tells us the relative value but does not tell us when the price of the stock should be expected to move to its fair price. That is, the model says that based on the inputs generated by the analyst, the stock may be cheap, expensive, or fair. However, it does not tell the analyst that if it is mispriced how long it will take before the market recognizes the mispricing and corrects it. As a result, a manager may hold a stock perceived to be cheap for an extended period of time and may underperform a benchmark during that period.

Moreover, as we pointed out at the outset of this chapter, while a stock may be perceived to be mispriced, an analyst must consider how mispriced it is in order to take the appropriate action (buy a cheap stock and sell or sell short an expensive stock). The stochastic dividend discount model described later in this chapter will allow an analyst to express the degree of confidence he has that a stock is mispriced.

Practitioners rarely use the DDM as given by equation (3). Instead, the specialized deterministic DDMs described below are used.

Deterministic Constant Growth Models

If it assumed there is a constant growth in dividends over the life of the stock, then the finite-life dividend discount model assuming a constant discount rate can be modified further.

Deterministic Geometric Growth Model

Dividend growth can be assumed to be geometric or additive. If future dividends are assumed to grow at an assumed rate (g) and a single discount rate is used, then the dividend discount model given by equation (3) becomes

$$P = \frac{D_1}{(1+r)} + \frac{D_1(1+g)^1}{(1+r)^2} + \frac{D_1(1+g)^2}{(1+r)^3} + \ldots + \frac{D_N(1+g)^N}{(1+r)^N} + \frac{P_N}{(1+r)^N} \qquad (4)$$

and it can be shown that as N approaches infinity, equation (4) reduces to:

$$P = \frac{D_1}{r-g} \qquad (5)$$

Equation (5) is called the *deterministic constant growth model*. It also referred to as the *Gordon model*, named after Myron Gordon who was one of its earliest advocates.[3] An equivalent formulation for the constant growth model is

$$P = \frac{D_0(1+g)}{r-g} \qquad (6)$$

where D_0 is the current dividend and therefore D_1 is equal to $D_0(1+g)$.

Let's apply the model as given by equation (6) to estimate the price of three utilities, Bell Atlantic, Bell South, and Cincinnati Bell, as of 1994. The discount rate for each telephone utility was estimated using the capital asset pricing model assuming (1) a market risk premium of 5% and (2) a risk-free rate of 6%. The beta estimate for each telephone utility was obtained from Value Line (0.90 for Bell Atlantic, 0.80 for Bell South, and 0.95 for Cincinnati Bell). The discount rate, r, for each telephone utility based on the CAPM was then:

Bell Atlantic $r = 0.06 + 0.90\,(0.05) = 0.105$ or 10.5%
Bell South $r = 0.06 + 0.80\,(0.05) = 0.100$ or 10.0%
Cincinnati Bell $r = 0.06 + 0.95\,(0.05) = 0.1075$ or 10.75%

The dividend growth rate can be estimated by using the compounded rate of growth of historical dividends. The dividend history for the three telephone utilities ending in 1994 is shown in Exhibit 1. The data needed for the calculations are summarized below:

	Starting in	Dividend	1994 dividend	No. of years
Bell Atlantic	1984	$1.60	$2.80	10
Bell South	1984	$1.72	$2.88	10
Cincinnati Bell	1977	$0.22	$0.84	17

---

[3] Myron J. Gordon, *The Investment, Financing and Valuation of the Corporation* (Homewood, IL: Richard D. Irwin, 1952).

Exhibit 1: Annual Dividend and Dividend Changes for Bell Atlantic, Bell South, and Cincinnati Bell

	Bell Atlantic		Bell South		Cincinnati Bell	
Year	Dividend	% Change[*]	Dividend %	Change[*]	Dividend %	Change[*]
1977					0.22	
1978					0.27	22.73
1979					0.30	11.11
1980					0.32	6.67
1981					0.33	3.13
1982					0.34	3.03
1983					0.35	2.94
1984	1.60		1.72		0.37	5.71
1985	1.70	6.25	1.88	9.30	0.42	13.51
1986	1.80	5.88	2.04	8.51	0.44	4.76
1987	1.92	6.67	2.20	7.84	0.48	9.09
1988	2.04	6.25	2.36	7.27	0.56	16.67
1989	2.20	7.84	2.52	6.78	0.68	21.43
1990	2.36	7.27	2.68	6.35	0.76	11.76
1991	2.52	6.78	2.76	2.99	0.80	5.26
1992	2.60	3.17	2.76	0	0.80	0
1993	2.68	3.08	2.76	0	0.80	0
1994	2.80	4.48	2.88	4.35	0.84	5.00

* The percent change is found as follows:

$$\frac{\text{Dividend in year } t}{\text{Dividend in year } t-1} - 1$$

The compound growth rate, g, is found using the following formula:

$$\left(\frac{1994 \text{ dividend}}{\text{Starting dividend}}\right)^{1/\text{no. of years}} - 1$$

Substituting the values from the table into the formula we get:

$$g \text{ for Bell Atlantic} = \left(\frac{\$2.80}{\$1.60}\right)^{1/10} - 1 = 0.0576$$

$$g \text{ for Bell South} = \left(\frac{\$2.88}{\$1.72}\right)^{1/10} - 1 = 0.0529$$

$$g \text{ for Cinc. Bell} = \left(\frac{\$0.84}{\$0.22}\right)^{1/17} - 1 = 0.0820$$

The value of D_0, the estimate for g, and the discount rate r for each electric utility are summarized below:

	D_0	g	r
Bell Atlantic	$2.80	0.0576	0.1050
Bell South	$2.88	0.0529	0.1000
Cincinnati Bell	$0.84	0.0820	0.1075

Substituting these values into equation (6) we obtain:

Bell Atlantic estimated price $= \dfrac{\$2.80 \; (1.0576)}{0.105 - 0.0576} = \$62.47$

Bell South estimated price $= \dfrac{\$2.88 \; (1.0529)}{0.10 - 0.0529} = \$64.38$

Cinc. Bell estimated price $= \dfrac{\$0.84 \; (1.0820)}{0.1075 - 0.0820} = \$35.64$

A comparison of the estimated price and the actual price is given below:

	Estimated price	Actual price
Bell Atlantic	$62.48	$61
Bell South	$64.38	$60
Cincinnati Bell	$35.64	$22

Notice that the simple constant growth model gives a decent estimate of price for Bell Atlantic and Bell South, but is considerably off the mark for Cincinnati Bell. The reason can be seen in Exhibit 1 which shows the annual percentage change in dividends for the three utilities. The dividend growth pattern for none of the three utilities appears to suggest a constant growth rate. However, the Bell Atlantic and Bell South appear to be more in conformity with a constant growth than Cincinnati Bell. We'll return to this issue later in this chapter when we look at a more realistic DDM that can handle dividend patterns such as those of Cincinnati Bell.

Deterministic Additive Growth Model
It is also possible that dividend growth follows an additive process. For instance, suppose the current dividend is D_0 and the dividend in one period's time is $D_0 + d$ where d is the dollar change in dividends. The dividend in two period's time is $D_0 + 2d$, the dividend in three period's time is $D_0 + 3d$, and so on, *ad infinitum*. The present value of this dividend stream is

$$P = \frac{D_0 + d}{r} + \frac{d}{r^2} \tag{7}$$

Equation (7) is termed the *deterministic additive growth model*.

More Complex Growth Models
Most multiperiod dividend growth models try to model the life cycle concept. In the simplest case, a model may recognize a finite period of accelerated growth followed by a more stable growth phase. An extension to this approach is to allow for a period of transition between the high and stable growth phases. These approaches are called the *two-phase model* and *three-phase model*, respectively.

Two-Phase Model

The two-phase geometric growth model recognizes that high growth rates can only be sustained for a finite period (say until the end of period N), and then the firm will face more stable growth prospects from period $N + 1$ to infinity. Hence we suppose that dividends grow at a geometric rate g_1 over the first N periods and, thereafter, at a geometric rate g_2. Under this assumption, the present value of future dividends can be shown to be:[4]

$$P = \frac{D_1}{r - g_1}\left[1 - \left(\frac{1 + g_1}{1 + r}\right)^N\right] + \frac{1}{(1 + r)^N}\left(\frac{D_N(1 + g_2)}{r - g_2}\right) \tag{8}$$

where $D_N = D_1 (1 + g_1)^{N-1}$

The first term in equation (8) gives the value of the dividends paid during the high growth phase, while the second term gives the value of the dividends paid from period $N+1$ to infinity.

Three-Phase Model

A simple variation of the two-phase model incorporates a transition phase in recognition of the fact that changes in growth rates are gradual and not abrupt. This is the three-phase growth model. Hence, suppose that dividends grow at a high geometric rate g_1 over the first N periods, at a geometric rate g_2 over the next M periods, and, thereafter, at a long-run steady state geometric rate g_3. Under this assumption, the present value of future dividends is[5]

$$P = \frac{D_1}{r - g_1}\left[1 - \left(\frac{1 + g_1}{1 + r}\right)^N\right] + \frac{1}{(1 + r)^M}\left(\frac{D_N(1 + r)^N}{r - g_2}\right)\left(1 - \frac{(1 + g_2)^M}{1 + r}\right)$$

$$+ \frac{1}{(1 + r)^{N + M}}\left(\frac{D_{N + M}(1 + r)^N}{r - g_3}\right) \tag{9}$$

where

$$D_N = D_0 (1 + g_1)^N$$
$$D_{N+M} = D_0 (1 + g_1)^N (1 + g_2)^M$$

The three-phase model is reasonably intuitive if one recognizes that the first term in equation (9) grosses up the original dividend at the high growth rate, the second term (the transition period) increases the dividend at a decreasing rate, and the third term is again the constant growth model discounted back to the present.

---

[4] This model and its derivation are from Eric Sorensen and David Williamson, "Some Evidence on the Value of Dividend Discount Models," *Financial Analysts Journal* (November-December 1985),pp. 60-69.

[5] This model, also from Sorensen and Williamson ("Some Evidence on the Value of Dividend Discount Models"), is most closely associated with Nicholas Moldovsky. (See, Nicholas Moldovsky, Catherine May, and Sherman Chattiner, "Common Stock Valuation — Principles, Tables, and Applications," *Financial Analysts Journal* (March-April 1965).)

Different companies are assumed to be at different phases in the three-phase model. An emerging growth company would have a longer growth phase than a more mature company. Some companies are considered to have higher initial growth rates and hence longer growth and transition phases. Other companies may be considered to have lower current growth rates and hence shorter growth and transition phases.

In the typical investment organization, analysts supply the projected earnings, dividends, growth rates for earnings, and dividend and payout ratios using fundamental security analysis. The growth rate at maturity for the entire economy is applied to all companies. As a generalization, approximately 25% of the expected return from a company (projected by the DDM) comes from the growth phase, 25% from the transition phase, and 50% from the maturity phase. However, a company with high growth and low dividend payouts shifts the relative contribution toward the maturity phase, while a company with low growth and a high payout shifts the relative contribution toward the growth and transition phases.

A three-phase model is used by Salomon Brothers Inc. This organization is a broker/dealer that provides research to clients. The three-phase model that it developed is called the E-MODEL (E for earnings).[6]

STOCHASTIC DDM

As we noted in the illustration of the constant growth model, an erratic dividend pattern such as that of Cincinnati Bell can lead to quite a difference between the estimated price and the actual price. In the case of Cincinnati Bell the estimated price of $35.74 was considerably greater than the actual price of $22, suggesting that this telephone utility was trading significantly below its true value.

William Hurley and Lewis Johnson have suggested a new approach to dividend discounting modeling.[7] Their work differs from conventional dividend discount models discussed earlier in this chapter in that they assume that the future dividend stream follows a stochastic process. They then find the expected discounted value of this random dividend stream.

In this section we analyze the distribution of this discounted value for various assumptions about the stochastic process generating dividends. Processes with a Markov property are employed. This is a reasonable property for time series like dividends. Generally history will be unimportant for the valuation process — we care only about the current dividend and the probabilistic way in which uncertainty will unfold. Hence the memoryless property of Markov processes is suitable.[8]

---

[6] For a discussion of this model, see Eric H. Sorensen and Steven B. Kreichman, "Valuation Factors: Introducing the E-MODEL," Salomon Brothers Inc., May 12, 1987.

[7] Hurley and Johnson, "A Realistic Dividend Valuation Model," and "Confidence Intervals for Stochastic Dividend Discount Models."

[8] In addition, this general assumption gives rise to functional equations which are relatively straightforward to solve.

The models we describe below are divided into two types: *binomial dividend growth models* and *generalized Markov dividend growth models*. For the binomial dividend growth models it is assumed that the dividend will either stay the same in the next period or change in the next period. The change is either an increase or a decrease, but not both. Typically, a dividend increase is assumed. In contrast, for generalized Markov dividend growth models, dividends can stay the same in the next period, increase in the next period, or decrease in the next period.

Furthermore, within each type of stochastic model, the type of dividend change can be specified. As with the deterministic dividend discount models, the dividend can be assumed to follow a geometric growth pattern or an additive growth pattern. In the discussion below, we will begin with a discussion of the binomial stochastic DDMs and then describe the generalized Markov growth stochastic DDMs.

The Binomial Growth Stochastic Model

In the additive version of the binomial growth stochastic model, dividends are assumed to increase by a constant dollar amount or stay unchanged. This formulation of the model is called the *binomial additive growth stochastic model* and expressed as follows:

$$D_{t+1} = \begin{cases} D_t + d \text{ with probability } p \\ D_t \text{ with probability } 1 - p \end{cases} \quad \text{for } t = 1, 2, \ldots$$

where

D_t = dividend in period t
D_{t+1} = dividend in period $t+1$
d = dollar amount of the dividend increase
p = probability that the dividend will increase

The expected discounted value of the stock based on the additive stochastic DDM can be shown to be:

$$P = \frac{D_0}{r} + \left[\frac{1}{r} + \frac{1}{r^2}\right]dp \tag{10}$$

For example, consider once again Cincinnati Bell. In the illustration of the constant growth model, we used D_0 of $0.84 and g of 8.2%. For the probability of an increase in dividends, the historical percentage of annual dividend increases can be used. The estimate for d is obtained by calculating the dollar increase in dividend for each year that had a dividend increase and then taking the average dollar dividend increase. For the 15 years in which there was a dividend increase, the average dividend increase was $0.041. Since dividends increased 15 of the 17 years, a value of 15/17 or 88.24% was used. Substituting these values into equation (10), we find the estimated price to be:

$$P = \frac{0.84}{0.1075} + \left[\frac{1}{0.1075} + \frac{1}{(0.1075)^2}\right](0.041)(0.8824) = \$11.28$$

This result is still quite different from the actual price. The reason for this difference is that the additive model still does not reflect the pattern of dividends. We'll return to this point shortly when we discuss a different stochastic DDM.

The additive binomial growth model given by equation (10) assumes that the dividend will either increase or not change. There is also the possibility that the firm goes bankrupt. Given this possibility, a lower bound for the price of the stock (P_L) can be determined as follows. Letting p_B be the probability of bankruptcy then:

$$D_{t+1} = \begin{cases} D_t + d \text{ with probability } p \\ D_t \text{ with probability } 1 - p - p_B \quad \text{for } t = 1, 2, ... \\ 0 \text{ with probability } p_B \end{cases}$$

and it can be demonstrated that the lower bound for the price of the stock is:

$$P_L = \frac{D_0(1 - p_B)}{r} + \left[\frac{1}{r + p_B} + \frac{1}{(r + p_B)^2} \right] dp \tag{11}$$

Now let's look at the corresponding geometric growth model. Letting g be the growth rate, then the geometric dividend stream ignoring the probability of bankruptcy is

$$D_{t+1} = \begin{cases} D_t(1 + g) \text{ with probability } p \\ D_t \text{ with probability } 1 - p \end{cases} \quad \text{for } t = 1, 2, ...$$

The price of the stock is then:

$$P = \frac{D_0(1 + pg)}{r - pg} \tag{12}$$

Let's apply equation (12) to Cincinnati Bell. The growth rate used here is the geometric average of the percentage dividend increases for those years in which dividends increased.[9] Based on the figures reported in Exhibit 1, g is 7.63%. Using a growth rate of 7.63% and the previous values for D_0, r, and p, the estimated price using equation (12) is:

$$P = \frac{0.84[1 + (0.8824)(0.0763)]}{0.1075 - (0.8824)(0.0763)} = \$22.32$$

The estimated price based on a geometric stochastic DDM comes close to the actual price of $22 and is a far superior estimate than that derived from the additive stochastic DDM and the deterministic constant growth model.

Incorporating the probability of bankruptcy into the geometric stochastic DDM allows for the calculation of a lower bound estimate for the price. The formula is:

---

[9] Letting g_t be the percent change in dividend (in decimal form) and N+ the years of years of a dividend increase, then the geometric average is found as follows: $[g_1 \times g_2 \times g_3 \times ... \times g_{N+}]^{1/N+}$

$$P_L = D_0 \left[\frac{1 + pg - p_B}{r - (pg - p_B)} \right] \tag{13}$$

From the difference in estimates between the additive and geometric stochastic models it can be seen that the selection of the assumed dividend pattern is critical.

Trinomial Markov Growth Model

The binomial stochastic models allow for two possibilities: an increase in dividends and no change in dividends. A lower bound for the stock's value can be determined by allowing for bankruptcy. It is not uncommon for companies to cut dividends temporarily. For example, an examination of the dividend record of the electric utilities industry as published in *Value Line Industry Review* found that in the aggregate firms cut dividends three times over a 15-year period.[10] The generalized Markov growth stochastic dividend discount model can accommodate dividend cuts.

The additive model version of the stochastic DDM is as follows:

$$D_{t+1} = \begin{cases} D_t + d \text{ with probability } p_U \\ D_t - d \text{ with probability } p_D \\ D_t \text{ with probability } 1 - p_C = 1 - p_U - p_D \end{cases} \quad \text{for } t = 1, 2, \ldots$$

where

p_U = probability that the dividend will increase
p_D = probability that the dividend will decrease
p_C = probability that the dividend will be unchanged

The theoretical value of the stock based on the generalized Markov additive growth stochastic model then becomes:

$$P = \frac{D_0}{r} + \left[\frac{1}{r} + \frac{1}{r^2} \right] d(p_U - p_D) \tag{14}$$

Notice that when p_D is zero (that is, there is no possibility for a cut in dividends), equation (14) reduces to equation (10). Since the model deals with three possibilities for dividends next period, it is called a *trinomial additive growth model*.

Allowing for the possibility of bankruptcy, the lower bound for the theoretical price is determined as follows:

$$P_L = \frac{D_0(1 - p_B)}{r + p_B} + \left[\frac{1}{r + p_B} + \frac{1}{(r + p_B)^2} \right] d(p_U - p_D) \tag{15}$$

where $p_B = 1 - p_U - p_D$.

---

[10] Yulin Yao, "A Trinomial Dividend Valuation Model," *Journal of Portfolio Management* (Summer 1997), 99-103.

For the trinomial geometric stochastic model that allows for a possibility of cuts, we have:

$$D_{t+1} = \begin{cases} D_t(1 + g) \text{ with probability } p_U \\ D_t(1 - g) \text{ with probability } p_D \qquad \text{for } t = 1, 2, \ldots \\ D_t \text{ with probability } 1 - p_C = 1 - p_U - p_D \end{cases}$$

and the theoretical price is:

$$P = \frac{D_0[1 + (p_U - p_D)]}{r - (p_U - p_D)g} \tag{16}$$

Substituting zero for p_D, equation (16) reduces to equation (12) — the binomial version assuming dividends are not cut. The model given by equation (16) is the *trinomial geometric growth model.*

The lower bound price for this version of the generalized Markov growth model allowing for bankruptcy is:

$$P_L = D_0\left[\frac{1 + (p_U - p_D)g - p_B}{r - (p_U - p_D)g + p_B}\right] \tag{17}$$

Application of the Stochastic DDMs

Yulin Yao applied the stochastic DDMs to five electric utility stocks that had regular dividends from 1979 to 1994 and had a temporary reduction of dividends in some periods: Rochester G&E, United Illum., Ohio Edison, Montana Power, and Sierra Pacific.[11] The historical dividends and the beta for each electric utility is reported in Exhibit 2. The discount rate is determined from the capital asset pricing models assuming a market risk premium of 5%, a risk-free rate of 6%, and the beta for the electric utility shown in Exhibit 2. The value for the dollar amount of the dividend change and the growth rate are estimated from the past pattern of dividend changes. The probabilities are based on the number of years of dividend increases, decreases, and no changes.

The results of the estimates are reported in Exhibit 3. For all five electric utility stocks, the trinomial growth stochastic models provide a better estimate of the price than the binomial growth stochastic models. Notice that there was no superiority of the geometric or additive models. In the case of Montana Power, the pattern of dividends reported in Exhibit 2 is best described by a geometric model; the geometric model was the best fit. For Sierra Pacific, the pattern of dividends payments is best described by an additive model and the additive model in fact provided an estimate closer to the actual price.

Confidence Intervals

One of the most useful properties of stochastic DDMs is that the discounted value of dividends is a random variable. Hence we ought to be able to specify a distribu-

---

[11] Yao, "A Trinomial Dividend Valuation Model."

tion for the discounted value. This then would allow an analyst to use the theory of statistical inference to judge whether a valuation is sufficiently far away from its market price to justify a buy or sell recommendation.

Unfortunately, it is not easy to specify the form of this distribution, much less estimate its parameters. Fortunately the technique of Monte Carlo simulation can be used to generate an empirical distribution and estimates of important parameters such as expected discounted value and the variance of expected discounted value. The calculation of a confidence interval can be obtained by making the simplifying assumption that the discounted value is normally distributed. Monte Carlo simulation can also be used to do the same thing.

Exhibit 2: Dividend History and Beta for Five Electric Utilities

Year	Rochester G&E	United Illum.	Ohio Edison	Montana Power	Sierra Pacific
1979	1.33	2.62	1.76	1.03	1.28
1980	1.40	2.68	1.76	1.06	1.43
1981	1.49	2.76	1.76	1.17	1.46
1982	1.75	2.92	1.76	1.27	1.46
1983	1.84	3.08	1.80	1.46	1.50
1984	2.04	2.30	1.84	1.30	1.57
1985	2.20	2.08	1.88	1.00	1.63
1986	2.20	2.32	1.92	1.26	1.69
1987	2.03	2.32	1.96	1.34	1.74
1988	1.50	2.32	1.96	1.35	1.77
1989	1.52	2.32	1.96	1.39	1.81
1990	1.58	2.32	1.73	1.44	1.84
1991	1.62	2.44	1.50	1.50	1.84
1992	1.68	2.56	1.50	1.55	1.48
1993	1.72	2.66	1.50	1.55	1.12
1994	1.76	2.76	1.50	1.59	1.12
Beta	0.60	0.60	0.75	0.75	0.60

Source: Exhibit 2 in Yulin Yao, "A Trinomial Dividend Valuation Model,"
Journal of Portfolio Management (Summer 1997), p. 102.

Exhibit 3: Valuation and Actual Prices of Five Electric Utilities Using the Stochastic DDM Ignoring the Probability of Bankruptcy

Company	Actual Price	Ignoring Dividend Cuts		Allowing for Dividend Cuts	
		Additive Model	Geometric Model	Additive Model	Geometric Model
Rochester G&E	$23	$27.91	$40.50	$24.63*	$28.39
United Illum	35	40.63	46.87	36.79*	39.09
Ohio Edison	19	19.74	19.82	18.73	18.74*
Montana Power	24	19.68	33.02	17.40	21.91*
Sierra Pacific	19	21.88	24.60	19.58*	20.27

* Indicates the best fit model.
Source: Adapted from Exhibit 3 in Yulin Yao, "A Trinomial Dividend Valuation Model,"
Journal of Portfolio Management (Summer 1997).

Assuming that the distribution of discounted value follows a normal distribution, the true value of the stock ought to be in the interval

Expected value $\pm\, 3 \times$ standard deviation of stock value

with probability 99.7%

The expected value for the discounted dividends is obtained from the equation above for the specific stochastic DDM. The standard deviations for each stochastic DDM can be derived mathematically.[12] However, obtaining a closed-form solutions for the standard deviation of a discounted Markov dividend stream is tedious, even for the simplest processes.

By way of example, consider a firm which currently pays a dividend of $2.50 ($D_0$) and suppose an analyst has estimated the following parameters for the binomial geometric growth model: $r = 0.15$, $g = 0.10$, and $p = 0.6$. Using equation (12), the expected value is:

$$P = \frac{\$2.50(1 + 0.6 \times 0.10)}{0.15 - 0.6 \times 0.10} = \$29.44$$

The variance for the discounted dividends for the binomial growth model has been derived mathematically and is as[13]

$$\text{Var}(P) = \frac{g^2 p(1-p)}{(1+r)^2 - (1+pg)^2 - g^2 p(1-p)} \left[\frac{(1+r)^2 D_0^2}{(r-pg)^2}\right] \qquad (18)$$

Using equation (18), the variance in our example can be shown to be equal to 12.46 and therefore the standard deviation is $3.53. An approximate 99.7% confidence interval is then:

$$[\$29.44 - 3\ (\$3.53)\ \text{to}\ \$29.44 + 3\ (\$3.53)] = [\$18.85\ \text{to}\ \$40.03]$$

In fact these results were confirmed with Monte Carlo simulation. Ten thousand random dividend streams consistent with the assumed random process were generated.[14] Each dividend stream consisted of 200 periods. Each of the dividend streams was discounted, and hence, 10,000 random values were generated. The mean value was $29.45 and the sample standard deviation was $3.55 (the theoretical standard deviation is $3.53). Hence the simulation results are consistent with the theory.

However the assumption of a normal distribution does not appear to be justified. In Exhibit 4 a plot of the frequency distribution of the simulation is shown. This distribution is skewed to the right. Hence the calculation of more accurate confidence intervals requires the computation of higher order moments. One way around this problem is to use Monte Carlo simulation. We detail this approach below.

---

[12] See William J. Hurley, "An Introduction to Stochastic Dividend Discount Modeling," unpublished manuscript, July 1997.

[13] The derivation is provided in Hurley, "An Introduction to Stochastic Dividend Discount Modeling."

[14] Hurley, "An Introduction to Stochastic Dividend Discount Modeling."

Exhibit 4: Frequency Distribution for the Binomial Geometric Growth Stochastic Model

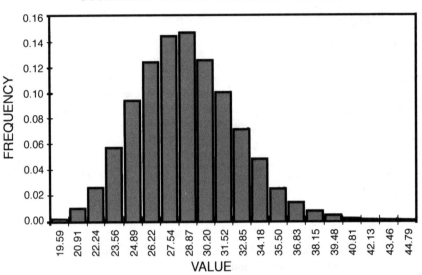

Obtaining Confidence Intervals Using Monte Carlo Simulation

As noted above, it is not simple to obtain a closed-formed solution for the variance of a discounted Markov dividend stream even for the simplest processes. The problem is compounded by the fact that the distribution of the discounted value tends to be non-normal. Hence estimation of confidence intervals will be difficult. A much simpler approach is to simulate the distribution of the discounted value. The following procedure using Monte Carlo simulation can be

1. Generate a truncated random dividend stream according to the assumed stochastic process.
2. Discount this truncated dividend stream to the present.
3. Repeat steps 1 and 2 a large number of times.

In terms of the parameters of the simulation, there are two issues. The first is where to truncate the dividend stream. This will depend on what discount rate is being used, but the experience of one of the authors suggests that truncating at 200 periods will give extremely accurate discounted values. The second is the number of discounted values to generate. Obviously, the more observations, the more accurate the discounted value and associated confidence interval will be. Again, based on the experience of one of the authors, 10,000 observations is more than sufficient.

Exhibit 5: Frequency Distribution for the Trinomial Simulation

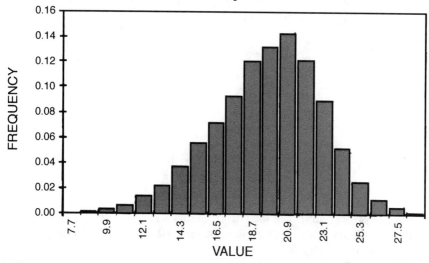

Consider the following example. Given the past dividend history and beliefs about the future, suppose an analyst believes that a firm's dividend stream is subject to the following trinomial process: the current dividend will remain unchanged with a probability of 50%; it will increase by 8% with probability 45%; and there will be a 25% cut with probability 5%. The current dividend is $2.50 and the discount rate is 15%. Based on these beliefs the analyst needs to determine the expected discounted value and its associated confidence interval.

A simulation in an EXCEL spreadsheet using the add-in @RISK was executed.[15] Ten thousand observations of discounted value were generated. This sample gave the following summary statistics:

Mean Observation	$20.23
Standard Deviation}	$3.23
Minimum Observation	$7.73
Maximum Observation	$29.72
Skewness	−0.323

A frequency plot of discounted value is shown in Exhibit 5. Note that this distribution is skewed to the left, which is consistent with the sample skewness of −0.323.

---

[15] About the only difficulty in setting up the model is the logic associated with determining the dividend each period. To accomplish this the following nested IF statement was used:

$new = \text{IF}((r < 0.05, old \times (1 - 0.25), \text{IF}(r < 0.05 + 0.50, old, old \times (1 + 0.08)))$

where *new* is the calculated dividend, *r* is a pseudo-random number drawn from a uniform distribution on [0,1], and *old* is the previous dividend.

An empirical confidence interval can be obtained from @RISK output in the following way. Based on 10,000 iterations, @RISK gives the percentile distribution shown in the following table:

	Percentile
5%	14.541
10%	15.821
15%	16.725
.	.
.	.
.	.
85%	23.479
90%	24.153
95%	25.151

We can get a 90% confidence interval from this table by taking the 5% and 95% percentiles. Hence the true discounted value will lie in the interval [$14.54 to $25.15] with probability 90%.

The @RISK percentile output is nice for another reason. It allows the analyst to estimate the probability that a stock is undervalued or overvalued. For instance, in the example above, suppose the stock is trading at $15.80. From the percentile table above we see that 10% of the sample observations of value were less than $15.821. Hence we can conclude that there is approximately a 90% chance that the true stock value is at least $15.80, and hence a 90% chance that the stock is undervalued.

DDM ASSUMPTIONS

We conclude this chapter with a discussion of the implicit assumptions when a DDM is used. The first assumption is that there is no attribute bias. Attribute bias means that stocks preferred by the DDM tend to be biased toward certain equity attributes. Examples of equity attributes are low price-earnings ratios, high dividend yield, high book value ratio, or a particular industry sector. To test for such biases, Jacobs and Levy conducted a study.[16] They analyzed over 1,000 stocks on a quarterly basis for five years (mid-1982 to mid-1987) and estimated the expected return for each stock using a DDM. Given the expected return, they then used multiple regression analysis to estimate the relationship between 25 equity attributes and 38 industry categories and the expected return. What Jacobs and Levy found is that expected returns from a DDM are related to equity attributes such as low price-earnings ratio, book-value-to-price ratio, dividend yield, beta,

---

[16] Bruce I. Jacobs and Kenneth N. Levy, "On the Value of Value," *Financial Analysts Journal* (July-August 1988), pp. 47-62.

and firm size. Thus, while the DDM assumes no attribute bias, this is not supported by empirical research.[17]

Second, the DDM assumes that the investor's horizon matches the time horizon used in the model. In practice, this is often not true. Users of DDMs typically hold stocks for much shorter time periods than those implied by the model. Finally, when applying any quantitative model such as a DDM there is the problem of estimating the required inputs.

---

[17] Another study that has suggested such attribute bias is Richard Michaud, "A Scenario-Dependent Dividend Discount Model: Bridging the Gap Between Top-Down Investment Information and Bottom-Up Forecasts," *Financial Analysts Journal* (November/December 1985), pp. 49-59.

Chapter 8

Normal Portfolios: Construction of Customized Benchmarks

Jon A. Christopherson, Ph.D.
Research Fellow
Investment Policy and Research Group
Frank Russell Company

INTRODUCTION

It is axiomatic that investment manager portfolios returns should be compared against benchmarks composed of securities in the same asset class from which the portfolio was selected. Investment managers, though, will often specialize in subsets of a universe of securities, rather than consider the entire universe. This has come to be widely recognized, and the institutional investing industry has moved away from judging all equity managers against the S&P 500 index and toward the use of more manager-specific benchmarks. The choice of proper benchmarks to evaluate manager performance is a continuing problem for fund managers. One of the better known types of specialized benchmark (or index) for a specific manager is the normal portfolio.

Our purpose in this chapter is to discuss not only how to create normal portfolios but how to use them. We will show how to identify one that is well-constructed and how to properly apply it to fund management. The virtues and limitations of different methods will not be explored in great detail; however, we will address some of those virtues and limitations. The examples that follow are taken primarily from U.S. equities; however, the framework for developing normal portfolios presented here is applicable to other asset classes or to funds of different classes.

DEFINITION OF A NORMAL PORTFOLIO

The notion of a normal portfolio was first introduced by Barr Rosenberg and the BARRA organization. The choice of the word "normal" to describe a portfolio is intended to capture the idea that for each money manager there exists a habitat of securities whose composition is very similar to the manager's average portfolio over time. In this sense, the normal portfolio is long-term "typical" or "average."[1] But average or typical of what? It is not clear that there should be a unique or single normal portfolio for a manager. There is more than one reasonable average in which we might be interested; hence, there might be more than one normal portfolio we could construct. One useful definition of "normal portfolio" is:

> A normal portfolio is a set of securities that contains all of the securities from which a manager normally chooses, weighted as the manager would weight them in a portfolio. As such, a normal portfolio is a specialized index.

To get an idea of how we can approach the construction of normal portfolios, let us identify two basic dimensions of "desirability" in constructing normal portfolios. Benchmarks can be designed that are desirable in terms of closely matching the actual portfolio holdings of a manager. Alternatively, benchmarks can be designed that are desirable in terms of closely matching the available factors of return and risk in the marketplace to which the manager's portfolios are exposed. And more recently, benchmarks have been created from weighted combinations of asset class component indexes which themselves are composed of factors of return and risk. Each approach to creating benchmarks will produce portfolios and return series against which a manager's portfolio and performance can be evaluated.

The object of using a normal portfolio as a benchmark is to improve one's understanding of a manager's investment activities. This is accomplished by comparing the manager's performance against a passive investment alternative (such as a portfolio of securities from which the manager actually selects) that approximately matches the manager's investment activity. The aggregate of the normal portfolios for a mix of managers can be used to manage the total risk exposure of a fund. It is simple to identify over or underexposed sectors or risks by comparing such a combination of normal portfolios to a target asset class benchmark. Thus, a properly constructed normal portfolio may be used as a performance measurement benchmark and as a tool for constructing manager mixes. Let us examine each of these purposes in turn.

NORMAL PORTFOLIOS AS MANAGER PERFORMANCE BENCHMARKS

The normal portfolio is normal or neutral because it includes all of the securities in the manager's investment habitat or the manager's opportunity set. Although the

---

[1] See Mark Kritzman, "How to Build a Normal Portfolio in Three Easy Steps," *Journal of Portfolio Management* (Summer 1987), pp. 21-23. The BARRA methodology is discussed in *The Normbook* (Berkeley, CA: BARRA, September 1988). For a discussion of more philosophical issues see Arjun Divecha and Richard Grinold, *Normal Portfolios: Issues for Sponsors, Managers, and Consultants* (Berkeley, CA: BARRA, February 1989).

Russell 3000 index or the S&P 500 could be a manager's normal portfolio, often this is not the case. Managers tend to specialize in different segments of the market, and broad market indicators are not generally useful for evaluating their stock selection and sector allocation skill. Broad market indexes are also inadequate as benchmarks for most managers because they contain many stocks managers would normally not even consider, much less choose. They also contain stocks in proportions managers would normally not hold. As a result, the average equity characteristics of many managers' portfolios can be quite different from a broad market index.

In fact, as Richard Roll pointed out, inappropriate use of broad market indexes can cause us to make incorrect judgments regarding a manager's riskiness and skill.[2] For example, a manager who specializes in defensive stocks will often outperform a broad market index during bear markets and underperform it during bull markets. In other words, when a manager's style is in favor he appears to be skillful, and when the style is out of favor his returns indicate a lack of skill. Without an adequate normal, it is difficult to determine if the manager has skill.

Therefore, to produce useful performance benchmarks, we must create a portfolio whose characteristics can be used to determine a manager's stock selection capability and, if appropriate, sector allocation skill. Presumably, the manager adds value by selecting the better performing stocks and/or the better performing sectors of his normal universe. If his portfolio return is worse than his normal universe return, then the manager made mistakes in choosing stocks, in departing from his normal weighting scheme, in choosing sectors, or all three.

The normal portfolio will also be useful not only if it is representative of the universe of securities that constitute the manager's "normal habitat," but if it holds these in proportions the manager normally holds. Furthermore, the normal portfolio's equity characteristics should closely resemble the manager's typical equity characteristics over time. Note however, that a manager's observed portfolio may vary considerably at any point in time — deviations from the normal are not unusual. This latter point is a constant source of difficulty because we are never really quite sure whether the observed current portfolio's deviation from the normal portfolio is merely the result of short-term tactical bets or a sign of a major shift in investment philosophy and style.

HOW TO CREATE A NORMAL PORTFOLIO

Approaches to Normal Portfolio Construction

There are several methods for creating normal portfolios. The most easily created is a list of stocks derived from an analysis of the manager's past behavior and is the approach most commonly used. A second approach is to base the list of stocks on factor risk exposures. A third approach, taking advantage of the advent of

---

[2] Richard Roll, "A Critique of the Asset Pricing Theory's Tests," *Journal of Financial Economics* (March 1977), pp. 129-176.

equity style indexes, is to create a simple weighted combination of indexes to match the manager portfolio. The first two approaches are the same in that they require reducing a broad universe of securities, such as the Russell 3000 index list of stocks, based on some characteristic(s) of the securities (e.g., price/earnings ratio or factor exposure) to obtain a subset of the broad universe. The resulting list of stocks is then weighted to produce a normal portfolio. The two approaches differ in the manner in which they derive screening and weighting rules. The third approach sacrifices portfolio membership accuracy but is easy to do. These benchmarks can all be used for performance and other portfolio comparisons.

If our interest is whether or not a manager picks the best stocks out of his "normal universe of stocks," where "normal universe" means the subset of all stocks that the manager actually considers for investment, then we can create a *manager-specific stock-matching benchmark*. In the approach advocated by Russell, the screening rules are determined by obtaining the proper screen criteria from the manager directly or from his written materials as augmented by an examination of his equity profiles over time. The resulting normal portfolio is used as a benchmark to determine performance attribution using the Russell standard analytic tools.

If our interest is to isolate macroeconomic sources of return and risk, we can create a *manager-specific factor benchmark*. A normal portfolio in this conception reflects the prominent financial characteristics the manager's portfolio would exhibit in the absence of active investment judgment. Given a credible factor model of stock returns and risks, our task is to create a portfolio of stocks similar to the manager's choice set and with factor exposures similar to the manager's average exposures. Such a benchmark allows us to evaluate how efficiently the manager chooses stocks given the exposures the manager undertakes.

In a factor model approach, the screening criteria are derived by examining the risk factor exposures over time.[3] The factor model approach analyzes the manager's average exposure to the various risk indexes of the BARRA risk model and assigns typical or average risk index exposures for the manager. Then the manager's performance is subsequently compared to the return that would have been generated by the hypothetical portfolio with the risk exposure of the normal.

If our interest is whether or not a manager can outperform a combination of readily available style indexes, then we can create a *manager-specific conditional style weighted benchmark*. There are two competing methods for obtaining the style weights. One is called "effective mix" and is based on the convariance of manager returns with style index returns.[4] The other method is called "portfolio characteristics analysis" and is based on the conditional evaluation of manager

---

[3] A procedure for factor normals is outlined in BARRA, *The Normbook* and Divecha and Grinold, *Normal Portfolios: Issues for Sponsors, Managers, and Consultants.*

[4] William F. Sharpe, "Determining a Funds Effective Asset Mix," *Investment Management Review* (December 1988), pp. 59-69 and William F. Sharpe, "Asset Allocation: Management Style and Performance Measurement," *Journal of Portfolio Management* (Winter 1992), pp. 7-19.

market relative equity characteristics.[5] The resulting normal portfolio is used as a benchmark just like the other two normal portfolio creation methods.

All three approaches provide useful, if somewhat different, information and all can be used profitably. However, the manager-specific stock-matching benchmark approach is somewhat easier to understand, implement, and provides the least ambiguous results. This approach will be the primary focus of this chapter.

MANAGER-SPECIFIC STOCK-MATCHING BENCHMARK

The Beginning Universe of Securities

In the manager-specific stock-matching benchmark the central goal is to capture stocks from which the manager normally chooses and on which one can obtain information reliably and readily. One could begin with all possible U.S. equities, which number over 6,000. The difficulty with this strategy is that sufficient data are often not available for many of the small capitalization stocks in this group. Furthermore, few investors in the United States actively trade the very small stocks which make up the tail end of the equity market.

There are a number of ways of isolating the beginning universe. Choosing subsets on the basis of capitalization is an easy first cut. A practical starting list would include the stocks in the Russell 3000. Using the Russell 3000 index list of stocks will provide coverage of nearly all U.S. stocks with capitalization above $20 million. One could also choose the list of stocks of the S&P 500 or some other major index; however, most of these are subsets of the Russell 3000.

Choosing the Securities for the Normal

Assuming the chosen universe contains all or most of the stocks from which the manager is likely to select, the next step is to reduce the list of stocks to those from which the manager actually does select. This is usually accomplished by subsetting the universe using screening criteria consistent with the manager's stock selection habit patterns. Decision rules are required for this process (i.e., it is necessary to have a numeric basis for deciding whether or not a stock belongs in the normal). Exhibit 1 is an example of the kind of information one needs to know in order to build a normal portfolio. This example comes from materials distributed by a well-known money management firm with a growth orientation. Note that these screens may not be used in any order. Sometimes the sequence of decision screens can make a great deal of difference.

The screens (as shown in Section A of Exhibit 1) must accurately capture the sub-universe of stocks from which the manager actually chooses. These

---

[5] Jon A. Christopherson and Dennis J. Trittin, "Equity Style Classification System," Chapter 4 in T. Daniel Coggin and Frank J. Fabozzi (eds.), *The Handbook of Equity Style Management,* (Frank J. Fabozzi Associates, New Hope, PA; 1995) pp. 69-98.

screens may be determined through communication with the manager or developed independently based on the fund manager's assessment of the manager's key selection criteria. In either case, the content of the screens is critical. Since, in our example, the manager will choose among large rather than small capitalization stocks, we would choose the broad, large capitalization market as the beginning universe (i.e., the Russell 1000). We would then subdivide or screen the universe on such criteria as those listed in Section A of Exhibit 1.

Exhibit 1: Example of Normal Portfolio Specification

Section A: Screening Procedure
Choose all stocks that meet the following criteria:

1. Capitalization	$\geq$	$350,000,000
		(i.e., large capitalization)
2. Yield	$\leq$	5.00%
3. Book Price	$\leq$	0.5 Std. Deviation
		(translates to Price/Book Ratio 1.00)
4. Dividend Payout Ratio	$\leq$	Market
		(translates to less than or equal to the mean of the distribution)
5. Historical Beta	$\geq$	0.85
6. Earnings Variability	$\geq$	(0.5) Std. Deviation
		(translates to one-half standard deviation below the mean of the distribution)

Section B: Weight Scheme
Equal Weight Within the Following Parameters

	% of Portfolio
$350 Million - $1 Billion	15%
$1 Billion - $3 Billion	30%
$3 Billion - $6 Billion	35%
$6 Billion and up	15%
IBM	5%

Section C: Rebalancing Scheme
Prior to 1989, the manager ran the screens semiannually and rebalanced position sizes monthly. After 1989, they do not rebalance monthly, rather they let the positions run for the full six months.

Of course, "average" can mean either the mean or median of the distribution, depending on the skewness of the underlying distribution. The equity portfolio statistics of the Russell 1000 or 3000 are useful market mean values since they are capitalization-weighted means. One could divide the universe in half by using the median, since the distributions of many characteristics are skewed, but there is the problem of whether to use weighted or unweighted medians. Where possible, the breakpoints should be set on the basis of the manager's behavior, either as described by the manager or as it has been observed. If the manager's decision criteria are not known, it may be desirable to try several screening values and examine how representative the resulting sub-universes are.

There are no unambiguous rules about setting screening values. The only good check is the reasonableness of the resulting sub-universe given the manager's style of investing. Two ways to judge the reasonableness of a sub-universe are (1) by evaluating how well the manager's return patterns fit the normal and (2) by evaluating how well the normal fits the manager's portfolio characteristics. If we had to choose between the two criteria, we should be more concerned with the portfolio characteristics than with similarity of performance because of the role of noise in stock returns. However, we would expect to find, on average, significantly higher correlations between the manager's performance and the normal than with the broad market and also a lower residual variance relative to the normal than to other indexes. The size of these differences is a function of the differences between the normal universe and the broad market as well as the noise introduced by the size of the bets the manager makes relative to his normal.

Conditional Decision Making and Manager Universe Misfit

If stock characteristics used in screens are independent (i.e., they are not correlated or causally related), then the sequence in which the variables are taken does not matter. However, the variables many managers use to choose stocks for their normal universe are not independent, and the sequence in which the screens are applied often makes a great deal of difference. For example, in screening the Russell 1000 stocks, the top 10% (of stocks based on return on equity) of the bottom 10% (based on price/earnings) is not likely to be the same set of stocks as the bottom 10% (based on price/earnings) of the top 10% (based on return on equity).

Most people do not stop to think that linear models, such as factor models, simultaneously evaluate all variables in the model at any given point in time. For example, in a factor model equation, each factor is a potential contributor to security returns. A factor exposure cannot be conditionally included in an equation; that is, included only if some condition is met as in our example above.[6] Optimizing on key portfolio characteristics cannot effectively portray a manager's selection process when conditional decision making matters. Ignoring conditional

---

[6] One can approach this through reformulation and imaginative use of dummy variables.

decision making can lead to choosing stocks for the normal portfolio that are not considered by the manager, and universe misfit will be the result.[7]

Weighting the Securities

Once the normal sub-universe of stocks has been specified, the critical problem of how to combine them into an index remains (i.e., the weights that should be applied to each stock). Broad market indexes such as the Russell indexes and the S&P 500 are capitalization-weighted indexes. Managers, on the other hand often do not capitalization-weight their portfolios. An example will demonstrate the importance of choosing a correct weighting scheme when creating normal portfolios.

Let us assume we have screened our universe in such a way that we end up with the same four stocks held in the manager's portfolio and the normal portfolio. Assume also that we choose to weight the normal portfolio on a capitalization basis even though our manager chooses an equal-weighted basis. Finally, let us assume that at the end of the quarter, the security return numbers shown in Exhibit 2 emerge. As can be seen, the normal portfolio has a much higher return than the manager's portfolio even though their holdings are identical. This example highlights the importance of the choice of weighting scheme. It always makes a significant difference in total performance. Generally, the normal portfolio and the manager's current portfolio will not include exactly the same stocks, so the weighting scheme can easily become a source of confusion and/or contention.

Bear in mind that while one wants to choose a weighting scheme that fairly reflects the manager's behavior, the fund manager also needs to evaluate other aspects of the manager's behavior that can affect overall performance, such as sector weighting and other bets. Note that when a manager equal-weights his portfolio there is an implicit bias against large capitalization stocks and toward smaller capitalization stocks.

Exhibit 2: Example of the Importance of Choosing a Correct Weighting Scheme when Creating Normal Portfolios

Stock	Cap Weight	Security Return	Stock Impact on Return	Manager Security		Stock Impact on Return
A	50%	15%	7.50%	25%	15%	3.75%
B	30	10	3.00	25	10	2.50
C	15	5	0.75	25	5	1.25
D	5	5	0.25	25	5	1.25
Total Returns			11.50%			8.75%

---

[7] See Jon A. Christopherson, "Selecting an Appropriate Benchmark: Problems with Normal Portfolios and Their Uses," *Russell Research Commentary* (April 1993, Frank Russell Company, Tacoma WA), pp. 4-6.

Weighting Alternatives

One can choose from a variety of weighting schemes. Here are three examples of weighting schemes based on capitalization:

1. *Equal weighting:* the same portfolio percentage for each stock regardless of stock capitalization
2. *Capitalization weighting:* each stock weighted according to its percentage of the total market value of the portfolio
3. *Capitalization weighting with break points:* each stock weighted according to its percentage of the total market value of the portfolio, down to a certain capitalization size; below the breakpoint each stock is equal-weighted (e.g., equal weight below $1 billion in market capitalization)

Other weighting schemes are feasible, such as the complex scheme shown in Section B of Exhibit 1. One might assign percentage weightings based on the logarithm of capitalization to compensate for the high degree of skewness in the distribution of capitalization (i.e., to give the smaller companies a larger percentage of the portfolio).

Of course, one is not confined to assigning portfolio percentages on the basis of capitalization. Weighting could be a function of other data. The treatment of such stocks as IBM often causes membership and weighting problems for normal portfolios. No "maybes" are usually allowed in portfolio membership — a stock is either in or out — but partial weighting can be obtained through controlling weights of classes of stocks. For example, value managers will often restrict the percentage of the portfolio that can be in utilities.

Advantages and Disadvantages of Capitalization Weighting

When choosing a weighting scheme for normal portfolios, one should be aware that capitalization weighting has certain advantages and disadvantages. Unlike an equal-weighted normal portfolio, a capitalization-weighted normal portfolio need not be rebalanced because of fluctuations in the price of the stocks in the portfolio. Also, since one is purchasing a percentage of each company in a capitalization-weighted portfolio, liquidity problems tend to be minimized. This makes them easier to passively replicate, if desired. Capitalization weighting also makes a buy-and-hold strategy easier to pursue.

The disadvantages of capitalization weighting are not inconsequential. As mentioned earlier, managers tend to not capitalization-weight their portfolios for a variety of reasons. The most often cited reason is related to the manager's aversion to putting too much money in any one basket (such as IBM) — they want stock name diversification. When compared against a capitalization-weighted portfolio, this aversion can be seen as a bet against certain sectors and stocks.

Finally, capitalization weighting tends to weight some sectors of the market more than would the average institutional money manager. In our experience, capitalization weighting will cause differences between the average characteristics of the manager's portfolio and his normal portfolio, as well as differences in performance.

Note, however, that weighting other than by capitalization is fraught with theoretical difficulties. For example, not every investor can purchase equal-weighted portfolios. Second, these types of benchmarks make passive management difficult. Furthermore, if one creates a noncap-weighted normal portfolio, a cap-weighted portfolio will also have to be created so that the user can understand the performance effect of underweighting large capitalization stocks. This is not a moot point. In the latter part of 1996 and early 1997, the large cap stocks performed much better than the overall market; managers who did not cap-weight their portfolios were negatively affected by their capitalization bets. It seems reasonable that the fund manager would want to know the extent of this bet against large cap stocks. As a general rule, for simplicity of passive management and to retain all market opportunities available to investors, capitalization weighting for normal portfolios is desirable.

Style-Weighted Normal Portfolio

A relatively new approach to creating normal portfolios takes advantage of readily available style indexes for segments of asset markets and newly developed methods that portray manager portfolios as weighted combinations of style indexes. For example, a value manager that has tight sector controls so that his portfolio has market-like sector exposures might have weights of 60% value and 40% growth, which can be described as market oriented with a value tilt.

As previously mentioned, there are two methods currently used to determine style weights — return pattern analysis and portfolio characteristics analysis. When an analysis of style is performed on a manager's portfolio using the methods described in the appendix for a given time period, a set of weights are obtained that represent the manager's style as of the end of that time period. A return that an investor can obtain over the next quarter (or month) as an alternative to purchasing the manager portfolio under investigation is a portfolio formed by purchasing passive style indexes in proportion to the weights suggested by the style analysis. The portfolio called the *style weighted normal portfolio* or *poor man's normal portfolio* is a realistic alternative because the investor could have purchased this portfolio rather than the portfolio under investigation. The argument is that the manager portfolio ought to be able to outperform this basic normal portfolio.

The style weighted normal portfolio is computed as follows:

$$R_{Nt} = w_{1t-1} S_{1t} + w_{3t-1} S_{2t} + \ldots + w_{nt-1} S_{nt} + \varepsilon_{nt}$$

where

R_{Nt} = style weighted normal portfolio return at time t

w_{nt-1} = style weight of style index n at the beginning of the time interval or at the end of the last time period

S_{nt} = style index n return at time t or over the interval from t-1 to t
ε_{nt} = residual return not correlated with the n style indexes
n = the number of style indexes in the analysis

The portfolio R_{Nt} can be used as any other benchmark for performance evaluation and fund management purposes as discussed herein. Note that any alpha the manager may have is confounded in the error term e_t with any specific risk. If return pattern analysis methods are used to compute the style weights, the alpha may be embedded in the weights assigned to the style indexes. Any return that is not captured in the style indexes is forced into the error term; hence these methods are inherently inferior to the manager-specific stock list method of creating normals.

ISSUES TO CONSIDER WHEN CREATING NORMAL PORTFOLIOS

Limitations of the Stock List Model

There are certain implicit assumptions about normal portfolios that one should bear in mind when creating and using normals. For example, the assumption inherent in the methodology described above is that the universe of securities from which a manager chooses can be determined by the fundamental stock characteristics used in screens. Hence, some styles of management such as market timing behavior would represent bets against a normal portfolio. If the manager has the discretion to move funds out of equities and into cash or other assets, this cannot be captured in a normal portfolio of equities only. A normal portfolio for market timers must also have a "normal" weight in the type of securities which the manager uses in market timing (e.g., cash).

Limitations of Factor Model Approach

There are several potential fit problems for factor-model normals when managers choose stocks on a basis other than the factors in the factor model. First, when a manager's key decision characteristics for each stock are not found in the multifactor model, the missing characteristics are matched by the factor model through a weighted combination of factors the model does have. Second, since the starting point is past portfolios, a persistent incidental and unintentional bet on factors could be misinterpreted as a normal bet (e.g., the sometimes high P/E of contrarian managers' portfolios that typically results from low earnings due to distress). Third, if a manager seeks exposure to a particular factor, stocks that have large exposures to that factor can easily be preferred by an optimizer. Hence, the optimizer might select an issue that "helps out" in optimizing several factor exposures.[8]

---

[8] For a discussion of normal portfolios and the problems managers and sponsors have tended to have with factor-based normals, see Christopherson, "Selecting an Appropriate Benchmark," pp. 8-15.

Limitations of Weighted Style Index Approach

There are several logical problems for weighted style index normals. First, style indexes by their nature are generally more broad lists of securities than the other two types of normal portfolios. If a manager is 90% large value and 10% large growth, then 100% of the security names, their weights and their equity characteristics are included in the benchmark. This will obviously lead to misfit between the manager's portfolio and the benchmark. This, in turn, means that evaluating the sector bets the manager takes is inherently more difficult. Because the stock lists of the normal and the manager do not match, explaining the inevitable difference in performance becomes problematical. These faults exist for either effective mix or portfolio characteristics methods of style determination. Although, the portfolio characteristics method is less likely to suffer less from these problems than return pattern analysis due to the nature of their methodology. The primary utility of the weighted style index approach to normal creation is the relative ease in creating these benchmarks and their concomitant low cost.

Communication Prior to Measurement

It is important to choose a normal portfolio in advance of the performance measurement period so that the manager and the sponsor both know the investment objective. The manager may be unclear concerning his most appropriate equity style. One should negotiate or otherwise determine before the performance period what characteristics the manager feels are a "fair" description of his universe. Such an *a priori* agreement can go a long way toward avoiding the "it doesn't fit me" argument.

NORMAL PORTFOLIOS AS
INVESTMENT STRATEGY TOOLS

So far we have examined how to create and use normals for the purpose of manager performance measurement. We will now turn to the second purpose of normals — the use of normals as investment strategy tools.

Normal Portfolios and the Policy Portfolio

The aggregate of the normal portfolios can be used to show the total equity exposure of the fund — the "policy portfolio." For example, a comparison of total exposure in the normal portfolios to a market benchmark such as the Russell 3000 will help identify over- or under-exposed sectors or factors. Passively managed "completeness" funds can be created to fill the gaps in exposure if needed. Of course, each of the multiple normal portfolios can be matched against one or more managers to help effectively mix multiple managers. Note also that normal portfolios can be seen as policy portfolios at the manager level.

Difficult Management Questions

While combining normals to achieve a policy portfolio appears simple on the surface, the decision to use normals presupposes the answers to several difficult, interrelated management questions.

Why Do We Create Normal Portfolios?

We create normals to provide an *ideal benchmark* against which to measure individual manager performance. In other words, we want to see how well he picks stocks within the group from which he normally chooses. We also want to see how well he allocates funds across industrial sectors and company sizes, and perhaps how well he covers a portion of the market.

Another, equally valid answer is to provide a tool for fund management. The sum of our normal portfolios across a fund can tell us what portion of the market has been covered. The sum of the normals plus a completeness fund can tell us how close we are to our policy portfolio or target portfolio. In this way normal portfolios can be used to guide our selection of managers and control the fund's exposure to market risks (i.e., to manage the fund).

These two answers are in conflict in certain ways. For example, in creating an ideal benchmark we would weight stocks in the normal portfolio exactly the way the manager does, but in using normals to manage a fund, capitalization weighting is desirable to minimize fund complexity and to determine the effects of capitalization bets. Also, we may capitalization weight the normal because we may like to think of it as an investable alternative, in which case capitalization weighting is essential. So the sponsor's purpose in creating normal portfolios is crucial to how they are constructed.

As for "ideal benchmarks," highly customized normal portfolios may provide much less useful tools for measuring performance than generic normals. It may very well be that the manager's returns correlate with a generic style index as highly or more highly than with a customized normal. In such a case the question naturally arises about whether the expense and effort of creating individual normal portfolios are worthwhile.

For What Should a Manager Be Given Credit?

The second question is related to the first. If, for example, a manager through intuition or research arrives at the contrarian investment strategy in which he buys only out-of-favor or undervalued stocks, then how much value added over a broad market benchmark should the manager be accorded — all of the contrarian style performance above or below the benchmark or only that portion not explained by a contrarian normal portfolio? This question, of course, moves the previous question of why we hire active managers in the first place. Presumably, we do so because we think managers can add value over a passive alternative. To the extent that active managers do not add excess return above their normal portfolios, the fund manager "could" or "should" create a passive portfolio of the securities in the normal portfolio and save a portion of the active management fees. Is this fair? Managers, want the credit for the wisdom of their style of investing. If we capture most of the manager's alpha by creating and subsequently passively investing in a normal portfolio, what is our moral obligation to the manager? Are we stealing the manager's alpha?

How Close to the Manager's Ideal Portfolio Do We Wish to Come?

Does the sponsor want a customized normal portfolio which matches the manager's style as closely as possible or a more generic normal which captures the manager's general style of management? The virtue of a close match is that it allows us to know more precisely where the manager added value (i.e., how well he chose securities). The virtue of the more generic normal is that we can judge how well the manager's variation on a theme — his skill in security weighting, sector allocation, and security selection — added value. A more generic normal portfolio also makes it possible to judge the skill of other managers of a similar style. The broader the normal portfolio, the more useful it will be for measuring opportunity costs, i.e., answering the question of how much better off would the sponsor be with Manager A rather than Manager B (given that the generic normal portfolio fairly accurately captures the investment style of both). The answer to this third question falls out of the answer to the first two, but it might very well be the first issue a fund manager decides.

How Much Cooperation is Necessary from the Manager?

The fourth question is more of a personnel management issue. Does the fund manager need and want the cooperation of the portfolio manager in creating the normal portfolio? If we know the securities from which a manager tends to choose and we do not care much whether or not the manager likes being compared to a normal which we feel represents his universe and/or strategy, then we can proceed without the manager's cooperation. The virtue of this approach is that it allows greater flexibility in fund management. The sponsor can define a set of "target" normals that come close to a policy portfolio and hold managers accountable for doing or not doing their part. In this context, normals may be seen as analogous to management by objective.

On the other hand, developing a customized normal for performance measurement usually requires the close cooperation of the manager to obtain the correct subset of securities for the normal and the correct weighting rules; hence, the closer we want to fit the normal to the manager's investment behavior, the more cooperation from the manager is required. Furthermore, a manager must know the basis of his evaluation, and to force a normal portfolio down a manager's throat can be seen as an arrogant, presumptive, and unfriendly act.

The resolution of this question has implications for all the other questions. If we decide the generic normal is close enough for our fund management purposes, then the manager's cooperation is less critical. This decision in turn is related to the question of giving credit for a manager's style. The more credit the sponsor wants to give the manager for his style and active management within his style, the less closely the normal will fit the manager's portfolio and the more closely it will fit the broad market. And, of course, the further away the normal is from the manager's typical portfolio, the less useful it is as a benchmark to measure manager skills within his universe — bringing us back to the question of what purpose the sponsor has in mind.

In summary, how the fund manager intends to use normal portfolios in fund management has much to do with the critical decisions the sponsor must make about the nature of each normal portfolio. Making any one decision has implications for all the other decisions, and the cumulation of them determines the overall usefulness of the normal portfolios.

CONCLUDING REMARKS

As we have seen, normal portfolios provide useful tools for fund managers to evaluate their money managers' performance and behavior as it relates to the overall fund structure. Some users of normal portfolios advocate producing normal portfolios that mirror as closely as possible the average portfolios of their managers. While this is a perfectly legitimate purpose for normal portfolios, we should also consider the merits of using normal portfolios to manage the fund structure. This provides a better basis for creating a set of normal portfolios. In other words, in addition to providing a close benchmark for performance measurement, the normal should also be created with opportunity costs in mind. This decision means that strict cooperation will not be required from the manager, and that the manager will be given credit for the nuances of his implementation of the investment style. It also recognizes that so long as it is reasonably close, the normal will be an effective benchmark for measuring not only security selection, but also sector allocation and capitalization bets.

While one could create normals that model a management firm so precisely they can pick up the differences between portfolio managers within one firm, it is more realistic to create normal portfolios that reflect the average portfolios of managers one could have chosen instead of the manager selected. In this way, the fund manager can evaluate the opportunity cost of hiring this manager rather than another or buying a passively managed alternative. At the same time, the sponsor can create a flexible instrument for fund management purposes.

APPENDIX

Return Pattern Analysis of Style

The object of return pattern analysis is to find a set of weights which, when applied to the indexes selected, minimizes the residual squared errors or differences between the optimal weighted set and the input portfolio's return series. In the least squares sense, this problem is similar to standard multiple regression but differs (and becomes non-linear) because the weights cannot be less than zero or greater than one and must sum to one. The method was first proposed by Sharpe.[9]

The number of optimizations depends on the length of the window used to set up the inputs for the optimization. The recommended choice is 60 months or 5 years of data. The first 60 months of index and manager data are analyzed and the means, variances, and covariances (correlations) are passed to the optimizer to find the optimal set of weights. The 61st month is then added to the data set and the first month is dropped, essentially rolling the window one month ahead, and the optimization is repeated. This rolling of the window and analyzing the data sets continues until the last time point in the data set is reached. The number of optimizations or analyses that can be obtained is equal to the number of time points (of complete data sets) minus the length of the rolling window, plus one. For example a data set covering 75 time points or months, using a rolling window of 60 months, will yield 16 analyses or optimizations (75 − 60 + 1 = 16). The choice of indexes is critical to the results obtained. Adding or dropping an index such as Treasury bill returns can dramatically effect the results. Changing the window length can also dramatically effect the weights.[10]

Portfolio Characteristics Analysis of Style

The object in portfolio characteristics analysis is to find a weighted set of indexes that has the same equity characteristics as the portfolio being analyzed. No optimization to match portfolio returns is attempted. The returns are the returns to a portfolio with a blended set of equity characteristics. The interest in portfolio characteristics flows from the expectation that portfolios with certain key equity characteristics will tend to earn a certain pattern of returns in the marketplace. The RSC system used by Russell Manager Research conditionally evaluates manager portfolio characteristics using non-linear probability of style membership functions to build a style assessment. The logic behind this system was developed by Christopherson and Trittin.[11]

The market relative equity characteristics analyzed are (1) price/book, (2) dividend yield, (3) price/earnings, and (4) return on equity (5 years). The portfolio characteristics that are judged in absolute terms are (1) sector deviation and (2) percent of capitalization in the small segment of market capitalization. The characteristics are analyzed sequentially, or more precisely, conditionally, so that the assessment earlier in the chain of logic is refined using subsequent information. In this sense it is an artificial intelligence system.

---

[9] Sharpe, "Determining a Funds Effective Asset Mix," and "Asset Allocation."

[10] For a review of the issues one should bear in mind when using return pattern analysis see, Jon A. Christopherson, "Equity Style Classification: Adventures in Return Pattern Analysis," *Journal of Portfolio Management* (Spring 1995), pp. 32-43.

[11] Christopherson and Trittin, "Equity Style Classification System."

Chapter 9

Equity Style: What It Is and Why It Matters

Jon A. Christopherson, Ph.D.
Senior Research Analyst
Frank Russell Company

C. Nola Williams, CFA
Senior Investment Strategist
Frank Russell Company

INTRODUCTION

Today the concept of equity styles permeates the way investors think about the U.S. equity market and investment managers. What was once an arcane idea promoted by consultants and embraced only by their large corporate clients has spread so that the popular press promotes it to the small investor. The public at large now has access to the same measurement tools as the large investor and, like the large client, is able to invest in style index mutual funds as an alternative to active management. Further, the concept of equity investment style has resulted in a veritable explosion of indexes designed to measure different segments of the equity market. No longer can a manager count on being successful by beating the broad market averages; the manager is highly likely to be held accountable for exceeding the appropriate style proxy.

This introductory chapter covers a broad range of topics concerning equity styles, from basic style definitions to potential applications of style analysis. Our intent is to define the term "style," provide some historical perspective, discuss style-related tools, and apply the concept to asset deployment. Our contention is that equity styles exist and that style matters.

DEFINING EQUITY STYLE

The notion of differing equity styles began in the 1970s as members of the investment industry began more actively gathering and analyzing data on market averages and investment managers (the advent of computerization doubtless did much to facilitate this effort). Although style descriptions weren't as well defined as they are today, analysts noted clusters of portfolios with similar characteristics and performance patterns. Groups of managers shared certain ideas about the best way to approach investing. The data were a manifestation of philosophical views about key determinants of stock price movements.

To see this point, consider two investors who are evaluating the same statistic from two opposing perspectives. They assess a stock's prospects using a ratio commonly applied in the industry, the price/earnings ratio. The "growth" investor is primarily concerned with the *earnings* component of the ratio. If the investor believes the company will deliver a particular future growth rate, and if the price/earnings ratio remains constant, then the stock price will have to increase as earnings materialize, and the investor will be rewarded. The key risks for the growth investor are that the future growth does not occur as expected and that the P/E multiple declines for some unanticipated reason.

The "value" investor, on the other hand, is concerned primarily with the *price* component of the ratio and cares much less, if at all, about the future earnings growth of the company. For this stock to be of interest, the value investor must deem the P/E ratio "cheap" by some comparison. The value investor's assumption is that the ratio is too low (perhaps due to an overly pessimistic assessment of the company's future) and that the P/E multiple will revert to normal or market levels when others realize that prospects are not as bad as thought. If so, the stock price will rise. In this analysis, the investor is relying on movement in price, rather than earnings, to be the reward. The investor anticipates that the price/earnings multiple will rise, with little or no increase in the earnings portion of the ratio. The value investor's primary risk is that the stock's cheapness is misread, and that the market's concerns about the company are indeed correct.

These two investors may assess the same stock at different points in its price and earnings pattern and from the opposing perspectives as shown in Exhibit 1. Often the value investor is the earlier buyer of a stock. If investor predictions are right, the price increases. This may or may not be accompanied by earnings increases, although that is not the investor's primary motivation to buy the stock. As the price increases, the value investor becomes uncomfortable with what seem to be expensive multiple levels and sells.

By now the growth investor has noticed the improving fundamentals of the company, which prompt interest in its future growth potential. The growth investor will purchase the same stock the value investor viewed as too expensive, and retain it for as long as the growth pattern emerges as anticipated.

Both investors are following logical courses, and empirical evidence can be found to support the profitability of both approaches. Their views of what is important to investing are diametrically opposed, however; and at the same time they reach opposite conclusions about the same stock. They buy and sell the same stock at different points along the price and earnings curves, both of which offer investment potential so long as the stock follows its typical pattern.

Exhibit 1: Change in Price Versus Earnings

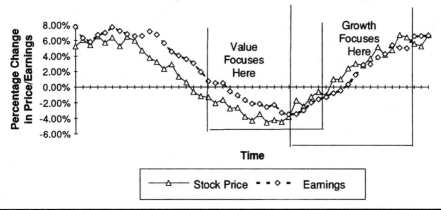

Note, however, in Exhibit 1 that there is a period of overlap when both the value and the growth investor may hold the same stock. An analysis of industry group performance also shows that stock groups often migrate from one group of investors to the other as equities experience a full business cycle.

To constitute a style, these investment philosophies must be held in common by a group of investors. While exact implementation of the shared philosophy may differ, the group agrees upon the factors that determine stock prices. If a philosophy is unique to a single manager, it is more appropriately called an investment "insight" that belongs to that firm alone. Such a firm would not rely on a certain factor, like growth or value, to add alpha and would have a set of portfolio characteristics different from a style group.

TYPES OF EQUITY STYLES

While industry terminology for U.S. equity styles varies somewhat, the style descriptions developed by the consulting firm, Frank Russell Company, typify those used today. Russell identifies four broad style categories:

- Value.
- Growth.
- Market-oriented.
- Small-capitalization.

Exhibit 2 depicts how these styles relate to different segments of the equity market.

Value

While value managers differ in how they define "value," they consider the stock's current price as critical. Some organizations focus on companies with low absolute or relative P/E ratios (price in the numerator), while others stress issues with above-market yields (price in the denominator). Additional valuation measures these investors often consider are price-to-book value and price/sales ratios. A stock whose price has declined because of adverse investor sentiment (i.e., price behavior) may also attract some of these managers. Their portfolios frequently have historical growth and profitability characteristics well below market averages, contrasting sharply with the characteristics of growth managers.

The value style can be viewed as consisting of three substyles:

- Low P/E.
- Contrarian.
- Yield.

Low P/E managers focus on companies selling at low prices relative to current, normalized, or discounted future earnings. These companies typically fall into defensive, cyclical, or out-of-favor industries.

Contrarian managers emphasize companies selling at low valuations relative to their tangible book value. They often favor depressed cyclicals or firms with virtually no current earnings or dividend yield. Contrarian investors purchase stocks in hope that a cyclical rebound or company-specific earnings turnaround will result in substantial price appreciation. The quality of companies owned is frequently below average, largely because corporate earnings are depressed and financial leverage is relatively high.

Yield managers are the most conservative value managers, focusing on companies with above-average yields that are able to maintain or increase their dividend payments.

Exhibit 2: Overview of Styles

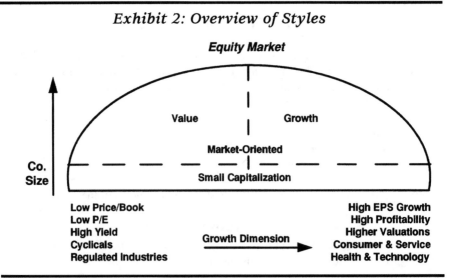

Growth

Growth managers attempt to identify companies with above-average growth prospects. They frequently pay above-market multiples for the superior growth rate/profitability they anticipate. Other typical characteristics of growth managers include selection of higher-quality companies; an emphasis on consumer, service, health care, and technology stocks; and lighter weightings in deep cyclicals and defensive stocks. Regardless of the source of expected future growth or the level of the current multiple, growth not reflected in the current price is the key focus.

There tends to be two substyles of growth managers:

- Consistent growth.
- Earnings momentum.

Consistent growth managers emphasize high-quality, consistently growing companies. Because such businesses have very predictable earnings and extensive records of superior profitability, valuation multiples are frequently well above the market. These managers typically underweight cyclicals, as they tend to purchase market leaders in consumer-oriented industries.

Earnings momentum managers, by contrast, prefer companies with more volatile, above-average growth. They attempt to purchase companies in anticipation of earnings acceleration. They are usually willing to purchase companies in any economic sector, as long as the equities offer the best potential earnings growth.

Market-Oriented

Market-oriented managers do not have a strong or persistent preference for the types of stocks emphasized in either value or growth portfolios; consequently, their portfolio characteristics are closer to market averages over a business cycle. A wide variety of managers with different philosophies fall into this category. Some may find a more "pure" growth or value orientation overly restrictive, and prefer selecting stocks wherever they might fall on the growth/value spectrum; others may purchase securities embodying both growth and value characteristics; or some wish to control nonmarket risk by reducing growth or value biases from their portfolio structures.

The managers in this group tend to follow four substyles:

- Value bias.
- Growth bias.
- Market-normal.
- Growth at a price.

Value-biased managers or *growth-biased* managers have portfolios with a tilt toward either value or growth. The tilts are not sufficiently distinct to put them in either the value or growth styles.

Many *market-normal* managers construct portfolios with growth and valuation characteristics that are similar to the broad market over time. Also included are those willing to make meaningful bets in growth or value stocks across time, but with no continued preference toward either.

Growth at a price managers seek companies with above-average growth prospects selling at moderate valuation multiples. Unlike managers in other market-oriented substyles, growth at a price managers generally do not offer wide diversification in portfolio structure or capitalization breadth.

Small-Capitalization

The major distinguishing feature of small-capitalization managers is a focus on small companies. Many investors are drawn to this market segment because they find more opportunities to add value through research, since the companies are less widely followed by institutional investors.

Typical characteristics of small-capitalization portfolios include below-market dividend yields, above-market betas, high residual risk relative to broad market indexes, and a thin following by Wall Street analysts. Just as in the large- and medium-capitalization segments of the market, managers in the small-cap arena focus on different stock characteristics. As a result, the substyles within small-cap closely resemble the broad categories of large-cap styles:

- Value.
- Growth.
- Market-oriented.

Small-cap *value* managers seek underresearched small companies that sell at low valuations relative to assets, earnings, or revenues. They correspond to large-cap value managers.

Small-cap *growth* managers focus on less seasoned companies with above-average growth prospects. They primarily invest in the technology, health care, and consumer sectors, and their portfolios exhibit high growth and valuation characteristics.

Small-cap *market-oriented* managers focus on small companies that, over time, exhibit growth and value characteristics similar to the broad small-cap marketplace.

EVIDENCE OF STYLES

Portfolio Characteristics

Different management styles produce different portfolio characteristics and performance patterns. Exhibit 3 gives a profile of fundamental data for representative value, growth, market-oriented, and small cap managers. Also shown for comparison is the Russell 3000® Index, a broad market benchmark. Note that all statistics shown are dollar weighted, so that they accurately reflect where the managers are investing their funds.

Capitalization Distribution The capitalization categories presented are determined by the rank ordering of companies within the Russell 3000 Index by market value, rather than by arbitrary capitalization cutoffs. The "large" category refers to the 50 largest companies in the market, the "medium/large" to companies 51 to 200, and so on. The Russell 3000 Index covers over 97% of the entire equity market.

As expected, the large-cap managers have the vast majority of their funds invested in the top 1,000 stocks in the market, which account for over 90% of the equity market's capitalization. The small-cap manager, by contrast, has the bulk of its money invested in the bottom 2,000 stocks in the market, which account for only 9% of the broad market.

Exhibit 3: Comparison of Equity Manager Style Characteristics as of December 31, 1993

Characteristic	Value	Growth	Market-Oriented	Small Cap	Russell 3000® Index
Capitalization Distribution					
% Large (Top 50 stocks)	16.2	30.9	26.6	0.0	34.4
% Medium/Large (51 to 200)	25.4	25.0	38.9	1.4	26.3
% Medium (201 to 500)	22.9	37.3	21.0	3.7	19.3
% Medium/Small (501 to 1,000)	24.3	5.9	11.0	33.6	11.2
% Small (1,000+)	11.2	0.9	2.5	61.4	8.8
Valuation Characteristics					
P/E on Normalized EPS	12.9	22.8	17.3	28.6	18.1
Price/Book	1.43	5.32	2.54	3.44	2.60
Dividend Yield	2.70	0.62	2.09	0.35	2.51
Growth Characteristics					
Long-Term Forecast I/B/E/S Growth	9.8	20.6	12.9	19.3	11.9
Return on Equity	12.7	25.5	17.2	12.7	16.3
Earnings Variability	88.8	62.4	56.5	84.5	48.5
Economic Sectors					
% Technology	6.2	25.8	13.7	18.3	11.6
% Health Care	8.2	9.8	6.1	11.2	8.8
% Consumer Discretionary	7.2	29.2	19.9	23.4	14.2
% Consumer Staples	3.5	0.0	7.3	0.0	9.0
% Integrated Oils	4.9	0.0	6.5	1.0	5.3
% Other Energy	6.2	3.6	3.8	2.7	2.7
% Materials and Processing	21.8	6.5	7.6	4.7	8.3
% Producer Durables	2.3	0.0	6.1	9.9	4.2
% Autos and Transportation	1.5	3.4	3.5	4.4	5.8
% Financial Services	29.6	15.6	18.7	16.1	14.8
% Utilities	7.5	6.1	6.7	6.4	14.8
% Sector Deviation	24	25	12	19	0

Valuation Characteristics Styles divide on valuation characteristics as expected according to our descriptions of investment philosophy. The value manager demonstrates below-market P/E and price-to-book ratios, and an above-market yield. The growth manager's characteristics are the opposite of those in the market. The market-oriented manager is close to market levels on these ratios. The small-cap manager shown here happens to have a growth substyle, so its valuation ratios are above-market; as discussed earlier, there is a full range of equity substyles in small-cap, so these characteristics are not necessarily representative of all small-cap managers.

Growth Characteristics Earnings growth characteristics (here noted as those forecasted by institutional investment analysts and historical return on equity) conform to expectations, given the differing investment philosophies. The earnings variability statistic refers to the historical behavior of quarterly earnings relative to long-term trend-line growth; the higher the number, the greater the cyclicality of earnings. We noted earlier that the value manager tends to have higher earnings variability relative to other large-cap managers, and that is evident here. This usually occurs because of the value manager's greater willingness to purchase companies with cyclical earnings. The small-cap manager also has a higher earnings variability number, but in this case it is due to the less seasoned nature of the companies held, rather than due to ownership of cyclicals.

Economic Sectors Economic sector exposure supports the other statistics shown in Exhibit 3 and confirms our sense of manager style. The value manager is overweighted relative to the Russell 3000 Index in financial services (typically a lower-multiple sector) and materials and processing, which in this case includes many manufacturing companies. The growth manager is overweighted in two traditional growth sectors, technology and consumer discretionary. The market-oriented manager has spread its bets the most among the sectors, as indicated by the sector deviation score. This score measures in aggregate the difference between the manager's overall sector allocations and those for the Russell 3000 Index; the higher the number, the more the manager's economic sector exposure differs from the market. Interestingly, the small-cap manager's bets relative to the broad market are smaller than those for all but the market-oriented manager. Often small-cap manager sector bets are larger since a small stock universe has different industry composition from a large-cap universe.

Performance Patterns

Differing portfolio characteristics result in different performance patterns, particularly over short time horizons. Exhibit 4 shows performance for manager universes for the four different styles. In this example, we have plotted excess returns net of the Russell 3000 Index for rolling five-year periods that shift quarterly; the Russell 3000 Index is represented by the horizontal line.

Exhibit 4: Five-Year Rolling Excess Returns
Growth/Market-Oriented/Small-Cap, and Value Accounts
Universe Means Versus Russell 3000 Index
Periods Through December 31, 1993

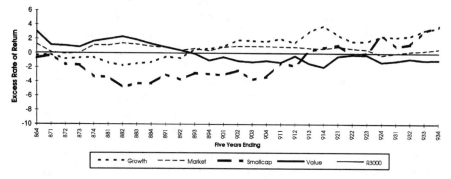

Exhibit 5: Growth in U.S. Equity Manager Style Membership

Style/Substyle	1980	1988	1990	1993	% Change 1980 to 1993
Growth	45	61	48	53	18
Market-Oriented					
Earnings Bias	13	16	15	18	38
Market Normal and Growth at a Price	58	50	51	42	−28
Price Bias	5	17	17	18	260
Value	18	58	70	67	272
Small-Cap	NA	48	70	99	NA
Growth + Earnings Bias	58	77	63	71	22
Value + Price Bias	23	75	87	85	270

Note the rotation of style performance over time, and the difference that style can make in shorter-term results. Growth lagged large-cap styles throughout much of the 1980s, but became the most dominant style in 1989, 1990, and 1991, ebbing somewhat thereafter. Value managers behaved in an inverse fashion from growth managers. Throughout all periods, the market-oriented group tracked market returns most closely, which would be expected, given their tighter factor bets relative to the market. The most prominent cycle is that of the small-cap style, which lagged significantly relative to large-cap styles in the 1980s, outperforming only recently.

HISTORICAL PERSPECTIVE ON STYLES

Interestingly, while the style definitions we describe are commonly used today, they have changed fairly significantly over the years. Exhibit 5 shows the growth and percentage of change in manager style universes over a fourteen-year period.

- In the 1970s (not shown in this exhibit), the vast majority of large-cap institutional managers used a growth investment approach; value managers were far fewer in number, and the term was much less frequently used. Value became more universally recognized as a style as more investors embraced it during the 1980s. Exhibit 5 shows the large increase in the number of value and price bias investors during that decade.
- Small-cap investing did not emerge as a separate style until the early to mid-1980s; instead, a more nebulous notion of style prevailed that was more aggressive in its use of high-growth and smaller-cap stocks. The idea that small-cap investing could encompass a full spectrum of investment styles did not fully emerge until a few years ago, and in fact, many investors still equate small-cap with high-growth investing. Exhibit 5 shows the large increase in small-cap managers in the early 1990s.

More recently, a new "style" has emerged in the marketplace called "mid-cap" investing. The argument for this style is that medium-cap stocks have different performance patterns from their large- and small-cap counterparts.

While statistical analysis supports the case for medium-cap stocks as a differentiated segment of the *market*, it is debatable whether it is an actual investment *style* according to the criteria set forth in this chapter. Recall we have said: (1) managers adopt a style because they have a guiding philosophical belief that it will add value, and (2) many investors need to share a belief in order for adherence to it to constitute a style. Finally, a style should result in a clustering of factor tilts or portfolio characteristics among portfolios that share that style.

The mid-cap example is the first time that a style concept may have been introduced *before* broad adoption among investment managers. The differing behavior of medium-cap stocks in the equity market was noted in research and press articles, yet few investment managers had produced portfolios with a mid-cap profile. While they have typically owned a broad array of medium-cap securities (and many certainly have a medium-cap bias relative to cap-weighted benchmarks), managers had not adopted this concept separately as an investment philosophy.

A simple screen for mid-cap portfolios (defined as 70% exposure or more to stocks in the Russell Midcap Index) resulted in only 28 managers when this style started appearing in the press. This contrasted with 89 small-cap managers and 183 large-cap managers.

Whether mid-cap investing is truly a style or not, history and its appearance demonstrate that style concepts evolve over time, and undergo refinement in the process.

CAPM, FACTOR MODELS, AND STYLE INDEXES

One might sensibly ask how styles and style indexes behave in light of capital asset pricing model (CAPM) theory and the assumption of efficient markets. If the equity market is efficient, then all stocks are correctly priced, given all available information. By extension, any choice of a market subset will yield a market return subject to variation due to sample size and the random character of specific risk. Yet this is true only if the CAPM determines the prices of assets, that is, if all stocks are driven by the same single factor, the market. As a consequence, all stocks will move up or down depending on their beta, and all other return will be specific return.

In such a world, no stock characteristic would lead to differential return. The implication of the one-factor CAPM is that stocks are not differentially sensitive to changes in interest rates or industrial production or any other economic variable. It is just this limitation of the CAPM that lead Barr Rosenberg and associates to develop their fundamental factor model and Stephen Ross to develop the APT factor model. Multifactor models recognize stock differential sensitivity to forces that can change stock prices above and beyond the effect of the market.

A few points follow from this discussion. If styles exist, then certain other things must also exist. First, the returns to style portfolios and style indexes must be significantly different for the market. Second, the style portfolios and index style returns must be significantly different from each other. Third, style portfolios and style indexes should have on average different factor exposure patterns from the market as a whole and from each other.

The existence of universes of managers created according to style characteristics suggest that it is possible to create indexes based on the types of stocks the managers typically select. The virtues of an index are that (1) it is unbiased and not subject to the vagaries or fads of managers implicit in universes, and (2) it offers a passive alternative to purchasing managers when active management is not perceived as productive.

Chapter 2 will review the growing number of indexes that have been created over the years since Russell first introduced its indexes in 1988-1989. The variety and diversity of style index definitions are covered there, and we do not review all style indexes here. We do use the Russell 1000 Growth and Value Indexes to demonstrate the presence of style cycles that are somewhat independent from manager portfolios.

Briefly, the Russell Growth and Value indexes are created by rank ordering all stocks in the Russell 1000 by price/book. The capitalization-weighted median is computed. All stocks above the median breakpoint have greater weights in the Russell 1000 Growth Index, and all stock below the median have greater weights in the Russell 1000 Value Index. The choice of price/book is the result of extensive research.[1] While it is a simple rule, it is not simplistic and is supported by subsequent academic research.[2]

---

[1] For a discussion of the research paths explored see Kelly Haughton and Jon A. Christopherson, "Equity Style Indexes: Tools for Better Performance Evaluation and Plan Management," *Russell White Paper* (Frank Russell Company, Tacoma, WA 1989). Stocks above the third quartile of P/E are 100% in the Growth index and 0% in the Value index while stocks below the first quartile of P/B are 100% in the Value index and 0% in the Growth index. Stocks between the first and third quartiles are in both indexes to some degree. Stock at the median P/B are 50% in both indexes.

[2] Eugene F. Fama and Kenneth R. French. 1993. "Common Risk Factors in the Returns on Stocks and Bonds, " *Journal of Financial Economics* (February 1993), pp. 3-56.

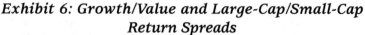

Exhibit 6: Growth/Value and Large-Cap/Small-Cap Return Spreads

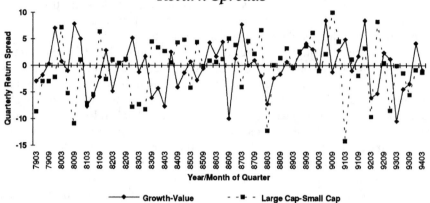

Exhibit 7: Cumulative Growth/Value and Large-Cap/Small-Cap Returns

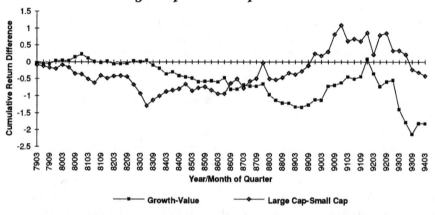

The returns of these indexes begin in 1979. As shown in Exhibit 6, the spread in quarterly returns between the Russell 1000 Growth and Value indexes and the spread between the Russell 1000 and 2000 is often different from zero. Over the period, large-cap stocks outperformed small-cap stocks much of the time. The same can be said for value stocks, which outperformed growth stocks about twice as often.

Exhibit 7 shows the cumulative return differences from 1979 through first quarter 1994. Returns will look different depending on the beginning date, but over this period the advantage of value over growth has been about 2%. At the end of the fourth quarter of 1991, however, the cumulative return differential since first quarter 1979 was essentially zero. From second quarter 1989 through fourth quarter 1991, growth recovered all the return differential it had lost from 1983 through 1989.

This raises the issue of whether we can expect any one style to underperform consistently for a long period of time. If one believes that value outperforms growth in the long run (as has been suggested by Fama and French and others), then the recovery of growth is an anomaly. If, on the other hand, one believes in efficient markets, then no market segment such as growth should be consistently underpriced. Hence, we would expect to see the type of recovery seen in the 1989 to 1991 period to happen again. Being able to time when growth becomes undervalued provides an obvious investment opportunity.[3] In any case, the index returns demonstrate that the style segments of the market behave differently from the market as a whole and do so consistently.

Style indexes are useful for performance evaluation of individual managers and combined manager mixes. In this sense, they can be used as normal portfolios.[4] If the style indexes accurately measure manager style, we would expect that the mean returns of universes of managers would behave more like the style indexes than broad market measures.

Exhibit 8 shows the regression statistics of the means of Russell Style Universe returns against the appropriate Russell style indexes. A benchmark that matches the universe of stocks from which the managers choose (i.e., its normal portfolio) will have a beta close to 1.0 (risk that is the same), an alpha close to zero (no abnormal excess return), and an R^2 close to 1.0 (a tight fit in return space).

For each style universe except market-oriented, the Russell style index has a beta closer to 1.0 than the alternative broad market benchmarks, the Russell 3000 and the S&P500.[5] The alphas of the style indexes are also closer to zero, except for market-oriented. For the market-oriented managers, the Russell 3000 and 1000 are all alternative broad market measures. The market-oriented betas are all less than 1.0, which is due to cash holdings.

We conclude from Exhibit 8 that using style indexes allows us to separate out style effects from manager universe group behavior, manager skill, and manager risk. Knowing the riskiness of small-capitalization versus the market as a whole, we can manage the plan to take this into account.

Style indexes by their nature also provide a passive alternative when hiring one or more active managers is problematical. Small pension plans may not have sufficient funds to hire a diversified set of active small-cap managers to man-

---

[3] For a discussion of the valuation compressions between growth and value stocks that suggested in 1989 that growth was undervalued, see Jon A. Christopherson, Natalie LaBerge, and Dennis Trittin, "Has Growth Become Value?" *Russell Research Commentary* (Frank Russell Co.: Tacoma, WA, September 1989).

[4] For a discussion of Normal portfolio construction and the role of style indexes in providing more precise manager benchmarks than broad market benchmarks, see Jon A. Christopherson, "Normal Portfolios and Their Construction" in Portfolio and Investment Management, Frank Fabozzi (ed.) (Probus Publishing: Chicago, 1989), pp. 381-397.

[5] While recognizing that the S&P 500 has serious drawbacks as a broad market benchmark because of its sector biases and capitalization biases, we include it in these analyses because of its familiarity.

age their plan. Rather than hire one manager with a style bias, they may wish to simplify management and hire a passive fund manager or manage the money in-house. Alternatively, some large funds have so much money that to place all their funds they would have to hire an extremely large group of managers. Rather than deal with the headaches of managing all these managers, they often choose to index part of their money.

STYLE MANAGEMENT: PRACTICAL APPLICATIONS

Performance Measurement

It should be apparent that taking style into account can make a difference in evaluating manager results. Look at Manager X's performance compared to a broad market index like the S&P 500:

	Annual Periods (%)					Annualized Periods Ending December 31, 1990		
	1986	1987	1988	1989	1990	3 Years	4 Years	5 years
Manager X	11.2	1.4	24.6	16.4	−11.5	8.7	6.8	7.6
S&P 500	18.2	5.2	16.5	31.4	−3.2	14.0	11.7	13.0

Given only this information, one would conclude that Manager X had not performed well. Yet when the manager's performance is compared to an appropriate benchmark (verified first by an analysis that the portfolio has small-capitalization characteristics), the conclusion regarding results changes markedly:

Exhibit 8: Benchmark Comparisons Manager Universe Means versus Style Indexes 10 Years Ending December 31, 1993

	Beta	Quarterly Alpha	Annualized Standard Error	R^2
Growth:				
Versus Russell 1000® Growth Index	0.992	0.368	3.210	0.970
Versus S&P 500	1.136	−0.043	5.208	0.922
Market-Oriented:				
Versus Russell 1000® Index	0.962	0.158	1.308	0.993
Versus Russell 3000® Index	0.945	0.256	1.178	0.994
Versus S&P 500	0.975	0.113	1.982	0.984
Value:				
Versus Russell 1000® Value Index	0.969	−0.110	2.474	0.970
Versus S&P 500	0.882	0.145	3.690	0.934
Small Capitalization:				
Versus Russell 2500™ Index	1.033	0.249	3.586	0.971
Versus Russell 2000® Index	0.924	0.769	4.462	0.955
Versus S&P 500	1.211	−0.418	8.958	0.819

	Annual Periods (%)					Annualized Periods Ending December 31, 1990		
	1986	1987	1988	1989	1990	3 Years	4 Years	5 years
Manager X	11.2	1.4	24.6	16.4	−11.5	8.7	6.8	7.6
Russell 2000®	5.7	−8.8	24.9	16.2	−19.5	5.3	1.6	2.4

Applying a benchmark that more closely embodies the stock universe in which the manager invests yields more information about manager skill.

One might ask (and many do) why comparisons that take investment style into account should be of such importance. The thinking is if investors cannot hire managers to outperform the broad market, then what is the point?

Over the very long term, managers should be able to beat the market regardless of style biases, or else they are not earning their fees. But in defining "long term," it is necessary to go beyond the typical five-year time horizon many investors choose. Style cycles can last, and have lasted, that long and longer.

One of the longest style cycles in recent years was the underperformance of small-capitalization stocks in the 1980s, which was shown in Exhibit 4. Small stocks grossly underperformed their large-cap counterparts for the better part of seven years, beginning in 1984 and ending in 1990 (there was one short-lived period of outperformance in 1988, but this quickly reversed). Managers who invested in that sector of the market were clearly underperforming the market consistently.

In a much broader context, the cycle of underperformance in the 1980s is not unheard of. While this period is certainly at the higher end of the range for small-stock underperformance cycles, similarly long cycles have occurred before.

Exhibits 9 and 10 show long-term data for the Ibbotson-Sinquefield Small Stock Index versus the S&P 500 from 1926 to 1993. These data demonstrate how much longer-term one needs to think in evaluating performance.

Exhibit 9: Performance of Small Stocks versus Large Stocks
Ibbotson and Sinquefield Index Relative to the S&P Index
Annual Rates of Return from 1926 to 1959

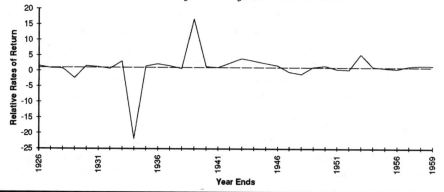

Exhibit 10: Performance of Small Stocks versus Large Stocks
Ibbotson and Sinquefield Index Relative to the S&P Index
Annual Rates of Return from 1960 to 1993

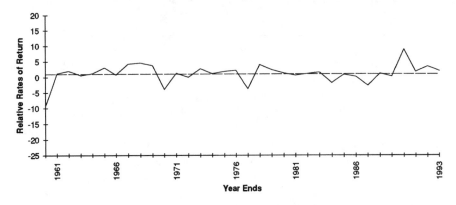

Unfortunately, the normal temptation is to use shorter time horizons. Also, it is unusual to find managers with 20-year track records where style effects would diminish in importance. This is why style analysis is so important. If investors select managers on the basis of historical performance versus a broad market benchmark, they may unknowingly hire a manager at a peak in performance that may be due solely to a style cycle. Conversely, they will be sorely tempted to fire a manager who has experienced underperformance solely because the manager's style category has lagged. These decisions can translate into a "buy high/sell low" pattern, which can be extremely damaging to performance. Of course, this analysis assumes that the managers being evaluated perform the way they do solely for style reasons and that other factors are not also at work.

Achieving Target Equity Returns

The ramifications of style analysis go beyond merely selecting individual managers. Style orientation can play a critical role in the performance of an entire equity plan.

The first step in constructing a coherent equity strategy is to determine not only the investor's goals, but, more importantly, how the investor defines risk. While this sounds like an obvious statement, this step is often overlooked. Most investors prefer to think of themselves as having long-term investment horizons and a fairly high tolerance for risk. But not many have examined equity performance patterns in detail and considered what their response would be to potentially long periods of underperformance due to style biases. As we noted above, style cycles may not fit the general notion that "long-term" is five years.

Risk is often also misdiagnosed. In the investment industry, risk is still often referred to as volatility of total return (i.e., standard deviation), when the investor really may be most concerned with a result that falls short of the overall equity market return (i.e., downside semivariance and/or probability of shortfall). Increasingly, the alternative investment is some passive instrument, so investor focus is appropriately on how an equity plan performs versus an index. For volatility reduction, the investor looks to other asset classes, with allocations according to long-term goals. Thus, investors may not rely on individual equity managers as the primary source of risk reduction, but instead, to deliver a better than equity market return.

Once an investor's risk tolerance has been defined, the second step is to diagnose the aggregate equity investments already held for potential structural biases versus the overall market. This step is important in determining whether there are *unintended* biases in overall structure. For example, an investor may have unknowingly built in a bias toward a certain capitalization segment of the market or a tilt toward growth or value. This may be particularly true if current manager selection has been made primarily on the basis of short-term historical performance without regard to style. Such a structure will subject the entire plan to underperformance from *unintended* style bets. An appropriate discussion for the investor in this case is whether these biases are appropriate for the risk tolerance level, and whether they should be modified.

Note these biases are separate from *intended* bets taken because of a conviction that they will pay off or a belief that the investor has hired the best possible managers regardless of style. But in either of these cases, presumably the investor knows the consequences of these choices and will not be alarmed at short-term underperformance because of this style structure.

Assuming investors have no preconceived ideas about style structure and are concerned with shorter-term risk, they can construct a style-neutral portfolio from managers with offsetting biases. The goal then becomes to produce outperformance from stock selection, rather than relying on a style bias to win over time. Style analysis plays a critical role in forming an accurate sense of manager portfolio structures and whether they indeed have diversifying performance patterns.

Regardless of the type of equity strategy selected, style analysis delivers, at a minimum, a key benefit in enhancing investor understanding of their investments. This should lead to better implementation of any change to an overall equity portfolio, as the reasons for the change and its potential performance impact will be better understood.

BEYOND STYLE DIVERSIFICATION

A style-diversified approach is best for investors who have no special insights into the equity markets, have multiple parties to whom they must explain performance results, have shorter time horizons, or have low risk tolerance. The style-diversified choice does not answer the question of whether one style is "best." All styles have their proponents, as anyone who has met investment managers will testify. But should any one style consistently perform better than the others over time?

The answer is "maybe." There are many studies that support the concept of value investing, and a recent article in particular provides some support for this approach.[6] Presented with such evidence, one feels compelled to consider it as "proof" that value and/or small cap must be the best style. Whenever one is confronted with such data, however, several issues need to be settled in order to structure an equity strategy around it.

- What sort of portfolios result from the criteria used to define "value"? How would the investor involved react to their structure? If the style definition used results in concentrated economic sector exposure (e.g., a heavy tilt toward value sectors like financials or utilities), would the investor feel comfortable holding that portfolio through potentially significant short-term performance volatility?
- Does the performance derive from the factor being studied? Or are there other effects that need to be "disentangled" in order to determine that value is really what is driving the study results? Could some other effect be a factor?
- How many investors employ the approach today compared to the time the study was performed? The number of value investors has increased dramatically over the last decade, for instance, which may have increased efficiency in that market segment, making it more difficult to find mispriced assets. A similar trend has begun to emerge in the small-cap sector, although indications are that there is still far less institutional research available in that arena.
- Finally, why should history necessarily repeat itself? What is the relevance of the test period to the current market? While this type of analysis poses some risk of rationalizing whether markets are truly "different this time," some attention to the economic and market backdrop of the historical analysis is appropriate. Otherwise, there is a risk for assuming parallels exist where there are none.

Beyond obtaining the highest absolute return, risk adjustment can also influence the answer for investors for whom risk reduction is important. Over its history, the Russell 1000® Value Index has outperformed the other style indexes. Perhaps more importantly, it has superior risk characteristics relative to the other indexes. To those concerned with volatility of absolute returns (rather than performance deviations from the broad market), this risk adjustment is worth something. Even if value had underperformed the other styles, to some degree an investor might be willing to give up superior performance for a superior risk position.

In summary, even though there are no clear answers to the question of which style is best, the numbers alone point toward value as the superior style. These numbers, however, beg a host of qualitative considerations.

---

[6] Fama and French, "Common Risk Factors in the Returns on Stocks and Bonds," op. cit.

SUMMARY

In this chapter we have defined certain styles of equity investment. We have shown that portfolios based on style concepts have different equity characterisitcs from each other and from the market. Style portfolios also behave differently from each other and from the overall market. These consistent differences in performance have implications for equity plan structures. Failure to pay attention to the equity style of a manager can lead the investor to take unintended factor bets and lead to unnecessary plan risk. Styles exist and style matters.

Chapter 10

Fundamental Factors in Equity Style Classification

David R. Borger, CFA
Director of Research
Wilshire Asset Management

INTRODUCTION

In recent years the term "style" has been prominent among equity practitioners in the areas of performance evaluation, manager selection, and product description. This usage gives just recognition to the well-known fact that certain categories of stocks perform differently than others, often over extended time periods. Within the last decade it has also been recognized that a manager who is hired to invest within the bounds of a particular category should not be reviewed favorably (unfavorably) if his returns exceed (fall short of) an arbitrary benchmark, the characteristics of which differ meaningfully from that of the type of portfolio that the manager can be expected to hold. To do so is unfair to both the manager and the sponsor and regardless of whether the manager's performance is made to look better or worse than a fair benchmark would make it appear, the resulting biased evaluation is likely to lead to an incorrect judgment on the part of the sponsor or consultant and an inappropriate feeling of satisfaction or dismay on the part of the manager. This can lead to a perverse system of rewards and punishments wherein a manager who has performed well but is perceived — by himself, his organization, the consultant and the sponsor — to have performed poorly is motivated to change a system which is, in fact, living up to expectations; at the same time a poorly performing but well perceived manager may well be rewarded with additional funds.

There are a number of ways of categorizing stocks, of course, but the paradigm which has gained greatest acceptance is a two-dimensional view in which size represents one dimension and some measure or measures of growth and value represent the second. There is some ambiguity in the terminology used to describe this breakdown. On the one hand, in describing the two dimensions it is common to refer to them as "size" and "style," the latter referring to the growth-value continuum. On the other hand, one also hears of the entire two dimensional approach as being "style" investing. As an example of the latter, below we shall make reference to the Large Growth "style" of investing. Clearly this refers to a management approach which focuses on companies with above average market capitalization

— the size dimension — and which have a growth orientation — the former use of the term "style." While this situation is perhaps unfortunate, it has emerged as somewhat standard and the reader is advised to let the context determine the proper interpretation. (In this chapter when we feel it is necessary to emphasize or clarify the second meaning we will use the terms "style/size" or "size/style.")

Looking at the universe of equity investments through the lens of size and style we see at least four possible investment categories: Large Growth, Large Value, Small Growth and Small Value. Of course, one may choose to have finer sub-divisions and include, perhaps, Mid Cap Growth and Mid Cap Value; or a neutral area between growth and value. Alternatively, sometimes it will be useful to aggregate these categories along one dimension, considering, for example, Large Growth and Large Value together as Large or Large Value and Small Value as "Value."

THE SIZE DIMENSION

What remains is to specify the criteria for membership in each of these categories. The easiest partition is the size partition. While there are numerous differences among the practitioners in the specifics of this division, the variable universally used to determine size breakpoints is market capitalization. One way of making the large/small split is to insist that the total market capitalization of each size category be the same (or as close to the same as is possible without having a single stock split between the two groups) as of a particular date.

The approach we took was somewhat different. First of all, we decided to focus our efforts on the largest 2,500 stocks from within the Wilshire 5000 Index. This subgroup represents about 97% of the market capitalization of the full index and we felt it was more representative of the type of stocks found in most institutional portfolios. It has the additional advantage of being more liquid and the stocks in the Top 2500, as we call it, are more likely to have complete and reliable financial data than are their micro cap brethren.

Since capitalization levels change over time, we decided to let our definition of "large" be reflective of this. Accordingly we defined "large" to mean the largest 750 stocks (Top 750) from the Top 2500 Index. We chose the largest 750 stocks to represent our large company universe because of a series of studies produced over the years by Wilshire's Institutional Services/Equity Division analyzing the performance profile by market capitalization over several market cycles. It was between the 700 and 800th stocks that we typically saw substantially different performance and since performance distinction by styles was a prime motivation for this endeavor, we felt this was an appropriate way to make the size cut. The remaining stocks in the Top 2500 were designated as small (Next 1750).

Subsequent to the initial creation of Wilshire's style indexes, an interest began to develop among some in the money management community in a Mid Cap category. Standard & Poor's Corporation was probably as responsible as anyone for fueling this interest when they introduced their Mid Cap 400. Perhaps the most natural way to define Mid Cap would be to divide the investment universe into three categories by using two breakpoints rather than a single one. Simply because we already had a vested interest in the Top 750/Next 1750 demarcation, we chose to approach Mid Cap as an overlay of our existing size categories. So for us Mid Cap consists of the 250 smallest stocks in the Top 750 and the 500 largest in the Next 1750.

DEFINING GROWTH AND VALUE

What makes a growth manager a growth manager? A reasonable and clearly intuitive answer would be: A growth stock manager is one who owns primarily growth stocks. What, then, is a growth stock? A growth stock is a stock which a growth stock manager would consider for purchase. This frustratingly circular attempt at defining growth illustrates the difficulty in trying to become specific about a term which has been used extensively, yet vaguely, and about which different investors have different ideas. Nonetheless, it does provide a helpful starting point if we try to focus on what is common among these alternate points of view and at the same time not try to satisfy everyone 100%. In particular, it should be kept in mind that there are different reasons investors may have in mind in the creation of style categories. Some, for example, may primarily be interested in the creation of a style index; others may be looking for a benchmark for performance measurement or performance attribution; still others may be primarily concerned with developing a disciplined model for investment management. These different perspectives may result in somewhat different approaches to one's definition of "style."

Expectations

In practice most equity managers, whether their orientation is to growth or value, construct their buy and sell lists based in part on expectations — either their own, consensus expectations, or the expectations of others. Even managers with relatively passive approaches occasionally design products which incorporate consensus earnings expectations. In our work with style we have chosen to base our models entirely on historically reported fundamental data. This approach is rooted in the belief that the historical ratios and growth rates correspond more closely with classic definitions or interpretations of growth and value. Furthermore, while all accounting numbers include a degree of subjectivity as well as noncomparability across time and possibly across industries, we believe that all of these problems exist to a greater extent with consensus forecasts and are still more problematic with specifically sourced (i.e., other than consensus) forecasts. But all this having been said and realizing, as mentioned above, that different investors may have different reasons for and different uses of style analysis, there is no reason why one could not legitimately include expectational data as part of a style model.

Growth

To determine what kind of stocks a growth stock manager might purchase, we can either examine the stocks that show up in growth stock portfolios or we can look at the process the growth stock manager uses to create his portfolio. The former approach does have the appeal of directness. However, the ability to get representative manager holdings data across a broad range of firms on a timely basis makes whatever analysis would result from this approach difficult to apply on a prospective basis. It also leaves unanswered the question of determining which managers are growth managers whose holdings should be considered representative of growth stocks in general. Not all managers who describe their approach as growth hold stocks which upon cursory review appear to be growth stocks. This is born out by Morningstar's recent decision to adopt a new fund classification scheme based on what managers actually own rather than on how they choose to describe their process. Additionally managers' styles drift overtime. Most likely the primary cause of this is performance pressure coupled with short time horizons. The result is a tendency to chase the style in favor and in the process move from a consistent style exposure.

Looking at what a growth manager does can also be said to suffer from the same lack of definition in the determination of who is a growth manager and who is not and hence whose actions it is that we should monitor. When Wilshire Asset Management created its style indexes in 1987, this was part of the dilemma we faced. How should we define "growth," whether we're talking about growth stocks or growth managers? There simply was no standardized definition. (A decade later there is still no standard but now the cause is an abundance of alternative definitions.) We chose to approach the problem in reverse — what is *not* a growth stock?

Consider the following thought experiment: Suppose you have been funded with an initial investment of $100 million and directed to start up an investment organization to actively manage this money in domestic equities in a manner consistent with an active, fundamental, large growth philosophy. You are given the financial resources (within reason) to hire whatever staff and purchase whatever support-ware you feel is necessary to profitably create and manage this organization. What is your game plan for allocating these resources? Consider that there are approximately 7,000 companies with U.S. headquarters which trade in the United States, either on one of the major exchanges or over-the-counter, for which daily prices are readily available — this being the definition used to include stocks in the Wilshire 5000 Index. Certainly it does not make sense to turn your analytical staff loose investigating all of these. Since we are interested in large company growth stocks, you decide to begin by setting a capitalization range within which you will work. There are some exciting opportunities in small growth stocks and some of your analysts may have a keen interest in some of them, but your mandate is large company growth and so you exclude these companies from consideration. For purposes of illustration, we will assume that you decide on the Wilshire Top 750 Index as your large company universe.

Similarly we want to eliminate stocks which, because of their fundamental characteristics, are unlikely to be considered growth stocks. Note the shift in perspective here: Instead of trying to define what growth is, we are trying to specify what it probably is not. We might conclude, for example, that a growth company is unlikely to pay out more than half of its earnings as dividends. If a company is a growth company, we expect it to have numerous opportunities to invest in projects which will produce high returns and, as a result, earnings growth well above that of the average company. Such a company will likely choose to retain most of its earnings for investment in such projects rather than pay them out as dividends. So, as our next screen we eliminate from our large company list all stocks with five-year average payout ratios greater than 50%.

Several things should be clear here. First, we are not asserting that every company with less than a 50% payout ratio is a growth company. We intend to further screen this list to zero in on a more growth-oriented group of companies. Second, we do not claim that it is impossible to find companies that most analysts would agree are growth companies yet which just happen to have payout ratios greater than 50%. Rather we believe that we lose little in our attempt to construct a quality portfolio of large company growth stocks if we restrict our analysis to companies with lower payout ratios and gain to the extent that our efforts are directed at a segment of the market more likely to contain the type of securities we seek. And finally, we do not assert that there is anything magic about the choice of 50% as a threshold. It is simply a convenient and, we believe, reasonable cutoff point in our definition of growth.

We can continue in this fashion eliminating stocks based on criteria which are thought not to be associated with growth. It will be clear as we proceed that the choice of some specific factors rather than others as well as the cutoff level for each is a matter of individual taste and reflects the creator's own biases with respect to a particular definition of growth within the guidelines just described. With regard to our biases, when we defined large growth we were thinking of an "established growth" kind of growth rather than either cyclical growth or turnaround growth. As a result we included as our next screen measures of the historic five-year average earnings growth and variability. Stocks which lagged relative to their peers were eliminated. We also screened on five-year average sales growth and five-year average return on equity. While the exact fashion in which these screens interact and the parameters used in the screening process are proprietary, they certainly are not unique in their ability to represent style. In fact it is our position that most growth managers have been or continually go through similar exercises with their own set of criteria. As indicated by the structure of this exercise, our goal is simply to produce a *working* list similar to that produced by an active manager — or, in this case, an active manager with a large company growth mandate.

It is our contention that such an active manager could take our list in place of his and through the application of his various methodologies and analyses generate performance consistent with the validity and current status of the approach he used. That is, if his large company growth methodology "works" and is currently "in favor" then this should be apparent in above average returns when applied to the large company growth index we intend to produce. Nor should there, over time, be any indication that these methods worked less well simply because they were applied to this specific index rather than another which might have been created at the time the model was run and the portfolio created. This exercise is realistic in that most managers already are creating lists in similar ways. Ours is an attempt to represent what is common among them.

Small Growth When building the value categories below, we use a single set of criteria for both large stocks and small. In the case of growth, however, we found it necessary to take a slightly different approach. Because in our design of the large company growth model our focus was on established growth, we required that a company have enough history to compute certain five-year average rates and ratios. The mere fact that a company had four or five years worth of history lent some credibility to the notion of "established." When looking at small company stocks, however, such a rigid requirement seemed inappropriate, particularly in recent years with the emergence of a plethora of new companies many of which became immediately perceived as growth companies. Despite the rapidly rising enthusiasm for many of these, we felt that it was necessary to demand some evidence that real earnings and real growth were possible. So we modeled the small company growth criteria as much as possible after the large, adjusting primarily for the likely limited availability of historic data.

One additional point. Those who are tempted to include expectational data in their style definitions might find this an appropriate place to take the plunge. The very short fundamental history of many of the companies in this capitalization range makes a purely quantitative judgment riskier than with larger companies. Of course, because of the size and newness of many of these firms, the availability of expectational data — at least on a consensus basis — may also be limited.

Value Stocks

We next go through a similar exercise for value. Here we are looking for fundamental factors which those who manage according to a value approach would likely evaluate in the construction of their portfolios or which those who hire value managers would expect to find well represented in their portfolios. Note at this point that very few self-proclaimed value managers would consider their universe of stocks to be simply anything which was not selected by a growth manager. Rather they would develop their own set of criteria based on their own understanding and interpretation of the term "value."

As was the case with growth, there is a range of opinion on just what constitutes value. Some investors think of value in terms of income and expect a value portfolio to consist primarily of high yielding stocks. Others think in terms of standard measures of cheapness such as relatively high earnings/price (E/P), book/price (B/P) or cash flow/price (CF/P) ratios, while still others are expectations driven and consider a stock to be attractive if its expected growth justifies its price.

This latter definition has intuitive appeal and has been in use for some time. Investors who follow this approach would argue that regardless of how low a stock's E/P ratio might be, if the expected growth rate is high enough, the stock is attractive. This approach is sometimes called "growth at a reasonable price." Such an approach, if faithfully and consistently implemented, need not reflect any selection biases relative to any specific fundamental factor. In other words, assuming that the inputs to the model for technology stocks are consistent with and comparable to those for bank stocks, there is no reason to suppose that technology stocks will be ranked favorably more often than bank stocks; or that low E/P stocks will be selected more or less often than stocks with high E/P's; and so on for every factor or classification system that one might consider.[1]

Models of this type (dividend discount models, for example) are used by many managers with a great deal of success. These models may lack in the ability to precisely time entry and exit points, but over the long run many, supported by a strong research staff capable of providing the required inputs, have been quite successful. Our reason for not using this definition of value was based not as much on the fact that, as indicated above, we have taken an overall approach to style based only on historic data — one which does not rely on expectational inputs, but rather in the lack of bias in the outputs just described. This lack of bias by its very nature makes it impossible to categorize such stocks into distinct groups. Lack of bias implies lack of discrimination and in this case our goal is in fact to distinguish between two types of stocks/managers which we feel are in some sense quite different and are able to serve two vary distinct roles in a sponsor's aggregate portfolio.

Some may object to this on the grounds that the valuation approach just described does offer a very clear classification of stocks — namely "overvalued" and "undervalued" (and throw in "neutral" if you like). Again without intending to disparage managers who follow this approach, this is not the type of distinction which meets the needs of a true style paradigm as we have outlined it. According to this paradigm, we wish to classify stocks in such a way that each category (with the exception of the "other" category — the category of leftovers) is a potential working list or could be reasonably used as a working list for some group of equity managers. We have perhaps prejudiced the discussion by identifying these early on as growth managers and value managers; deconstructing things a bit more we might have (or might still) come up with other divisions. Nonethe-

---

[1] The terms "comparable" and "consistent" as used above to describe the technology and bank inputs are not intended to imply that there should be no difference in the inputs or that one can't be more optimistic about the growth prospect for technology stocks that for bank stocks. Rather we wish to factor out those situations where an analyst for one industry may be significantly more optimistic/pessimistic than his peers. This fact alone will cause that analyst's stocks to rank inappropriately high/low. We assume in this discussion the ideal situation where this is not the case.

less, there is not likely to be a group of managers whose *intended* strategy or "style" is to invest in overvalued stocks.

In identifying value candidates, we have taken an exclusionary approach similar to that taken for growth. While it may be the case that there are some stocks which it may be reasonably argued are underpriced or are value stocks in some other sense but which also have relatively low E/P ratios, we doubt if a classic value manager will have difficulty building a value portfolio *without* these names. Similarly for B/P and yield. Also, as was the case with growth, there will be some who will choose other factors than the ones which we chose and which will combine them in different ways. They will, of course, come up with a different list of stocks which will in turn have a different performance profile and different overall characteristics. Again, however, we have no reason to believe that a value manager would have difficulty working from our list or from any of a number of similarly constructed lists.

In the case of growth stocks, there was an explicit requirement that to be included in the growth index corresponding to the stock's capitalization range that some minimum amount of history be available. Any such seasoning requirement in value is only implicitly stated. The key elements in our value model are the latest 12 months of earnings (hence an implicit requirement of at least 12 months and perhaps a bit more to allow for reporting lags); book value (this is a point in time number and its existence does not guarantee any back history for the company — in fact a company has a book value as soon as it comes into being); dividend (again, point in time); and price (current data only). Furthermore in the case of our value models the exact same screening criteria are used for both large and small companies.

The "Other" Category

The process which we have just described for classifying stocks as growth or value is not guaranteed to assign every stock in our universe into one of these two categories. In fact a substantial number are not so classified based on the variables and parameters which we used. An acceptance of this fact is tantamount to an acceptance of the premise that, indeed, not all stocks are either growth or value. If it is agreed that the terms "growth" and "value" have some natural meaning within the investment community, both among practitioners and consumers, then this state of affairs should not only not be surprising, it should be expected. This is certainly consistent with the decision above not to define value as simply being non-growth.

There are a number of reasons why a stock might not be considered as either growth or value. The first of these is negative earnings. We classify a stock as value in part because of a relatively high earnings/price ratio, where "earnings" is the latest 12 months reported earnings and price is the price as of the date of the creation of the value list. Since stocks with negative earnings will rank low in an E/P ranking, it is unlikely that such stocks would be considered value stocks according to our criteria.[2] Furthermore, a stock with negative earnings for the last 12 months is unlikely to be ranked among the top growing companies over the last five years. And there is a good chance that it will also fail the earnings stability screen.[3] Given this perspective, it is difficult to see why a company should be forced into either of these style categories.

A second reason is the differential performance profile we see in using our criteria — differences in both return and risk. Our creation of style indexes and style funds was in large part motivated by the belief that managers which follow growth approaches perform differently from those who follow value approaches — that at any point in time one style may be in favor and the other out, and that neutral or biased benchmarks can distort not only performance evaluation but also the manager selection process. In order to address this issue we set two goals: we wanted our indexes to be broad enough to serve as reasonable working lists for managers with clear style orientation and we wanted to be sufficiently focused so that the stocks selected by our models were *clearly* representative of the indicated style. We considered it *a priori* possible that all stocks would be classified into one of our style categories; however, we did not feel that this was necessary. In fact, we find it somewhat satisfying that they are not, given our intuition, commented on elsewhere, that value and growth are different investment approaches and that managers who adhere to one or the other approach their jobs differently. This being the case, we were not prepared to *force* all stocks into one category or the other.

Stocks which are Value and Growth

Because the criteria used for growth and value are distinct and because the construction rules for these stocks rely on a completely different set of variables, there is no reason to suppose that there will be no overlap between growth and value. While it is unlikely that a stock with a high historic growth rate and which passes all of the other growth screens will also have a high E/P and pass the various value criteria, it is certainly not impossible. In fact we have found typically that somewhere in the range of six to eight companies will be classified as both growth and value. We have also examined the performance of these stocks thinking that perhaps we have found some rare jewels, namely cheap growth stocks. Unfortunately, there does not seem to be any advantage to owning this particular group of stocks.

Others have suggested that all stocks are part growth and part value and carry out their analysis of style from this point of view. We certainly agree with the hypothesis and, in fact, the style metric which we discuss below is based on this belief. However, as discussed in the previous section, at times it is useful to focus the analysis on those stocks which are clearly identifiable as belonging to one category or the other. Either starting point is possible and from either one can get to the other. The approach which we favor starts with a discrete categorization

---

[2] Others, however, may seek out exactly this type of stock as a turnaround/value stock.

[3] Again, this is based on our approach; others could legitimately choose to include cyclical growth stocks — which could well have negative earnings — in their growth indexes. We chose not to.

of stocks by size and style and develops a continuous measure (the style metric) from that. The other starts with a continuous measure and, by the selection of appropriate ranges, can be used to classify stocks into discrete style classes.

Weighting, Re-Weighting, and Other Issues

At this point we have proposed a methodology for screening a universe of stocks based on fundamental factors normally associated with growth and value styles. We have suggested that the criteria we used, while not the only criteria available, are relatively non-controversial. We would further expect that the result of the thought experiment described above, if applied by a large number of investors or investment organizations, would result in a wide range of specific rules and the use of a number of different variables and parameters. We do not expect that the end results would differ widely, nor that any of the differences would be perceived as beyond compromise.

Having built one such list we are now confronted with the issue of maintenance. In particular, how frequently do we run our model? While much of the data used change only quarterly, some, especially price data, change daily. Since even the data which changes quarterly may become available on any random day during the quarter, an argument can certainly be made for running the model on a daily basis. However, our intent in developing a style model was to enable us to manage style portfolios. As a result we were interested in selecting a rebalancing frequency which reached a modest balance between accurately reflecting current information and avoiding unnecessary turnover. We felt that a quarterly rebalancing frequency (at calendar quarter-ends) was appropriate for the inclusion of new fundamental data while an annual adjustment to the definition of "large" and "small" would properly avoid the marginal turnover which would result in the frequent reclassification of stocks as large or small simply due to short-term price fluctuation. As a result, our institutional universe, consisting of the largest 2,500 stocks by market capitalization, is reconstructed each June 30 and split into large and small based on the market capitalization of its constituents as of that same date.

Regardless of the applications one may have in mind for the development of a style categorization, one of the outputs of the process will undoubtedly be a time series of returns for each style. This effectively requires that a paper portfolio be created and that some attention be given to the issue of the weighting methodology and frequency. The most common approach here is to capitalization weight the lists as of each rebalance interval, in our case quarterly. On occasion one might see reference to equal-weighted returns, but the sensitivity to the rebalance period generally limits the usefulness of such series. There is also the issue of what shares should be used in the calculation of market capitalization. The various approaches to this, however, transcend the issue of style and so will not be discussed in detail here. Suffice it to say that a seemingly simple data item such as shares outstanding means different things to different people. Naturally these difference will have an impact on the performance of a benchmark or index. Capitalization weighting also aids in the management of a fund intended to track the index. Since larger capitalization names *tend* to be more liquid than smaller names, we will tend to own larger shares of companies for which it is easier to acquire larger amounts.

Sector Representation

When viewing the style categories individually, particularly after the component securities have been capitalization weighted, there are clear sector over- and underweightings present compared with the universe of all equities or even with the subuniverses of securities of comparable size. Historically, these sector bets are more prominent in the value indexes than in the growth indexes. Of course, it is not surprising that some of the factors which are strong style determinants are also correlated with industry membership. We expect, for example, that more technology stocks will be classified as growth than as value — particularly among small companies — and that more banks and utilities will show up as value.

The issue at hand is whether to attempt to neutralize these sector bets or not. The answer again depends on the use one wants to make of the resulting index. If the indexes are intended to be used as benchmarks for the purpose of performance based incentive fees, then the creator of the index should be careful not to include in the structure of the index characteristics which will motivate the manager to perform in an undesirable fashion. It has not been uncommon, for example, for the Wilshire Small Value Index to have a combined weight in the Finance and Utility sectors of 60% or more. It is unlikely that a sponsor or consultant would want to set that as a target for all small value managers.

Our purpose, on the other hand, was to design indexes with a very focused exposure to a particular style as represented by what we believe to be classic style factors. The industry and sector profiles which emerge from this tell us something about how these factors appear in various segments of the market. We would not propose that any sponsor invest all of his money in any of these indexes or the corresponding portfolios. Rather they can serve as extremely useful tools for diversification. Because of their focus, it requires less of an investment in one of these indexes to move one's aggregate portfolio toward a desired style/ size exposure. We would also argue — whether with regard to style management or portfolio management in general — that if each manager a sponsor hires individually attempts to diversify his own portfolio, then the sponsor's aggregate portfolio will be overdiversified. Better that each manager design a portfolio which represents his own best efforts in the style he manages and then the sponsor/consultant diversify among managers (as they already are attempting to do).

The Multifactor Approach

The minimum requirement for a factor-based style classification is a factor which one is willing to claim represents style. One can then rank stocks according to that factor and insert any number of breakpoints according to whatever rule one deems appropriate and claim to have created style categories.[4] But, in part, because the categories of growth and value have evolved over the years to mean different things to different investors, it seems unlikely to find a single, simple variable which will meet this need.

The consideration of multiple style factors proceeds in two directions. The first of these considers whether or not a single factor — or even a single group of factors — can be used for both growth and value. Below, where we discuss the development of the style metric, we will appear to answer this question in the affirmative. However, note that in that case we have really taken a somewhat different approach in developing a single variable which is itself a mathematical combination of several others, some of which are intended to represent growth and others to represent value. The variable itself, the "style metric," is not a naturally occurring or commonly used investment variable. Note too that the weighting scheme changes over time to reflect the predictive contribution of each of these factors and also that the weights are selected *ex post* to optimally represent an *ex ante* classification based on separate growth and value variables.

The notion of a single, "natural" variable, particularly an accounting-based one, which can distinguish between growth and value is an attractive one, but one which is probably counterintuitive to most managers as well as most plan sponsors. Growth managers and value managers have different approaches to stock selection as well as portfolio construction. Each of these uses a combination of variables/factors to evaluate the stocks in their universes and while there may be some overlap, it is unlikely that any of these managers would be comfortable reducing their process to the examination of a single variable, much less explaining or justifying the composition of their working lists in these terms. Our choice of different factors for growth and value stemmed from the desire to create indexes in much the same way as an active manager would create such a working list, using those variables normally associated with each particular style. It was not clear as we proceeded with our initial work that the end result of this process would be the creation of indexes/portfolios which differed not only in their composition but also in their return profile. As we will see below, the latter turned out to be the case.

Amongst those who nonetheless favor using a single variable, probably the most popular candidate is the book-to-price ratio (B/P), based in large measure on the work done by Fama and French.[5] We, too, have found B/P to be a very useful discriminator of *value* stocks, though we must admit to having some difficulty seeing why stocks with low B/P's should be considered growth. In addition to B/P, we also use E/P as mentioned above. As one might expect, selecting stocks

---

[4] Of course, one would hope that there was some rationale — either statistical or otherwise — for the selection of this factor and that the classes which resulted had some natural association with common investment classes.

[5] Eugene F. Fama and Kenneth R. French, "Common Risk Factors in the Returns on Stocks and Bonds," *Journal of Financial Economics*, 33 (1993), pp. 3-56, and "The Cross-Section of Expected Stock Returns," *Journal of Finance* (June 1992), pp. 427-465.

by B/P and alternatively selecting by E/P often produces a similar list. Often, but not always. There are times when the B/P effect is stronger and times when the E/P effect dominates and, to be sure, there are times when it is a toss up as to which one is the more important. Since each works well in identifying value candidates and because sometimes one works better than the other, we have chosen to include both (along with yield) in our value model and to include them in such a way that this complex interaction is reflected.

Having argued for the need for multiple variables (in our case three) to represent value, we observe that the style classification scheme would in some sense be simplified if we were able to find a way to identify growth stocks using the same variables. Unfortunately there does not seem to be any clear path to that end. While it is true that a classic growth portfolio, including our growth indexes, will on average have low E/P, low B/P, and low yield — the exact opposite of what one expects in a value portfolio, these are not the defining characteristics of growth. After all, such portfolios typically have other common characteristics as well. These factors are simply not the basis of growth stock selection by growth managers. Growth stock managers are more likely to look at direct measures of growth, either historic or projected, and if they have to tolerate low E/P's and B/P's, so be it; if they can find growth candidates with higher valuation ratios, so much the better.

The Performance Profile

It is one thing to create a classification system for stocks and another to establish that such a classification is meaningful. One could, for example, have classified stocks somehow based on the first letter of their ticker symbols or the age of their CEO, but one would not expect such schemes to have any useful application. Our selection of the variables which we used to define growth and value was admittedly based on preconceived notions of what these terms meant and clearly reflect some author's license in their selection and interaction. Others have created other factor based approaches which they aggressively defend. Some of the methodologies they use have been discussed above. Different investors will respond differently to the various rationales and explanations for each of these different style models. And the different models will suit different investors' various needs better or worse than others.

Having reviewed the construction process of factor based classification models and the reasonableness of referring to these as "growth" and "value," it remains to be shown that this breakdown is significant and should be viewed as such by managers and sponsors. The key issue here is performance. Do these two groups of stocks perform differently in any way which would be useful to a plan sponsor, a money manager, or a consultant? As Exhibit 1 shows, the answer is clearly, "yes." During the period for which we have constructed the style categories, there have been several easily discernible style trends. Such trends are of course best seen in hindsight, once one can determine whether a small reversal will develop into a total change of course or whether the old trend will resume shortly. Also, the meaning of the term "trend" changes depending on one's time horizon. It is quite possible that some will choose to look within the periods listed in Exhibit 1 to identify other, shorter term trends, while others will combine some or all of these into longer periods. With that caveat, Exhibit 1 presents one breakdown of the time period over which we have investigated style.

Exhibit 1 clearly shows that style, as represented by the factors used to define the Wilshire Style Indexes, has been a significant factor in the determination of performance over the last two decades. The compound annual return for switching to the best performing style in each of these time periods was 21.3%, compared with 11.5% for being in the worst performing style and 15.5% for staying in the Wilshire 5000 Index. Of course, this reflects perfect hindsight and does not include the transaction costs of implementing such a strategy. These returns are presented solely to illustrate the potential significance of style to total equity performance.

The implications for performance measurement are dramatic and have been reflected in the way that consultants measure and evaluate managers compared with a decade ago. Imagine being a growth manager in 1992-1993 and being benchmarked against the Wilshire 5000. You would have had to be very good or very lucky just to meet your benchmark. Stocks with classic growth characteristics simply did not perform well in that period. Of course, if you were a growth manager of another sort with less exposure to these factors than the Wilshire Growth Indexes, this, too, would have impacted your performance, for better or worse.

Or if you were a classic growth manager as characterized by these indexes but saw the strengthening performance of value stocks and as a result shifted your portfolio in that direction, you probably would have generated returns better than your peers in growth. Whether or not you were fulfilling your responsibility to your client who hired you to deliver growth, is another matter. This departure from style purity in response to external events is referred to as "style drift." Here, we should emphasize, we are referring to drift along both the size and style dimensions. It is not uncommon for managers with small company mandates to bump up the limits on their definition of "small" when mid cap and large companies seem to be taking the lead.

Exhibit 1: Equity Style Performance Profile
1978-1996/Q3

Period	Growth Return (%)	Value Return (%)	Wilshire 5000 Return (%)
1978-80	28.7	13.7	22.4
1981-88	10.7	19.5	13.1
1989-91	24.2	13.2	17.6
1992-1993	4.6	15.1	10.1
1994-1996/Q3	20.4	14.9	17.2

A STYLE METRIC

The methods outlined above for the creation of style categories have proven useful in a number of areas, including the development and management of style oriented portfolios as well as style related performance attribution. However, after managing style portfolios for a while, it became clear that it would be useful to have a continuous measure of style orientation rather than the discrete classifications we were working with. As things stood, any security in our universe was classified as either growth, value, or other. There was no way to determining whether a value stock was just barely a value stock or whether an "other" stock just missed being classified as growth. For some applications this did not cause a problem, but for real-life portfolio management where trading costs are an important component of return — particularly with small stock applications — we would like to avoid buying a stock which is only slightly value and at the same time selling one which just barely failed our screens. Ironically, it is our use of a multifactor model, which we feel is important for an accurate specification of style, which complicates the situation.

While in certain trivial cases it is possible to "eye ball" the model output to determine whether a passing stock passed with flying colors or not, in general this is not practical. Suppose a stock which shows up as a small value stock would not have if the E/P ratio had been slightly lower and another would have failed if the B/P had been slightly lower. Should these two cases be considered identical? Suppose a stock which failed would have passed if its E/P ratio had been slightly higher but has a B/P ratio which was in the top half of the universe. If this stock is currently held, should it be sold to purchase one of the previous two? What guidelines can be offered to assist in making these trade-offs? Any attempt to answer these questions is further complicated by the observation above that the relative importance of the model's factors is not constant over time.

To address these questions, Wilshire developed a style metric — a single measure of style which allows us to distinguish, based on fundamental data, those stocks which are most growth-like and those which are most value-like. The statistical technique used to accomplish this is discriminant analysis — a procedure for classification of objects based on properties of these objects and of similar objects whose proper classification is known. The original work in this area was done early in the century by Fisher who wanted to develop a methodology for classifying iris plants in general based on physical measurements on individual iris plants. He was able to accomplish this by taking a series of such measurements on plants whose classification was already known and through a Baysian strategy, discriminant analysis, to develop a linear weighting of the variables which was optimal in the sense of being able to classify the known plants properly with highest possible success rate of any such weighting. Another benefit of this methodology, which is particularly important in the development of the style metric, is the fact that the linear model produces a monotonic, continuous result, so as an individual's score toward a particular category increases, it is more and more likely to be a member of that category.

Exhibit 2: Sample Characteristics of Wilshire Style Indexes

	E/P	B/P	Five Year EPS Growth (%)	Five-Year Return on Equity (%)
Large Growth				
Mean	0.047	0.23	15.9	21.3
Standard Deviation	0.018	0.22	13.8	19.4
Large Value				
Mean	0.072	0.54	10.7	13.4
Standard Deviation	0.072	0.51	8.3	12.5

The application to style classification and the shortcomings of our discrete model are clear. We can use the fundamental variables from the original style classification as the measurements and the results of that classification as the basis for estimating the model. Understand that we are not changing the construction of our existing indexes; nor are we proposing a methodology which could be used as an alternative. The style metric is based entirely on the style indexes as we have already described them and relies on their existence for its computation. With these (or comparable) indexes in hand, we can calculate, using standard statistical software, for any security for which the requisite fundamental data are available, what the probability is that stock is a growth stock or a value stock. When we apply this computation to the stocks which have already been assigned to one of these two categories, we find that the "hit" rate — the number of stocks which are mapped to the proper category — is quite high. Of course this is not surprising since the nature of the discriminant model is that it will find the linear model of the input variables which produces the greatest number of "hits."

Suppose, for example, we select a stock at random from the union of our Large Company Growth and Large Company Value indexes. In other words, we know that the company has already been selected by either our growth model or our value model; however, we do not know which model is the reason for its inclusion in the union. (For simplicity sake we will rule out the possibility that it was selected by both.) We do, however, have available a complete listing of the stock's fundamental characteristics as well as those same characteristics (mean values and standard deviations) for the two indexes. Consider the two style indexes in Exhibit 2.

Now suppose that the stock which we selected had an E/P of 0.08. Is it a growth stock or a value stock? Admittedly this is very little information to go on and whatever our answer we will certainly have a limited amount of confidence in it. But that having been said, most people would probably say it is a value stock or that is more likely to be a value stock than a growth stock. If we were to select another random stock which happened to have an E/P of 0.10, most people would probably conclude that this is a value stock as well; and that it is more value like than the first, or perhaps that they have a higher degree of confidence that the second stock is a value stock.

Now suppose we add another variable, say B/P, and reconsider the first stock we picked. If it were to turn out that this stock had a B/P of 0.60, this would serve to reinforce our belief that the stock is a value stock, giving us a higher degree of confidence or causing us to assign a higher (subjective) probability to its being a value stock. However, what if the stock had a B/P of 0.40? That's not quite as value-like and might add to any doubts we might have had about this really being in the value index. Still it does have a B/P more like a value stock than a growth stock, so we'll stick with our original answer. But what if the stock had a B/P of 0.20? If this were all the information we had, we would call it a growth stock. But since it also has a value-like E/P, we're caught in the middle. Is one factor more important than the other? Are the answer to these questions valid always or just with this particular data set? If we add in five or six more variables and a few hundred securities, the problem becomes completely intractable using only *ad hoc* tools.

This is exactly the type of classification problem the discriminant model was designed to deal with and does so in the following ways: (1) normalize each stock's exposure to each factor so that we are dealing in units of standard deviations from the respective means; (2) for each stock compute a score which is a weighted average of the above exposures; (3) rank the stocks by this score and call the stocks ranked in the top half "growth-like" and the bottom half "value-like;" (4) calculate the percentage of stocks that are properly classified — i.e., growth-like stocks are in fact in the growth index; and, (5) determine the weighting scheme so that the percentage of correct classifications in step 4 is maximized.

The discriminant model is structured in such a way that the scores in step 2 above are in fact probabilities — namely the probability that any given stock is a growth stock. (We could equally well have specified the model in terms of value stocks.) So a score of 0.75 means that there is a 75% chance that the stock is a growth stock. Step 3 then selects all stocks with a better than 50% chance of being a growth stocks and calls them "growth-like." The scoring system — that is the weighting scheme — which does the best job of classifying stocks consistent with their membership in the growth and value indexes is the one which is used.

Since the results of the discriminant models are probabilities, it follows that they can be interpreted as a continuous measure of style orientation and since we have only two classifications (growth and value) in our sample, if a high (low) score represents growth then a low (high) score will represent value. We have scaled our style scores so that the equal-weighted average score for a stock previously identified as a value stock is −100 while the average growth stock has a score of +100.[6]

---

[6] This is a convention which we chose to give us a measure of comparability across time and a standard scoring system with which to describe a stock's or a portfolio's growth exposure. Some who have adopted this overall approach have chosen different scaling parameters, including forcing the style axes through a prespecified point, such as the Wilshire 5000.

The Style Metric and Portfolio Comparisons

In addition to aiding in the reduction of turnover and transaction costs by providing a means for avoiding marginal trades, the style metric is also useful in evaluating portfolios, both individual and aggregate. Because the style model is linear, the style score of a portfolio is simply the market value weighted average style score of the individual securities. Similarly the style score of a group of portfolios is the weighted average score of the components. This provides a useful measure of the style orientation of individual managers or groups of managers. It also provides a means of evaluating the consistency of a manager's style exposure over time or the consistency of the management of purportedly similar portfolios within an organization.

The style metric also yields itself readily to graphic representation. One graphic tool which has proven quite popular is the so-called "style map," a two dimensional plot which presents size on the vertical axis and style on the horizontal. Individual securities, portfolios, and indexes can then be graphed — either separately or in combination. By using such a map to view the style profile of their existing managers as well as their aggregate portfolio, a plan sponsor can quickly determine the net style bets that are being taken. By overlaying this graph with a plot of alternative investment managers or by hypothetically adding, deleting or re-weighting managers, the sponsor can easily see which actions would most easily address whatever style deficiencies exist.

Over time we have had the chance to review the results of the style metric model with investment managers as well as plan sponsors. The reception from each has been encouraging. Managers are frequently concerned with the consistency of results across accounts managed by different portfolio managers. Our metric analysis allowed us to view the exposure of these managers to style/size and to evaluate their resulting performance variability. In those cases where there were outliers, our analysis was supported by comments from these firms of the idiosyncrasies of the highlighted managers.

We were also able to show managers how the style exposure of their funds changed over time. Of course, with some managers there was a high degree of consistency — a fact which should be pleasing to their clients. Others, however, did show some variability, either a trend from a base style toward the other or a steady exposure to one style and then a rapid, perhaps temporary, jump to the other. Again, these moves were validated in discussions with these managers as they reflected on their changing strategies over this time.

ADVANTAGES OF THE FACTOR APPROACH TO STYLE

There are at least two major approaches to identifying equity style: the returns-based approach and the factor- (or portfolio-) based approach. Each of these has its proponents and each has its strong and weak points. Among the advantages of the factor-based approach is that it directly focuses on the very characteristics that the style-oriented manager focuses on in the construction and maintenance of his portfolio. This aids the manager in seeing where he might be taking bets relative to his style before the bets are taken. It also makes it possible for a manager to understand the reason for the over- or underperformance that comes out of an attribution analysis.

Another way of looking at this is that factor-based equity style analysis is security oriented — any portfolio level conclusions or observations flow directly from the aggregation of the security based results. There is total comparability between the interpretation of style at the security, portfolio or aggregate level, and it is straight forward to determine how one impacts the other. If a portfolio is not as value oriented as one would like, a candidate list of stocks and an optimizer — or for that matter any structured portfolio construction tool — could be used to create a portfolio with any target value profile, even subject to a wide range of construction constraints.

A second benefit of the factor-based style approach is that it is easier to determine style drift. A returns-based approach, requiring as it does some mean-ingful amount of history to compute its correlations, will not necessarily catch near-term composition changes which some managers will make in an attempt to profit by reacting to short-term trends. Factor-based style classification always focuses on the characteristics of the stocks which the manager holds right now, those which will impact future performance, not those which may have influenced the past. If the manager continues to hold stocks which no longer fit the desired style profile or begins to purchase "hot" stocks outside of his normal style, this will immediately become apparent using a factor-based model.

Finally, regression based models of style are subject to one of the poten-tial flaws of any regression based model, namely misspecification. One popular way of measuring a portfolio's style orientation is to regress the portfolio's returns over some time period against the corresponding return of a set of style indexes.[7] If, in fact, all managers fall into one of the styles included in the regres-sion, such an approach will show which managers' returns have been most corre-lated with which style. That of course is just what the regression does. The question then is how one interprets these results. In one of the early applications of this approach, one consultant attempted to classify the Wilshire Style Indexes. Because at that time there was no acknowledgement of small value as a separate category and because as a result it was not included in the regression model, our Small Company Value Index showed up with heavy exposure to Japanese equities, of which it held none.

Another way that this can happen is due to an individual manager's alpha. Suppose over the time period used in the regression a particular large value man-ager had a significant positive alpha, while remaining strict in his adherence to a value discipline. Suppose, too, that during this period large growth stocks outper-

---

[7] It is also common practice to constrain the coefficients to sum to one.

formed large value. Depending on a number of other factors (such as the volatility and correlation of the individual indexes over this specific time period) it could appear that this very strict value manager could be classified as growth based on a regression approach. (This is a real life observation, not a hypothetical.)

SUMMARY

Style is more than a fad. Ten years ago no one talked about portfolio construction or performance measurement in terms of style. Now you can't talk equities to a consultant without the term "style" popping up in the conversation. Style managers exist because stocks with different fundamental characteristics have different performance profiles. Sometimes one style is in favor, sometimes another. There are those investors who prefer to permanently position themselves in one size/ style quadrant or another in a belief that that style will outperform the others on a secular basis. Despite fairly long-term studies which support some of these strategies, that view of the market could well change in the future. It could well be that a century from now when all of our databases are overflowing with information and our time series encompass dozens of market cycles, that the very long-term performance results will show no difference in the performance of these styles "over the long run." But surely the patterns that we have seen over the shorter term will continue: namely, that the classic fundamental factors distinguish among stocks as well as among managers and that these will generate their own unique performance patterns into the future. So regardless of what apparent anomalies have or continue to exist, the need for diversification among equity styles will persist, and the successful investor will employ the various style tools in his stock/manager selection and review process.

Chapter 11

Value-Based Equity Strategies

Gary G. Schlarbaum
Partner
Miller, Anderson & Sherrerd, LLP

INTRODUCTION

As equity investors, we have certain bedrock beliefs that guide our investment decisions. These beliefs are based on our experience, that of our predecessors, and on findings from continuing research. In fact, one of our bedrock beliefs is that careful research is a major contributor to investment success.[1] To test our long-held belief that focusing on measures of value is very important in the investment process, we measured value using price/earnings ratios (P/E's). We also looked at the importance of near-term business dynamics, as measured by earnings-estimate revisions, and how those might affect the performance of value stocks. Then we looked at a combination of the two to see how that would have worked. As it turned out, a combination of the two — a value score — worked better than either by itself.

Our research has practical application. When we construct equity portfolios, we begin by looking for stocks with low expectations — measured by low-P/E's. Second, we look for stocks that have rising expectations — measured by positive earnings-estimate revisions.[2] Third, we subject the resulting candidate stocks to rigorous fundamental analysis by our experienced analysts and portfolio managers. Finally, we build diversified portfolios — in keeping with our experience that broadly diversified value portfolios are less volatile but provide comparable excess returns. This is a continuing process. We screen our database every week in search of inexpensive stocks whose fundamentals are turning. Screening is central to our stock-selection process.

Our research focused on the 500 largest U.S. companies over the period 1977 through 1994. We formed various 100-stock portfolios and examined the market-relative returns of those portfolios. The market-relative return is the dif-

---

[1] The research reported in this chapter was conducted at Miller, Anderson & Sherrerd in the fall of 1994. It is best viewed as an extension of research that was conducted by Paul Miller and Jay Sherrerd (two of our founding partners) back in the mid-1960's — even before our firm began. This work was continued by Robert Hagin, who did extensive work on value investing in the 1980's. Our 1994 results show, as did the earlier work, that investing in value stocks gives an investor an important edge, reaffirming one of the basic principles that lie at the heart of our equity-investment process.

[2] It is, of course, preferable to detect stocks for which expectations are about to rise by thoroughly analyzing inexpensive stocks. Our analysts spend much of their time looking for such stocks.

ference between the return on a particular portfolio and the average return on the universe. For the purpose of this research, we assumed that we rebalanced those portfolios quarterly. We developed results for portfolios of various types — equal-weighted, value-weighted, diversified, and nondiversified. The best results were obtained from equal-weighted diversified portfolios.

The results for portfolios formed using P/E ratios are reported first. Results for portfolios formed using estimate revisions and value scores are presented in the subsequent two sections. An examination of results within individual economic sectors is then presented. Finally, we look at the differences in results between diversified and nondiversified portfolios.

RETURNS FOR PORTFOLIOS
CONSTRUCTED USING P/E RATIOS

We have long believed that value is the central consideration in a sensible investment process. Although the P/E ratio is not the only possible measure of value, we believe it is the most effective. We have not undertaken a comparative evaluation of different measures of value in this study. Rather, we have focused on P/E ratios. We have found them to be a very effective tool for selecting stock portfolios over the period of the study.[3]

The effectiveness of value investing reflects the mispricing of financial assets at either end of the spectrum. Investors overvalue the prospects of the stocks they consider to be the best and undervalue the prospects of those they view as the worst. There is a tendency to project positive or negative developments of the past into the future. As a result, prices are pushed too far in the direction of recent events. Ultimately, however, there is reversion to the mean as the perceptions of investors change. The reversion to the mean can be more or less rapid, but overvalued (high-P/E) securities will tend to underperform on average, while undervalued (low-P/E) securities will, on average, deliver superior returns. The implosion of stock price when a high-multiple stock misses the consensus estimate by a penny or two in the reporting of quarterly results is a vivid example of a rapid change in perception and movement toward the mean.

The price/earnings ratios used to form portfolios for this study were based on current price and consensus estimates of earnings for the next 12 months. This choice is based on our view that the market focuses on and capitalizes earnings 12 months ahead. We did not do any tests to determine whether estimates of future earnings provide better results than trailing earnings. We consider estimates of future earnings preferable from a conceptual point of view. Furthermore, the estimates are clean and not clouded by extraordinary items.

---

[3] The findings are consistent with those developed by Paul Miller and Jay Sherrerd in the 1960's and with those obtained by various academic researchers in later years.

Exhibit 1: P/E Strategy — Using Sector-Neutral Equal-Weighted Portfolios*

	P/E Quintile	Annual Rate of Return (%)	Market-Relative Return (%)	Quarters of Outperformance
Lowest	1	17.6	3.1	46
	2	16.3	1.8	43
	3	14.0	-0.4	35
	4	12.6	-1.8	29
Highest	5	11.2	-3.3	25
Universe:		14.4		

* Period included 69 calendar quarters from the first quarter of 1977 through the third quarter of 1994.

Exhibit 2: P/E Strategy — Using Sector-Neutral Equal-Weighted Portfolios

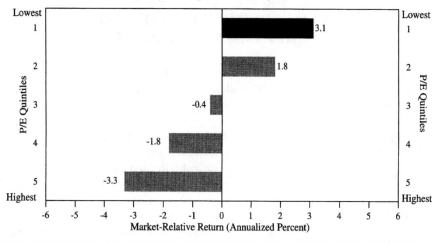

Absolute returns, market-relative returns, and a count of the number of the quarters of outperformance are shown for five portfolios in Exhibit 1. The market-relative returns are depicted in Exhibit 2 as well. The results for the lowest-P/E portfolio are shown on the top line of the table, those for the second-lowest-P/E portfolio are shown on the second line, etc. The bars in Exhibit 2 are shown in the same order.

The results included in Exhibits 1 and 2 are for equal-weighted, sector-neutral portfolios. The portfolios were formed in two steps. First, the stocks were grouped into 12 economic sectors. Then the lowest quintile of P/E's from each sector was selected for inclusion in the low-P/E portfolio. The same procedure with the appropriate quintiles was used to form the rest of the portfolios. The returns, then, are those of very well diversified value-based portfolios. (A comparison of the results for diversified and nondiversified portfolios is contained in a later section of this chapter.)

We found that, over this period, being sector neutral and picking the lowest-P/E portfolio from each economic sector led to 3.1% a year additional return relative to the 14.4% return for the universe. In contrast, the high-P/E portfolio had an annual return of 3.3% below that of the universe. Moreover, the low-P/E portfolio outperformed in 46 out of 69 quarters included in the study while the high-P/E portfolio outperformed in only 25 of the quarters. In other words, the low-P/E portfolio outperformed two thirds of the time, and the high-P/E portfolio underperformed about two thirds of the time.

The results reported in this section are consistent with our belief that value is the central consideration in a well designed investment process. P/E ratios were very effective tools for selecting stocks over the period studied here. Concentrating on low-P/E stocks and avoiding high-P/E stocks provided an important advantage for investors. We believe that focus on stocks with low expectations as measured by P/E ratios will continue to provide an advantage.

RETURNS FOR PORTFOLIOS CONSTRUCTED USING ESTIMATE REVISIONS

Stock prices are driven by the earnings generated by the underlying businesses. The question posed here is whether changes in expectations about earnings, as measured by analysts' estimate revisions, are useful in selecting a portfolio of common stocks.[4] Estimate revisions are important as representations of the near-term business dynamics of the companies being considered. We used 3-month smoothed revisions for the purposes of this study. More weighting is assigned to the most recent month in computing the estimate revision used for ranking stocks.

Estimate revisions provide a measure of the direction and magnitude of change in expectations about a company's earnings. The assumption is that rising expectations are associated with above-average stock returns and falling expectations are associated with below-average returns. Revisions tend to be positively serially correlated. Positive revisions tend to be followed by positive revisions, and negative revisions tend to be followed by negative revisions. It is difficult for analysts to judge how far a positive or negative trend may go once it has begun. Recent academic studies have shown that investors and analysts tend to respond sluggishly to new information (i.e., that markets are not totally efficient). Analysts react slowly to a change in the direction of the underlying fundamentals because of a natural unwillingness to believe the change. These studies opine that the effect may be stronger on the downside because of the reluctance of analysts to make negative comments about companies with which they have investment-

---

[4] I/B/E/S collects the earnings estimates of analysts and, in addition to reporting them, aggregates the estimates into summary measures such as the mean and median. A revision is a change in the mean estimate for a company. Changes for the three most recent months are combined to obtain the measure of estimate revisions used here.

banking relationships. As a result, the analysts issue frequent, minor revisions instead of marking their estimates down all at once.

There is also a strong relationship between estimate revisions and earnings surprises.[5] Positive estimate revisions are frequently followed by a positive earnings surprise. The positive earnings surprise will often be followed by subsequent positive estimate revisions. There is a kind of virtuous cycle when the fundamentals of a company are improving. Of course, the opposite is true when the underlying fundamentals are deteriorating. Disappointing earnings lead to negative revisions, which are followed by more disappointments, and so on.

We again formed five portfolios of 100 stocks each to ascertain the relationship between returns and estimate revisions. The stocks were grouped into 12 economic sectors. Then the stocks were divided into quintiles within the sectors on the basis of estimate revisions. The stocks from the highest quintile within each economic sector formed the first portfolio. The same procedures with the appropriate quintiles were used to form the rest of the portfolios.

Absolute returns, market-relative returns, and a count of the number of quarters of outperformance are shown for the five portfolios in Exhibit 3. Market-relative returns are also shown in Exhibit 4. The results for the best-revision portfolio are shown in the top line of the table, those for the second-best-revision portfolio are shown in the second line, and so on. The bars in Exhibit 4 are shown in the same order.

The sector-neutral portfolios with the best-revision stocks provided an extra 4.2% a year relative to the 14.4% return for the universe. The worst-revision portfolio, on the other hand, underperformed the universe by 4.3%. The returns were perfectly rank ordered by the revisions. Moreover, the best-revision portfolio outperformed the universe in 51 out of 69 quarters — nearly 75% of the time. Meanwhile, the worst-revision portfolio was nearly as consistent, trailing in 46 of 69 quarters.

Exhibit 3: Estimate-Revision Strategy — Using Sector-Neutral Equal-Weighted Portfolios*

	Estimate-Revision Quintile	Annual Rate of Return (%)	Market-Relative Return (%)	Quarters of Outperformance
Best	1	18.6	4.2	51
	2	15.8	1.4	39
	3	14.7	0.3	36
	4	11.9	−2.5	28
Worst	5	10.2	−4.3	23
Universe:		14.4		

* Period included 69 calendar quarters from the first quarter of 1977 through the third quarter of 1994.

[5] An earnings surprise is the difference between the actual quarterly earnings of a company and the consensus estimate at the time of the report.

Exhibit 4: Estimate Revision Strategy — Using Sector-Neutral Equal-Weighted Portfolios

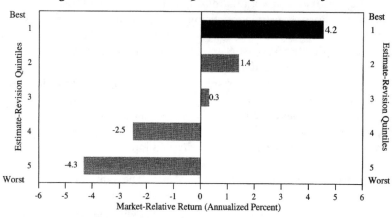

These results show the strong relationship between near-term business dynamics and equity returns. The results are consistent and powerful. (We should note that the extra returns based on near-term business dynamics are harder to capture than those based on measures of value because of the greater trading activity required.) It is clear that the direction of expectations is a powerful influence on stock performance.

We saw in the previous section that portfolios of low-expectation stocks outperform. This section demonstrated that portfolios of stocks with rising expectations also outperform.

RETURNS FOR PORTFOLIOS CONSTRUCTED USING VALUE SCORES

We have demonstrated in the previous two sections that both value as measured by P/E and fundamental business dynamics as measured by estimate revisions are effective as portfolio selectors. Stocks with low expectations, on average, outperform the market. Stocks with high expectations lag. Stocks with rising expectations, on average, outperform the market. Stocks with falling expectations lag. Seemingly a combination of good value and positive dynamics would be more powerful than either by itself in forming a portfolio. The question addressed in this section is whether this is in fact the case.

Each stock in the universe of the largest 500 stocks was assigned a percentile ranking based on P/E and a percentile ranking based on estimate revision. A value score was then computed for each stock by determining a weighted average of the percentile rankings. We assigned 70% of the weight to P/E and 30% to estimate revision. This was the only set of weightings that we tried. In fact, other combinations are undoubtedly very effective as well; investors with a stronger growth orientation might well choose to place more weight on estimate revisions.

We again formed five portfolios of 100 stocks each to discern the relationship between returns and value scores (combinations of P/E and estimate revisions). Stocks were divided among 12 economic sectors and ordered from high to low on the basis of the value scores. Those with the best (highest) value scores were assigned to the first portfolio, and those with the worst (lowest) value scores were assigned to the fifth portfolio. Equal weightings were used in forming the portfolios. The results shown below are, as a result, for equal-weighted sector-neutral portfolios.

Absolute returns, market-relative returns, and a count of the number of quarters of outperformance are shown for the five portfolios in Exhibit 5. Market-relative returns are shown again in Exhibit 6. The results for the best-value-score portfolio are shown in the top line of Exhibit 5. Those for the second-best-value-score portfolio are shown in the second line, and so on. The bars in Exhibit 6 are shown in the same order. The sector-neutral portfolio of stocks with the best value scores earned an extra 4.6% a year relative to the universe. The sector-neutral portfolio of the lowest-value-score stocks lagged the universe by 5.4%. The portfolio returns were perfectly rank-ordered. The best-value-score portfolio consistently outperformed the universe; the count was 49 out of 69 quarters, more than 70% of the time. The worst-value-score portfolio was even more consistent, lagging in 55 of 69 quarters.

A comparison of the results included in this section with those in the previous two reveals that the value score is a better selector than either P/E or estimate revision. The top-quintile portfolio's relative return was more than one and a half percent higher than that of the top-quintile-P/E portfolio and moderately higher than that of the top-quintile-estimate-revision portfolio. At the opposite end of the spectrum, the bottom-quintile-value-score portfolio lagged the universe by 5.4%, whereas the bottom-quintile-estimate-revision portfolio trailed by 4.3% and the worst-quintile-P/E portfolio by 3.3%. The advantage of the value score is most pronounced at the least attractive end of the range. Simply avoiding stocks in the fifth quintile of the value scores should significantly enhance performance. The comparisons of top- and bottom-quintile performance for the three selectors is shown in Exhibit 7.

Exhibit 5: Value Score Strategy — Using Sector-Neutral Equal-Weighted Portfolios*

	Value Score Quintile	Annual Rate of Return (%)	Market-Relative Return (%)	Quarters of Outperformance
Best	1	19.0	4.6	49
	2	16.3	1.9	45
	3	14.5	0.0	34
	4	12.8	−1.6	25
Worst	5	9.0	−5.4	14
Universe:		14.4		

* Period included 69 calendar quarters from the first quarter of 1977 through the third quarter of 1994.

Exhibit 6: Value Score Strategy — Using Sector-Neutral Equal-Weighted Portfolios

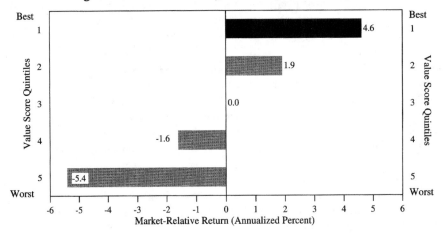

Exhibit 7: Performance Comparisons Using Three Strategies

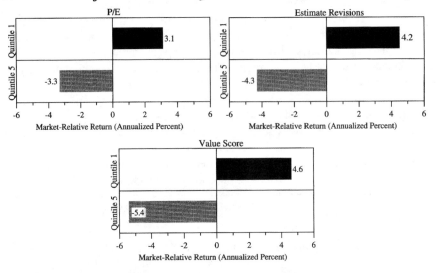

The results presented in this section (and the previous sections) do not take trading costs into account. The impact of trading costs is to mitigate the positive excess returns obtained by investing in the most attractive stocks. The question is by how much. The answer depends on both the cost of trading and the amount of portfolio turnover required to be continuously invested in the more attractive stocks.

Exhibit 8: Quarterly Turnover Using the Value Score

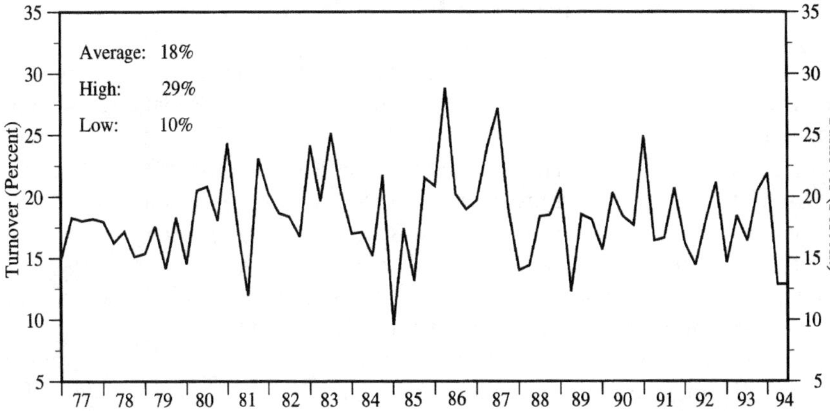

The cost of trading will depend on trading skills and on the kind of stock deemed attractive by the selector. It is reasonable to presume that both turnover and trading costs would be higher for an approach based on estimate revisions than for one based on P/E ratios. It is also reasonable to conclude that the value-score approach combining the two would fall somewhere in between. As long as the last statement is true, the value-score approach will be better than an approach based on revisions alone because of the superior discrimination power and lower trading costs of the value-score system. The value-score approach would be superior to one based on P/E ratios unless the turnover were much higher for the former.

We have examined turnover percentages for the value-score approach for the entire period of our study. Quarterly turnover percentages for a strategy that involved buying quintile-one stocks and holding them until they became quintile-three stocks are shown in Exhibit 8. Using the value-score, the average quarterly turnover was 18%. The highest turnover for any quarter was 29%, and the lowest was 10%. The average of 18% implies an annual turnover of 72%. This is not an extraordinarily high turnover ratio for an active manager. And the strategy should allow the investor to capture a combination of quintile-one and quintile-two returns with an emphasis on the quintile-one stocks.

The turnover ratio for the low-P/E approach was 12% — implying a 48% annual turnover. Assuming that transaction costs amount to two percent for a round trip, the difference in turnover ratios between the value-score approach and the low-P/E approach reduces the advantage of the value-score approach by 48 basis points — just about one half of 1%. This reduces the advantage from approximately 1.5% to 1.0% for first-quintile stocks. Nonetheless, the value-score approach retains a significant advantage. And it retains that advantage so long as round-trip costs are 6% or less.

COMPARISON OF SELECTION STRATEGIES
ON A SECTOR-BY-SECTOR BASIS

This section focuses on how well the three selectors considered in this study — P/E ratio, estimate revision, and value score (a combination of P/E's and revisions) — work within each of the 12 economic sectors employed in the study. Previous results cause us to expect that the value score will work most effectively in most sectors. However, there is no reason to believe that the same selector will work best in every sector. Furthermore, there is no reason for an investor to use the same approach in every sector of the stock market.

The within-sector relative returns for all quintiles for each selection are shown in Exhibit 9. Each chart in the exhibit shows the results for one of the 12 economic sectors. Review of the charts suggests that the value score was the most effective selector in eight of the twelve economic sectors while estimate revision was best in three and P/E was best in one. In most cases, the conclusions seem obvious, but there are several sectors in which performance of two of the selectors is very close. Note that the vertical scales in Chart 6 were selected to illustrate the return differences within each economic sector.

In those cases in which the first-quintile returns for a selector were higher than those for the others *and* in which the fifth-quintile returns were lower, the selector in question was deemed most effective. For example, the value score was clearly the most effective in the energy sector. The first quintile of value-score stocks produced a relative return of 7.0% while the first quintile of P/E stocks provided 6.8% and the first quintile of estimate-revision stocks only 3.4%. At the same time, the fifth quintile based on value score lagged the universe by 9.8% while P/E and estimate-revision fifth-quintile stocks lagged the universe by 8.0% and 5.8%, respectively.

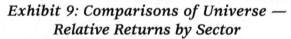

Exhibit 9: Comparisons of Universe — Relative Returns by Sector

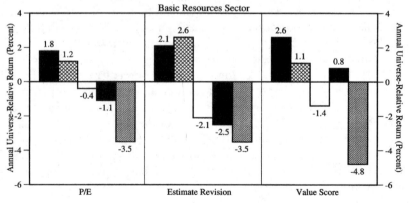

Exhibit 9: (Continued)

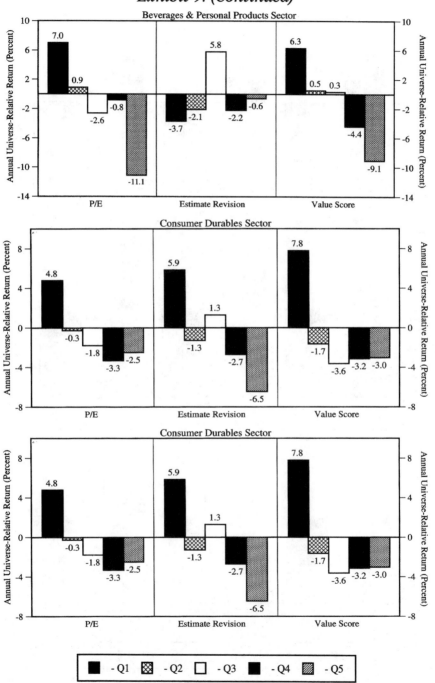

Exhibit 9: (Continued)

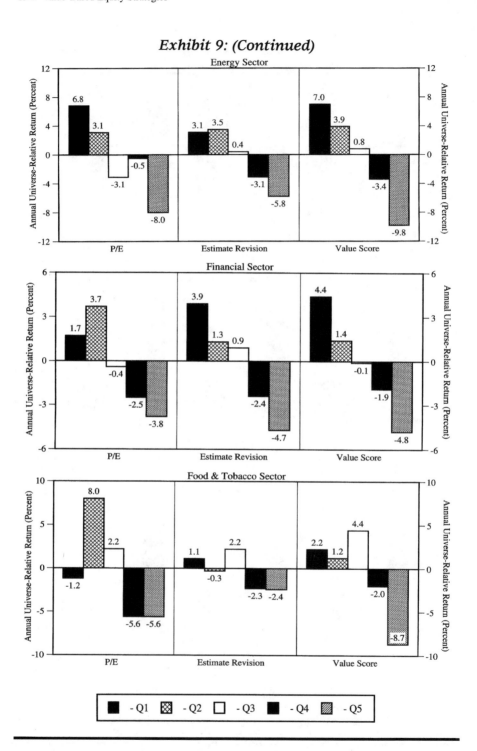

Exhibit 9: (Continued)

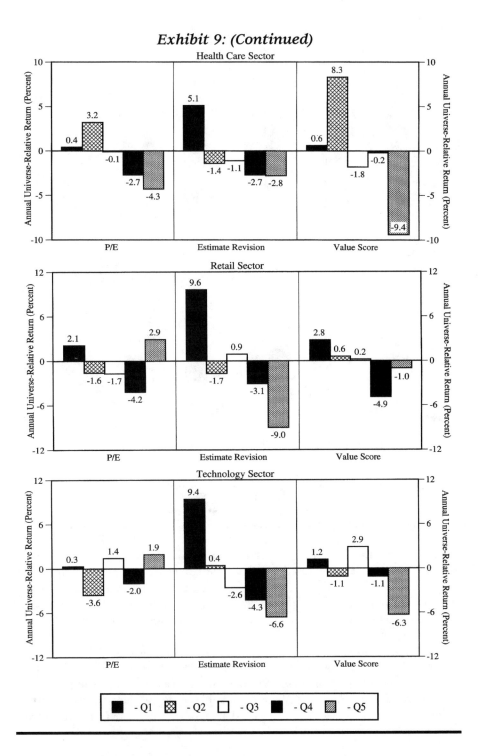

Exhibit 9: (Continued)

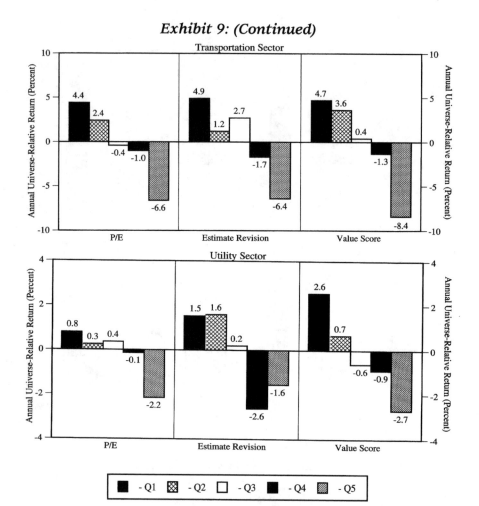

If we use the relative performance of first- and fifth-quintile stocks as criteria, P/E's worked best in the Beverage and Personal Products sector. Estimate revisions dominated in the Retail sector and the Technology sector. The value score was clearly most effective in Basic Resources, Consumer Services, Energy, Financials, Food and Tobacco, Transportation, and Utilities sectors. The Consumer Durables sector yielded mixed results; the value score was most effective on the upside, but revisions were relatively close on the upside and clearly were most effective in identifying laggards. On balance, we conclude that estimate revisions are most effective. The other controversial sector is Health Care. Estimate revisions best identified superior performers. But the value score was clearly dominant in identifying laggards. This fact — and the good performance of the first two quintiles based on value score — led to the conclusion that the value score is most effective.

Caution is warranted in interpreting the results contained in this section of the chapter. Too much weight should not be placed on empirical results for a specific period of time. One could argue, for example, that value scores should be used in all sectors because of their conceptual soundness and the power of the overall cross-sectional results. We have, in fact, chosen to sort stocks into quintiles by value score in 10 of the 12 sectors in our continuing analytical work on the stock market. Nonetheless, we do place more emphasis on estimate revisions in the Retail and Technology Sectors. The empirical results supporting this decision are very strong, as shown above.

Moreover, there are sound conceptual reasons for believing that near-term business dynamics will dominate in determining the winners and losers in the Retail and Technology sectors. Value is elusive in both cases. Take Technology, for example. The rate of change and obsolescence in Technology is very rapid. Once a product is obsolete, the equipment used to produce it has little, if any, value. As a result, stocks in the technology sector that appear cheap are not necessarily inexpensive at all. Often the companies are simply in a declining stage, and the usual measures of value provide no help in determining where stock prices might go. In Retail, too, it is not so much the value of the fixtures and physical space as the concept that counts. When a concept is working, the fundamentals move in a positive direction. When it is not, a decline in price and an apparently attractive measure of value do not mean that the stock is likely to do well in the future. Rather, when a concept is not working, the fundamentals move in a negative direction; that is the signal to avoid the stock.

DIVERSIFIED VERSUS NONDIVERSIFIED PORTFOLIOS

Throughout this chapter, we have presented returns from diversified portfolios. The purpose of this section is to compare the returns and risks of *diversified* portfolios and *nondiversified* portfolios. Each portfolio contains 100 securities. Diversified portfolios, are those that are spread across economic sectors so that the weighting of each economic sector in the portfolio is the same as the weighting of the sector in the universe. These portfolios are "sector-neutral." For example, the low-P/E diversified portfolio includes the low-P/E quintile of stocks *from each economic sector.*

Nondiversified portfolios are formed without regard to economic sector membership. The low-P/E, nondiversified portfolio contains the 100 stocks with the lowest P/E ratios in the whole universe. This low-P/E portfolio would typically have a larger weight in banks and utilities than the universe.

The focus of our attention is always the best portfolio — the top-quintile portfolio. We examined returns and risks for the best diversified and the best nondiversified portfolio in every instance. We found that diversified portfolios provided higher relative returns on average, and, at the same time, protected the investor on the downside in those instances in which the returns from the best portfolios lagged those of the universe. This was true regardless of the selector used in forming the portfolios.

Exhibit 10: Lowest P/E Strategy

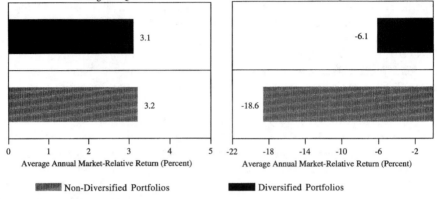

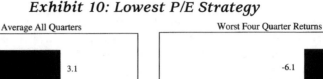

The average relative returns and the worst annual relative return for diversified and nondiversified portfolios are shown in Exhibits 10, 11, and 12. Exhibit 10 shows the results for portfolios based on P/E ratios; Exhibit 11 shows the results for estimate revisions; and Exhibit 12 shows the results for the value score. The average relative return was always higher for the diversified portfolios' and it was nearly one percent higher in the case of the value-score portfolios. Similarly, the worst annual return was always lower for nondiversified portfolios than for diversified portfolios. The difference was not large in the case of the estimate-revision portfolios. But it was dramatic for the low-P/E portfolios and the value-score portfolios; in each case the difference was over 16%.

The results reported in this section suggest that a diversified value approach is preferable to one that is highly concentrated. Diversifying across economic sectors does not reduce the extra returns provided by value portfolios. In fact, over the period of this study, diversification actually enhanced returns. More importantly, diversified portfolios provided significant protection against years of dramatic underperformance.[6] Clients may question their commitment to value investing after a year in which their portfolio trailed the universe by 1,000 basis points. It is easier to maintain their commitment after a year in which performance lagged by 100 to 200 basis points.

---

[6] We believe that broad diversification is desirable much of the time. Furthermore, we believe that systematic approaches must work within sectors to be effective overall. Nonetheless, these results do not imply that it is not possible to add value through making sector overweighting and underweighting decisions. In fact, our own experience has shown that it is possible to augment returns through sector-weighting decisions. Our results suggest that either (1) other tools are more valuable for making sector decisions than the selectors used to pick stocks within sectors here or (2) there were few opportunities to add value through sector selection over the time period of the study because sectors were fairly priced relative to one another most of the time. There is probably a degree of truth in both of these possibilities.

Exhibit 11: Highest Estimate-Revision Strategy

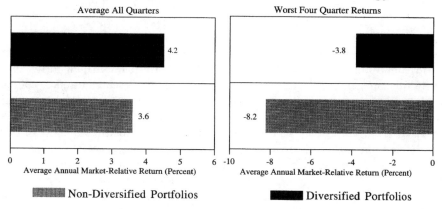

Exhibit 12: Highest Value-Score Strategy

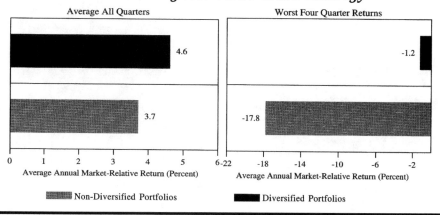

CONCLUSION

The research reported here has confirmed the bedrock beliefs upon which we construct equity portfolios. We have once again found that value investing leads to higher returns. We have shown that a value approach can be enhanced by judicious use of a measure of the underlying business's dynamics. We have further shown that a diversified approach to value investing is particularly effective at controlling portfolio risk — while not detracting from the benefit of the value-only approach.

Hence, when we build equity portfolios, we begin by looking for stocks with low expectations — measured by low-P/E's. Second, we look for stocks that have rising expectations — measured by positive earnings-estimate revisions. Third, we subject the resulting candidate stocks to rigorous fundamental analysis by our experienced analysts and portfolio managers. Finally, we build diversified portfolios — in keeping with our research findings that broadly diversified value portfolios are less volatile but provide comparable excess returns.

Our approach employs a systematic component wherein stocks are ranked within each economic sector according to our value score. The stocks are sorted into quintiles. Each economic-sector portfolio is the responsibility of a portfolio manager who devotes his research time and the research resources of his team to investigating those stocks ranked highest within the sector. Stocks within the first two quintiles are selected for the portfolios. Fourth- and fifth-quintile stocks are eliminated. In the end, we believe, the systematic elements of our approach, combined with the judgment of our experienced portfolio managers, constitute a very attractive approach to managing large equity portfolios.

We believe that a focused approach to stock selection built around this effective ranking system will produce superior investment results over the long haul.

Chapter 12

The Use of Derivatives in Managing Equity Portfolios

Roger G. Clarke, Ph.D.
Chairman
Analytic/TSA Global Asset Management

Harindra de Silva, Ph.D., CFA
Managing Director
Analytic/TSA Global Asset Management

Greg M. McMurran
Chief Investment Officer
Analytic/TSA Global Asset Management

INTRODUCTION

The growth of the derivatives markets in recent years has given the investment manager an important set of tools to use in managing the risk and return characteristics of equity portfolios. In this chapter we will discuss some of the common strategies available using three different derivatives contracts: index swaps, futures, and options. Each of these derivatives has their own special characteristics which make them useful for adjusting the payoff profile of the portfolio to reflect a manager's expectations or view of the market.

One of the main characteristics of derivatives contracts is that little, if any, up-front money is required to initiate the contract. This feature allows the manager to maintain the principal involved in the transaction in other securities while increasing or decreasing exposure to the market through the derivatives contract. This separation of market exposure from the need for immediate cash outlays is what makes hedging possible, for example. Market exposure generated by holding underlying securities can be hedged with a derivative without having to sell the underlying securities themselves.

A major difference between the types of derivative contracts is the shape of the payoff structure that results when the market moves. Both index swaps and futures contracts have linear payoff patterns. That is, the payoff is symmetric around current market levels. The payoff as the market goes up or down mirrors the movement of the market itself. As a result, swaps and futures are often referred to as *portfolio substitutes* since their effects can substitute for the market return on a well-diversified portfolio of stocks. However, options generate non-linear payoff patterns. Put options are more sensitive to down market moves while call options are more sensitive to up market moves. This asymmetry allows options to create special effects in managing the risk of a portfolio not available by using swaps or futures contracts. The choice of the optimal derivative strategy is naturally a function of the manager's objectives, risk preferences, and market view.

This chapter is organized as follows. We first outline the use of derivative strategies which have linear payoffs including swaps and futures. Call and put options, along with other combination strategies which have non-linear payoffs are reviewed in the next section. In the final section we discuss the typical framework used to price options and the limitations of using this approach to select an optimal derivative strategy. We illustrate a basic framework for selecting a particular strategy given a manager's risk and return expectations. Examples are provided for one of the more commonly used derivative strategies — the covered call strategy.

LINEAR PAYOFFS: SWAPS

The simplest index swap contract is structured between two parties where the counterparties agree to exchange the return between an equity index and a fixed interest rate (usually LIBOR) scaled by the principal or notional amount of the swap. We shall refer to the investor who pays the fixed rate and receives the market return as the swap buyer; the counterparty is the swap seller. The swap allows the investor buying the swap to gain exposure to the market without having to purchase the underlying equities themselves. The investor's funds can be left in cash reserves earning interest which is exchanged with the counter party who has agreed to pay the investor the return on the equity index.

This arrangement is illustrated in Exhibit 1. Investor A who has purchased the equity index swap receives the equity index return from Investor B while paying the agreed upon fixed rate. No principal is exchanged between the two parties, only the agreed upon return tied to the notional amount of the swap is exchanged. This allows the investors to achieve returns in one market without actually having to hold securities in that market. Swaps are usually negotiated, private-party transactions. Though the specific terms of a swap may vary, it is not unusual for the maturity or *tenor* of a swap to run for a year or more with returns being exchanged at quarterly intervals.

A simple way to look at the impact of using a swap to achieve equity market returns is illustrated in Exhibit 2. The purchaser of the swap holds the notional amount of the swap in cash which earns interest. When the return on the investor's cash reserve is combined with the return on the equity index less the payment of the promised fixed rate, the investor is left with the return on the equity index plus the difference in return earned on the underlying cash reserves less the fixed return paid to the counterparty. The purchaser of the swap has created a synthetic equity return on the investment without having to actually purchase equity securities.

The seller of the swap receives the fixed return and pays the return on the equity index. If the seller holds underlying stocks which mirror the return on the equity index, the net return to the seller will be the fixed rate received plus any difference in return between the actual return on the stocks and the return on the equity index. The seller of the swap has effectively created synthetic cash while the actual underlying portfolio is invested in equities as illustrated in Exhibit 3. This is part of the power of using derivatives to manage portfolios. Since derivative contracts do not require the exchange of principal, underlying assets may be held in one type of security but the net result may be the return on another type of security.

Exhibit 1: Equity Index Swap

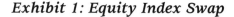

Buyer		Seller
Investor A	A pays fixed return → ← B pays equity index return	**Investor B**

Exhibit 2: Return Equivalency from the Purchase of an Equity Index Swap

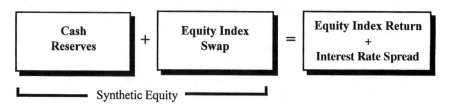

Cash Reserves	+	Equity Index Swap	=	Equity Index Return + Interest Rate Spread

Synthetic Equity

Exhibit 3: Return Equivalency from the Sale of an Equity Index Swap

Equity Portfolio	-	Equity Index Swap	=	Fixed Return + Equity Portfolio Spread

Synthetic Cash

Exhibit 4: Payoff of an Equity Index Swap as a Function of the Return on the Index

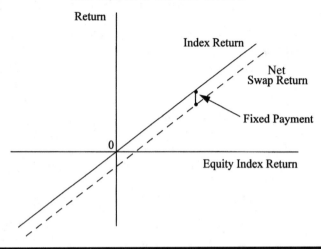

The return on the swap contract is referred to as being *linear* because it bears a straight line relationship to the return on the underlying equity index as shown in Exhibit 4. If the market goes up, the return on the swap contract will also go up. If the market goes down, the return on the swap contract also goes down. The difference between the index return and the swap return is the fixed rate the purchaser of the swap pays to the seller. When the swap return is added to the return the buyer earns on the underlying principal, the net result reflects the return on the equity index plus or minus the spread between what is earned on the cash reserve and what is paid to the seller.

Since swaps are usually entered into for an extended period of time, they are used primarily for either gaining or reducing market exposure. It may not be convenient or cost effective for the purchaser of a swap to buy actual equity securities. Entering into the swap agreement is an alternative for achieving equity exposure without the actual purchase of underlying equity securities. It has become popular in recent years to use swaps to create enhanced index funds. The investor may have a specific expertise in managing cash portfolios but no expertise in managing equity portfolios. If more can be earned on the cash portfolio than has to be paid to the seller of the swap, the investor ends up with an index-like return in the equity market but adds a spread generated by the difference in return between the actively managed cash portfolio and the fixed rate in the swap. This is sometimes referred to as *transporting alpha*. The alpha or differential return generated in one market can be converted to a differential return in another market.

Any type of equity index can be used in a swap as long as it is well defined and is agreed upon by both parties. It has become increasingly popular in recent years to use a swap on an international equity index. This saves the purchaser of the swap the difficulties of transacting in international markets and avoids directly paying for the accounting and custody fees. To the extent that the seller of the swap has potential economies of scale in assuming these costs and builds this reduced cost into the fixed return in the swap, the buyer of the swap may be able to generate international equity market returns at somewhat lower cost than purchasing the securities directly.

To illustrate an equity index swap transaction, suppose two investors agree to swap the return on the S&P 500 index in exchange for LIBOR plus 20 basis points on a $20 million notional value. The buyer of the swap pays the seller LIBOR plus 20 basis points in exchange for the total return on the S&P 500 index. If annualized LIBOR is 5.25% and the return on the S&P 500 index is 6.3% for the quarter, the buyer pays

$$\$20,000,000 \ (0.0545/4) = \$272,500$$

and the seller pays

$$\$20,000,000 \ (0.063) = \$1,260,000$$

In practice, the two amounts would usually be netted out against each other with the seller paying $987,500 to the buyer in this case.

Furthermore, suppose the buyer has invested $20 million in cash reserves earning an annualized rate of 5.85% for the quarter. The buyer of the swap has effectively earned a net return of

$$6.3\% + (5.85\% - 5.45\%)/4 = 6.40\%$$

or 10 basis points more than the index for the quarter. The extra 10 basis points comes from earning an annualized 40 basis points more per year than is required to be paid in the swap contract. If the seller of the swap has hedged the market obligation using a portfolio of stocks which has returned 6.5%, the seller's net return for the quarter will be

$$5.45\%/4 + (6.5\% - 6.3\%) = 1.56\%$$

or 6.25% at an annualized rate. The extra 100 basis points return over LIBOR with little market exposure is generated by receiving an extra 20 basis points from the fixed return in the swap plus an annualized differential return over the index of 80 basis points from the underlying equity portfolio.

LINEAR PAYOFFS: FUTURES

Futures contracts work much like swaps in their payoff pattern but there are some important institutional differences. One of the differences comes from the fact that futures contracts are traded on organized exchanges and are not negotiated directly between two counterparties. With a swap contract each counterparty is exposed to the credit risk of the other. With futures contracts the trading exchange and its members stand in the middle between two investors who have bought and sold futures contracts. The exchange plays the role of guarantor of the contract to ensure that all contract obligations are met. To help assure the financial integrity of the exchange and minimize the possibility that investors could build up losses beyond their ability to pay, investors initiating a position must deposit a performance bond with the exchange as *initial margin*. In addition, gains and losses are settled up on a daily basis between investors through the exchange (called *mark to market*) in contrast to swap contracts which are typically settled only quarterly. Finally, the interest rate which is fixed in the terms of a swap contract is embedded directly in the price of the futures contract so that it is not required to be independently specified up-front. The rate embedded in the futures contract is an implied market rate called the *implied repo rate* and matches the maturity of the contract in contrast to the fixed rate in the swap which usually resets each quarter when payments are exchanged

Exchange traded futures contracts typically carry a shorter term maturity than swap contracts. Maturities are usually staggered in three month segments with most of the liquidity found in the nearest maturity contract. There is often poor liquidity beyond the first two or three contracts. The shorter maturity of futures contracts allows them to be used with greater flexibility in managing equity portfolios, though like a swap, there are still only two things to do with a futures contract: buy it or sell it.

Applications of Buying Futures

The purchase of an equity index futures contract accomplishes the same thing as the purchase of an equity index swap. It adds equity exposure to the manager's portfolio. There are a variety of situations where a manager may want to add equity exposure. One of the most common is referred to as *cash equitization*. Equitizing cash through the purchase of futures contracts creates equity exposure synthetically without having to actually purchase underlying securities as illustrated in Exhibit 5. Many equity portfolios contain frictional amounts of cash that are difficult to keep fully invested. Dividends may be received from time to time or there may be new contributions that increase the cash in the portfolio. If the market moves up before these frictional amounts of cash can be invested in stocks, the portfolio performance will be exposed to *cash drag* and will not track the market as closely as it might. In a year when the market returns in excess of 25%, holding 5% cash would reduce portfolio performance by over 100 basis points. Since the market generally trends up over time, any frictional cash in the portfolio will tend to hurt performance.

Futures contracts might be purchased for more than just equitizing frictional amounts of cash. An entire portfolio could be left in cash reserves and futures contracts could be purchased to create a synthetic index fund. The combination of the cash reserve plus the futures contracts will behave as if a manager had purchased all of the stocks in the index. This creates tremendous liquidity in the portfolio. If funds are needed quickly, the futures contracts and the cash reserves are often easier to liquidate at lower cost than the underlying stocks. Furthermore, if the underlying cash reserve is actively managed to yield more than the implied repo rate in the futures contract, the index fund will have an enhanced return greater than the index itself. Futures contracts have been used to create enhanced index funds not only in the United States but in other countries that have actively traded equity index futures contracts. This achieves the same effect as purchasing a swap but with a shorter maturity.

Futures contracts are also useful in the trading process by helping manage the net market exposure of a portfolio as stocks are purchased or sold. It is not uncommon for slices of a portfolio to be traded involving multiple securities. These trades could be caused by the addition or withdrawal of funds in a portfolio or by a restructuring of positions internal to the portfolio. As long as the purchase or sale of securities leaves the portfolio temporarily overexposed or underexposed to the market while the trades are taking place, the portfolio manager can maintain market exposure until all of the security positions are in place by selling or buying the requisite number of futures contracts. The positions can then be closed out when they are no longer needed.

Applications of Selling Futures

The most common motivation for selling a futures contract in managing an equity portfolio is to temporarily hedge its market exposure. Like a swap, the sale of a futures contact against an underlying portfolio of stocks is equivalent to creating synthetic cash as illustrated in Exhibit 6. In essence, creating a hedged position is an attempt to counteract the market risk in the underlying securities and shift the risk to others willing to bear the risk. The risk can always be shifted by doing away with the underlying security position, but this may interfere with the nature of the investor's business or disrupt a continuing investment program. The futures market provides an alternative way to temporarily control or eliminate much of the risk in the underlying securities while continuing to hold the stocks.

Exhibit 5: Creating Synthetic Equity Exposure Using Index Futures Contracts

Exhibit 6: Creating Synthetic Cash Using Equity Index Futures Contracts: Hedging

Exhibit 7: Return Profiles for Hedged Portfolios

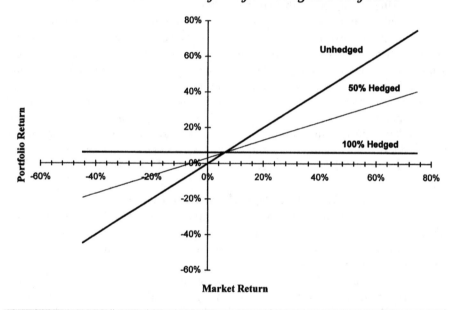

The impact of hedging can be seen by examining the effect of hedging on a portfolio's return profile and probability distribution. Exhibit 7 illustrates the return on the hedged portfolio relative to the return on the underlying market index. A partially hedged position reduces the slope of the return line, so that the hedged portfolio does not perform as well as the market when returns are high, but it also does not perform as poorly when returns are low. The greater the portion of the portfolio that is hedged, the less slope the line will have. A full hedge produces a flat line, indicating that the hedged portfolio will generate a fixed return no matter what the underlying market does. This fixed return should be equal to the riskless rate if the futures contract is fairly priced. The slope of the return line for an equity portfolio is often referred to as the portfolio's market sensitivity or beta. Hedging effectively reduces the market beta of the portfolio as it amounts to selling the equity exposure of the portfolio.

Exhibit 8: Return Distributions for Hedged Portfolios

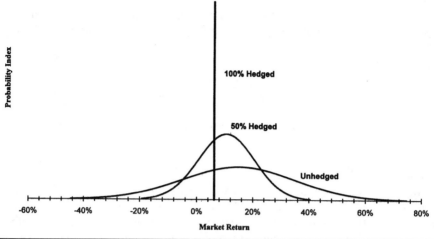

Exhibit 8 shows how the futures hedge changes the probability distribution of returns. If the return distribution for the market is symmetric with a wide dispersion, hedging the portfolio with futures gradually draws both tails of the distribution in toward the middle, and the mean return shrinks back toward the riskless rate. A full hedge draws both tails into one place and puts all of the probability mass at the riskless rate (the implied repo rate in the contract).

Hedging with futures will affect both tails equally. One of the main differences between options with their non-linear effects and futures is that options can affect one tail more dramatically than the other, so the distribution becomes quite skewed. Exhibit 9 illustrates the difference in the return distributions caused by a partial futures hedge versus a partial hedge created by using a put option. The put option hedge reduces the downside risk while leaving much of the upside potential. The use of options for hedging will be explained in more detail later.

Hedge Ratios Using Futures

A *hedge ratio* represents the amount of the futures used to construct a hedge relative to the amount of the underlying portfolio being hedged. In some cases there is a direct way to calculate the appropriate hedge ratio between futures and the portfolio. This technique can be used when the futures contract used for hedging is tied closely to the underlying portfolio being hedged as is the case when equity index futures are used to hedge a well diversified portfolio. Hedge ratios can be calculated easily because there is a direct link between the change in the value of the underlying portfolio and a change in the value of the associated futures contract.

To develop this idea, suppose an investor holds one unit of a portfolio containing securities *S* and wants to hedge it with a futures contract *F*. The change in the value of the combined position *V* as the portfolio value changes is

$$\Delta V = \Delta S + h\Delta F \tag{1}$$

where h (the hedge ratio) represents the number of units of futures F used to hedge portfolio S. Solving for the hedge ratio directly from equation (1) gives

$$h = \frac{\Delta V - \Delta S}{\Delta F} \tag{2}$$

For a complete hedge, or market neutral hedge ($\Delta V = 0$), the hedge ratio would be equal to the negative of the ratio of relative price changes between the portfolio being hedged and the futures contract. That is,

$$h = -\frac{\Delta S}{\Delta F} \tag{3}$$

To illustrate this concept suppose S is a diversified equity portfolio, F is a futures contract on the S&P 500 Index, and $\Delta S/\Delta F$ is assumed to equal 0.95. That is, when the S&P 500 futures contract moves by $1, the underlying equity portfolio moves by only $0.95, indicating that the portfolio is slightly less volatile than the broad market represented by the S&P 500 Index. For a market neutral hedge, the hedge ratio is

$$h = -\frac{0.95}{1.00} = -0.95$$

Exhibit 9: Return Distributions for Hedged Portfolios
Options versus Futures

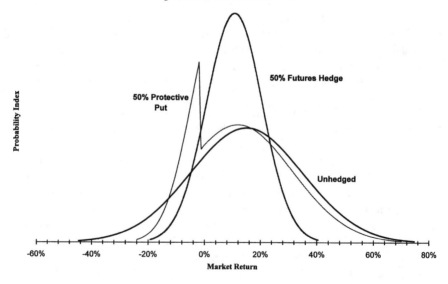

An investor would sell futures contracts worth 95% of the value of the equity portfolio to create the hedge. If the investor wanted only a partial hedge ($\Delta V = \frac{1}{3}\Delta S$, for example), the hedge ratio is

$$h = \frac{\frac{1}{3}\Delta S - \Delta S}{\Delta F} = \frac{-2}{3}\left(\frac{\Delta S}{\Delta F}\right) = -0.63$$

The investor would sell futures contracts worth only 63% of the value of the equity portfolio. With the hedge in place, the hedged portfolio would move only $\frac{1}{3}$ as much as the underlying portfolio.

Because the equity portfolio does not move one for one with the S&P 500 futures contract in the example, the investor does not want to use a hedge ratio of -1.0 to hedge the market risk in the underlying securities. A market-neutral hedge requires fewer futures contracts to be used because the underlying equity portfolio has only 95% of the movement of the futures contract.

The example above also shows what the hedge ratio must be if only a partial hedge is created to protect against the price movement in the underlying securities. If the combined hedged position is targeted to have $\frac{1}{3}$ of the movement of the underlying securities, a hedge ratio of -0.63 is needed. The investor would sell futures contracts worth only 63% of the value of the equity portfolio to create the partial hedge.

The arbitrage pricing relationship between the futures contract and the underlying market index links the two price changes together. This relationship can be used to calculate how the fair price of the futures contract will change as the price of the equity index changes. To see how this relationship can be used to estimate the hedge ratio directly, suppose that the price change of both the portfolio to be hedged and the futures contract are proportional to the change in the market index I in the following way:

$$\Delta S = \beta_S \Delta I, \text{ and } \Delta F = \beta_F \Delta I$$

where β_S and β_F represent the sensitivity to the index (market betas) of the portfolio being hedged and the futures contract, respectively.

Because portfolios and futures contracts are tied to the same underlying index, the hedge ratio is proportional to the ratio of their respective market betas. That is,

$$h = \frac{-\Delta S}{\Delta F} = -\frac{\beta_S}{\beta_F} \tag{4}$$

If the investor has an estimate of the market betas of the futures contract and the portfolio relative to the market index, the investor can calculate the appropriate hedge ratio directly.

For example, consider the calculation of the hedge ratio and the number of S&P 500 futures contracts required to hedge a $50 million equity portfolio with a beta of 1.05 relative to the S&P 500 Index. If the futures contract has a beta of 1.01 and the current level of the index is 900, the hedge ratio is

$$h = \frac{-1.05}{1.01} = -1.04$$

The contract size for the S&P 500 is 500 times the value of the S&P 500 Index, or $450,000 (500 × 900), so the number of futures contracts required to be sold is

$$n = \frac{h(\text{Hedge value})}{\text{Contract size}} = \frac{-1.04(50,000,000)}{450,000} = -116 \text{ contracts}$$

Notice that the hedge ratio is slightly less than the beta of the portfolio. The short-term hedge ratio accounts for the slightly larger volatility in the index futures contract caused by its arbitrage pricing relationship. This additional volatility will shrink towards zero as the contract gets closer to maturity, reflecting a beta for the futures contract which converges to 1.0 at expiration. For longer term hedges with an investment horizon equal to the expiration date of the futures contract, a futures beta of 1.0 is typically used to calculate the hedge ratio.

NON-LINEAR PAYOFFS: OPTIONS

Simple options come in two forms: put options and call options. Unlike futures contracts and swaps, options require a small premium to be paid when purchased. Depending on the maturity of the option and the exercise price, the premium may range from less than 1% to more than 10% of the value of the underlying security or index. The payoff from an option at expiration depends on whether the security is above or below the level of the exercise or strike price. This lack of symmetry creates a non-linear payoff for the option at expiration. Put options have a non-zero payoff when the security price is less than the exercise price and call options pay off when the security price is greater than the exercise price. To see how options can be used in managing equity portfolios it is useful to review the payoff profile of put and call options.

Payoff Profiles for Options

Insight into the characteristics of options can be obtained by looking specifically at how options behave and what value they have at expiration. The matrix below is a simple technique for showing the value of option positions at expiration where S represents the value of the individual security or index and K represents the exercise price of the option:

	Payoff at Expiration	
	$S < K$	$S > K$
Call	0	$S - K$
Put	$K - S$	0
Security	S	S

At the expiration of the put or call option, its payoff depends on whether the security price is less than or more than the exercise price. The value of the underlying security is the same, S, whether it is below or above the option's exercise price. These payoffs form the basic building blocks for option strategy analysis.

Exhibit 10 illustrates the payoff pattern at expiration for a call option. On the horizontal axis is plotted the security price. The vertical axis measures the payoff at expiration. The trivial case representing the security's value is shown by the dashed line. For example, if the security ends with a value of K dollars, then the security will have a payoff of K dollars. The call option has a value of zero until the security price reaches the exercise price K, after which the call option increases one for one in price as the security price increases. The investor, however, must first purchase the option. So the net payoff from buying a call option is negative until the security price reaches the exercise price, and then it starts to rise (the dotted line). This line represents the payoff the investor receives net of the cost of the option. The investor breaks even with zero net profit at the point where the security price equals the exercise price plus the call option premium, C.

Note that the call option has a kinked or asymmetric payoff pattern. This feature distinguishes it from a futures contract. The future has a payoff pattern that is a straight line, as does the underlying security. This asymmetry in the option's payoff allows the option buyer to create specialized return patterns that are unavailable when using a futures contract.

Exhibit 11 illustrates the behavior of a put option. The put option has an intrinsic value of zero above the exercise price. Below there, it increases one for one as the security price declines. If an investor buys a put option, the net payoff of the option is the dotted line. The investor breaks even, with zero net profit, at the point where the security price equals the exercise price less the put option premium, P.

Exhibit 10: Payoff Profile of a Call Option

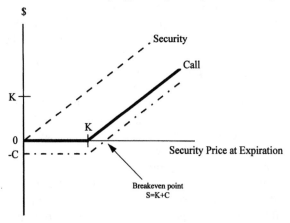

$-\cdot-\cdot$ Net of option premiums

Exhibit 11: Payoff Profile of a Put Option

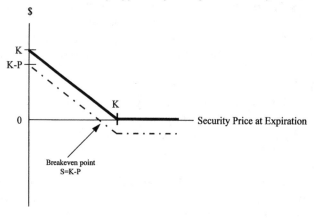

- · - · Net of option premiums

Selling Call Options: Exchanging Appreciation for Income

One of the most popular option strategies is known as a *covered call*. A covered call is constructed by holding the underlying security and selling a call option. The payoff matrix at expiration for this strategy is

	Covered Call Payoff at Expiration	
	$S < K$	$S > K$
Security	S	S
Short Call	0	$-(S - K)$
Total Payoff	S	K

The value of the security is S whether it finishes above or below the exercise price. The value of the call option is zero below the exercise price and $(S - K)$ above the exercise price. Since the call option has been sold by the investor, the payoff of the call option is owed and serves to reduce the total payoff below the value of the security itself. The total payoff of the covered call is found by adding up the value in each column. Below the exercise price, the portfolio is worth S dollars since the call has expired worthless. Above the exercise price, the portfolio is worth K dollars since the short call neutralizes the appreciation in the security above the exercise price.

The covered call strategy is shown graphically in Exhibit 12. The dashed line again represents the security value. The solid line represents the value of the security plus the payoff from the short call option. Below the exercise price the investor is left with the value of the security. Above the exercise price the security's appreciation is capped at the exercise price. In exchange for this limit on the security's appreciation, the investor receives the premium of the call option. The investor has traded the possibility of upside appreciation above the exercise price for income in the form of the option premium. The break-even point occurs when the security price is equal to the exercise price plus the call option premium. Below this point the covered call strategy gives a better payoff than holding the security by itself.

To demonstrate the result of a covered call strategy, consider an investor who holds a position in a stock worth $10 million. Assume that the current stock price is $100. The following example illustrates the effect of selling call options if the stock appreciates or depreciates 10% over the next six months.

	Stock Price	Underlying Portfolio Value	Portfolio Percentage Change
Current	$100	$10,000,000	
After six months	$110	$11,000,000	10.0
After six months	$90	$9,000,000	−10.0

Suppose the investor sells 100,000 6-month call options, each covering 100 shares with an exercise price of $105 to bring in premium income of $300,000. If the stock price declines by 10% to $90, the call options will expire worthless and the investor keeps the income from the sale of the call options giving a portfolio value of

$9,000,000 + $300,000 = $9,300,000

representing a decline of 7.0%. The value of the portfolio has declined by less than the 10% decline in the stock price because of the premium income received from the call options. If the stock price appreciates by 10%, the payoff of the call options owed by the investor will be

$100,000 (105 − 110) = −$500,000

Exhibit 12: Payoff Profile of a Covered Call

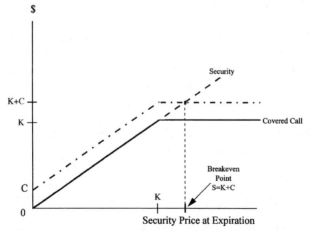

— · — · Net of option premiums

which when combined with the value of the stock and the premium income from the sale of the call options gives a portfolio value of

$$\$11,000,000 + \$300,000 - \$500,000 = \$10,800,000.$$

This represents a return of 8.0% on the value of the stocks in the portfolio compared to the stock price appreciation of 10.0%. The premium income from the call options has helped to offset the loss on the exercise of the options but the stock has appreciated beyond the break-even point so the net return on the portfolio is less than the appreciation in the stock itself.

Asymmetric Hedges: Protecting the Downside

The construction of an asymmetric hedge which responds to positive market returns differently than to negative market returns usually requires the use of an option. The most common strategies to hedge market exposure are (1) the protective put, (2) the protective put spread, and (3) the collar, range forward, or fence.

Protective Put

A *protective put* is constructed by holding the underlying security and buying a put option. The payoff matrix at expiration for this strategy is

	Protective Put Payoff at Expiration	
	$S < K$	$S > K$
Security	S	S
Put	$K - S$	0
Total payoff	K	S

The value of the security is S whether it finishes above or below the exercise price. The value of the put option is $(K - S)$ below the option's exercise price and zero above the exercise price. The total value of the protective put is found by adding up the value in each column. Below the exercise price, the portfolio is worth K dollars at expiration. Above the exercise price, it is worth S.

This strategy is depicted graphically in Exhibit 13. The dashed line again represents the security value. The solid line represents the value of the security plus the put option. Below the exercise price, the put option compensates for the decline in the security price. Once the original cost of the put option is accounted for, the net payoff is represented by the dotted line. The break-even point occurs when the security price is equal to the exercise price less the cost of the put option. Below this point, the protective-put strategy gives a better payoff than holding just the security by itself.

The benefit of this strategy occurs below the break-even point. If the security price falls below this level, the portfolio is always worth more than the security itself. This protection is of great benefit if the market is going down. The market does not give this protection for free, however. Above the break-even point, the protected portfolio is always worth a little bit less than the security. The price paid for the option results in a slightly lower return on the upside. This strategy has sometimes taken on another name, portfolio insurance, because the put option protects the value if the security price falls while maintaining some market exposure if the price rises.

To illustrate the impact of put options to hedge equity exposure, consider the same investor who holds a stock position worth $10,000,000. Assume that the current stock price is $100 and can appreciate or depreciate by 10% over the next six months. Suppose also that the investor hedges the market risk by purchasing 100,000 6-month put options, each covering 100 shares with an exercise price of $100 at a cost of $600,000. If the stock price declines to $90, the payoff of the put options at expiration will be

$$\$100,000 \ (100 - 90) = \$1,000,000$$

The net value of the portfolio will be

$$\$9,000,000 + (\$1,000,000 - \$600,000) = \$9,400,000$$

representing a decline of 6%. The value of the portfolio has declined by less than the 10% decline in the stock price because of the net payoff of the options. The options will finish in the money and contribute some value to the portfolio. Without the option position, the unhedged value of the portfolio would have declined by the full 10%.

Exhibit 13: Payoff Profile of a Protective Put

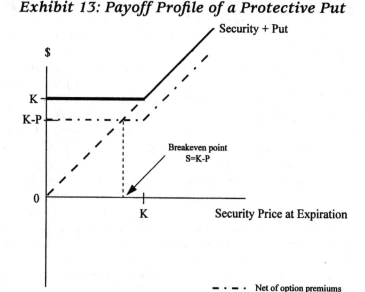

If the stock price increases to $110, the value of the put options at expiration will be zero giving a net value of the portfolio of

$11,000,000 – $600,000 = $10,400,000

representing an increase of 4%. Due to the cost of the options, the hedged portfolio will underperform the unhedged portfolio which returns a full 10.0%.

Protective Put Spread

The *protective put spread* is constructed by purchasing a put option and selling a put option farther out of the money. The payoff matrix at expiration for this strategy is

Protective Put Spread Payoff at Expiration			
	$S < K_l$	$K_l < S < K_u$	$S > K_u$
Security	S	S	S
Put Purchased	$K_u - S$	$K_u - S$	0
Put Sold	$-(K_l - S)$	0	0
Total Payoff	$S + (K_u - K_l)$	K_u	S

The total payoff of the protective put spread is split into three pieces corresponding to whether the security price is below the lower exercise price (K_l), in between the two exercise prices, or above the higher exercise price (K_u). Below the exercise price the hedged portfolio is worth the value of the stock plus the difference between the higher exercise price and the lower exercise price. If the stock price falls in between the two exercise prices, the payoff is just equal to the higher exercise price. Finally, if the stock price is above both exercise prices, the payoff is equal to the stock price since both put options expire worthless.

The strategy is shown graphically in Exhibit 14. The dashed line represents the security value. The solid line represents the value of the security plus the payoff from the two put options. In between the two exercise prices, the put spread protects the value of the portfolio as before. Below the lower exercise price the portfolio is again exposed to the decline in the market price of the stock. Once the net cost of the put option spread has been accounted for, the net payoff is represented by the dotted line. The break-even point occurs when the security price is equal to the exercise price of the protective put less the net cost of the put option spread. The cost of the protective put option spread is less than that of the protective put by itself because of the premium brought in from the put option which has been sold. As a result the break-even point is higher. The stock has to decline less in order for the protective put spread to be better than leaving the security unhedged.

The previous example can be expanded to incorporate the put spread. Suppose that 100,000 put options with an exercise price of $90 were sold to bring in premium of $100,000 to help pay for the cost of the protective puts. Now the net cost of the option positions would be $500,000. If the stock price rises 10% to $110, the payoff of the hedged portfolio will be

Exhibit 14: Payoff Profile of a Protective Put Spread

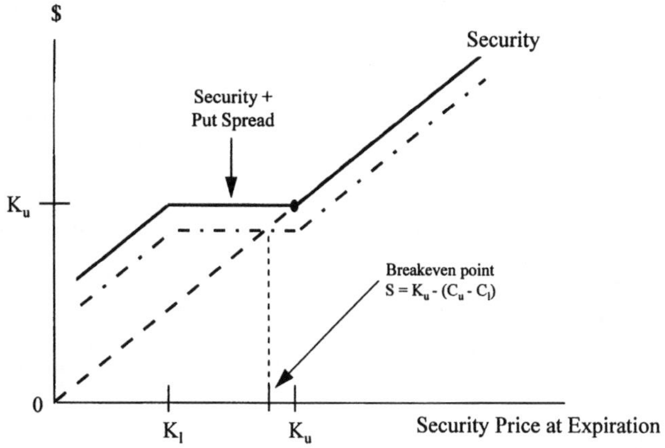

$11,000,000 - ($600,000 - $100,000) = $10,500,000$

resulting in a portfolio return of 5%. If the price of the stock falls 10% to $90, the payoff of the hedged portfolio will be

$9,000,000 + $100,000 (100 - 90) - ($600,000 - $100,000) = $9,500,000$

resulting in a portfolio return of –5% compared to the 10% decline in the stock and the 6% decline if only the protective put is used. The additional benefits resulting from the protective put spread come because the portfolio is not completely protected if the stock price falls below the lower exercise price. For example, a 20% decline in the stock price would result in a 15% decline using the protective put spread while resulting in only a 6% decline using the protective put by itself.

Collar (Range Forward or Fence)

The *collar, range forward, or fence* is constructed by selling a call option in addition to the purchase of a put option. The sale of the call again brings in cash which reduces the cost of purchasing the put option. The maturity of the call option is typically the same as that of the put, but has a higher exercise price. The sale of the call option eliminates the benefit of positive security returns above the level of the call's exercise price. If the exercise price of the call option is set close enough to that of the put, the cost of the put option can be offset entirely by the sale of the call option. This is typically referred to as a *zero cost collar.*

To accommodate the difference in exercise prices between the put and the call options, the payoff matrix must again be expanded. As a result, the payoff matrix for the collar is

Exhibit 15: Payoff Profile of a Collar

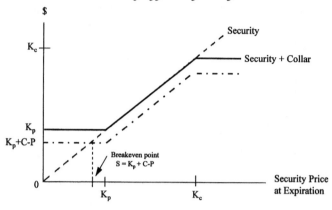

	Collar Payoff at Expiration		
	$S < K_p$	$K_p < S < K_c$	$S > K_c$
Security	S	S	S
Put	$K_p - S$	0	0
–Call	0	0	$-(S - K_c)$
Total payoff	K_p	S	K_c

K_p represents the put exercise price and K_c represents the exercise price of the call option. If the security is below the exercise price of the put at expiration, the payoff will be equal to the exercise price of the put. If the security is above the exercise price of the call option, the payoff will be equal to the exercise price of the call option. In between the two exercise prices the payoff will be equal to the underlying security price.

The payoff of the collar is shown graphically in Exhibit 15. The solid line represents the value of the security plus the payoff from the options. The dotted line represents the value of the strategy once the net cost of the options is considered. A zero cost collar would have no net option cost so the dotted line would converge to the solid line. The dashed line represents the value of holding the security unhedged. The benefit of this strategy occurs below the exercise price of the option similar to the protective put. The exact break-even point depends on the price of the call option sold to truncate some of the upside potential. This loss of upside potential beyond the break-even point of the short call position is the disadvantage of using the collar.

To continue the previous hedging example, suppose that call options are sold with an exercise price of $105 for $300,000 in addition to the purchase of put options with an exercise price of $100. If the stock price declines to $90, the put options will have value, but the call options will expire worthless. The net value of the portfolio will be

$$\$9,000,000 + \$100,000 \, (100 - 90) - (\$600,000 - \$300,000) = \$9,700,000$$

representing a decline of 3% compared to the stock price decline of 10%. The sale of the call option has helped offset the cost of the put option hedge which previously showed a decline of 6%.

On the other hand, if the stock price increases to $110, the put options will expire worthless and the value of the call option at expiration will detract from performance giving a portfolio value of

$$\$11,000,000 - \$100,000 \, (110 - 105) - (\$600,000 - \$300,000) = \$10,200,000$$

representing a net increase of only 2% compared to the 10% increase in the stock price.

Comparing the protective put strategy with the collar shows that the investor is better off using the collar if the stock price declines, but could be worse off if the stock price increases sufficiently beyond the exercise price of the call option. In the example here the loss on the value of the call option is more than the premium received when the option was sold so the investor has done slightly worse than the protective put strategy even though the stock price increased. In general, the collar or range forward works well as long as the market does not increase beyond the exercise price of the call option. If the market rallies much beyond that point, the investor will not participate in the upside market gains.

Buying Call Options: Creating Market Exposure

Two common option positions used to create market exposure are buying calls and buying call spreads. To add equity market exposure to a portfolio, the investor can buy call options on an equity index. If, for example, extra exposure to the U.S. equity market is desired, the investor can buy call options on the S&P 500. If the market appreciates, the option will increase in value. If the market declines, all the investor can lose is the cost of the option. The cost of the call option is the price the investor must pay to participate in the upside market potential while avoiding a loss in a declining market.

An alternative strategy would be to buy a call spread to create the market exposure. With a call spread, an investor buys calls with a lower exercise price than the call options sold. For example, if the market has only moderate upside potential, an investor might buy a call option with an exercise price at current market levels and sell a call option with a higher exercise price — at an exercise price above where the market is expected to be at expiration. Using a call spread, the investor participates in the market only up to a point, but at a reduced cost because the sale of the out-of-the-money call option offsets the cost of the long call option.

Exhibit 16: Payoff Profiles from Buying Calls and Call Spreads

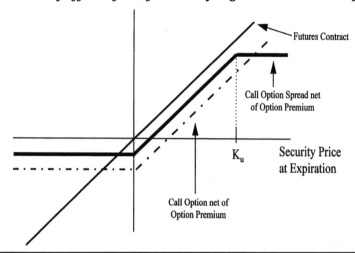

The payoff profiles at expiration for these two strategies, compared to buying a futures contract, are illustrated in Exhibit 16. If investors buy futures contracts, they will participate to the full extent of the market increase or decrease. If they buy a call option to create exposure, they participate if the market goes up, but if the market goes down, they will not suffer the full decline. The gap between the option and futures payoff on the upside represents the cost of the call option. If an investor's view about the market is positive, but not excessively bullish, the lower-cost call spread creates additional exposure but caps the market participation beyond a certain point.

Probability Distribution of Returns

In addition to using payoff diagrams to describe the effect of options, an investor can look at the probability distribution of returns for various strategies. Consider first the covered call strategy. Exhibit 17 shows the probability distribution of returns for an underlying security with and without the sale of call options. Note how the shape changes as an increasing proportion of call options are sold relative to the underlying security position. Selling call options draws the portfolio distribution back gradually on the right side and increases the chance that an investor will receive only moderate returns. Selling call options on 100% of the portfolio completely truncates the right-hand side of the probability distribution: the investor has a high probability of receiving moderate returns and no probability of receiving high returns. Most of the probability of receiving low returns is preserved, however.

Next consider the protective put strategy. Exhibit 18 shows the probability distribution of returns for an underlying security with and without the use of put options. Note how the shape changes as an increasing proportion of put options are purchased relative to the underlying security position. Purchasing put options draws the portfolio distribution back gradually on the left side and increases the chance that an investor will receive only moderate returns. Buying put options on 100% of the portfolio completely truncates the left-hand side of the probability distribution: The investor has a very high probability of receiving moderate returns and no probability of receiving low returns. Most of the probability of receiving high returns is preserved, however.

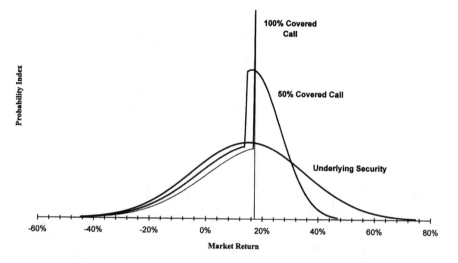

Exhibit 17: Return Distributions for Covered Calls

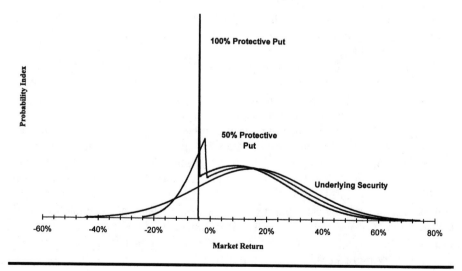

Exhibit 18: Return Distributions for Protective Puts

Exhibit 19: Return Distributions for Collars

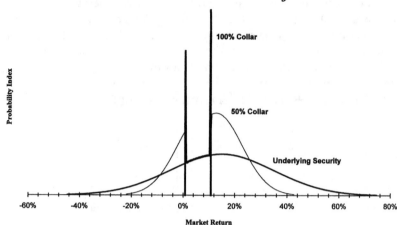

Exhibit 20: Creating a Synthetic Cash Reserve Using Options

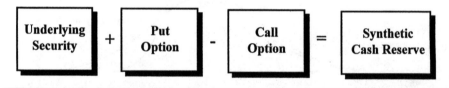

Exhibit 19 illustrates the effect of selling call options and buying put options simultaneously (a fence or collar). The combination causes quite a severe misshaping of the probability distribution in both tails. The distribution is no longer smooth and symmetric. The asymmetry of options allows an investor to shape and mold the probability distribution by truncating some parts and adding to others. Call options affect the right-hand tail most dramatically, while put options affect the left-hand tail.

Notice that the collar provides similar downside protection but loses its upside participation if the security return is positive beyond the level of the call's exercise price. Selling the call option with the same exercise price as the put option would protect against downside losses but would also eliminate any upside participation. This would make the hedge symmetric similar to selling a futures contract or swap. Indeed, the short call and long put position with the same exercise price creates a synthetic futures contract which produces a symmetric hedge. This can be seen from the stylized put/call parity relationship in Exhibit 20 which indicates that a combination of the underlying security, the purchase of a put option, and the sale of a call option with the same exercise price and maturity will behave the same as a cash reserve. The short call option and the long put option work to create a synthetic futures contract which offsets the risk in the underlying security resulting in a cash equivalent position.

Exhibit 21: Creating Synthetic Equity Exposure Using Options: Put/Call Parity

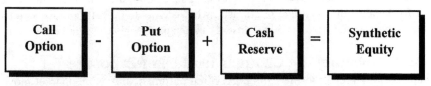

Exhibit 22: Creating a Synthetic Covered Call Strategy: The Collateralized Put

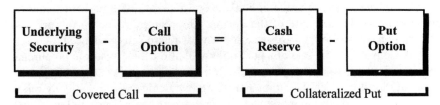

Exhibit 23: Creating a Synthetic Protective Put

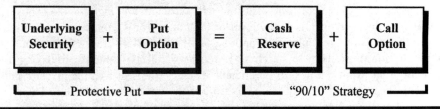

Rearranging the relationship to create a synthetic security instead of a synthetic cash reserve indicates that the combination of the cash reserve minus a put option plus a call option creates a market position as shown in Exhibit 21. In this case the long call option and the short put option work to create a synthetic futures position which adds market exposure to the cash reserve creating a synthetic security.

One last comment about the put/call parity relationship. Rearranging the components allows us to create the same payoff for the covered call and the protective put strategies in another way than previously described. The covered call strategy is normally constructed by purchasing the underlying security and selling a call option. An equivalent way to achieve the same payoff is to sell a put option and invest equivalent funds in an interest bearing cash reserve as shown in Exhibit 22. This alternative is sometimes referred to as a collateralized put and produces the same return profile as a covered call. In like manner, an equivalent way to create the same payoff as the protective put strategy is to purchase a call option and invest the remainder of the funds in an interest bearing cash reserve as illustrated in Exhibit 23.

This alternative is sometimes nicknamed the "90/10" strategy since roughly 90% of the investor's funds are held in a cash reserve with 10% used to purchase call options to give upside market participation. These configurations give equivalent payoffs because the arbitrage relationships between put and call options with the same maturities and exercise prices ensure that the payoff patterns will be preserved.

Automatic Changes in Market Exposure

Changes in market exposure can be triggered automatically as the market moves by selling options. The sale of a call option will truncate market participation above the option's exercise price. Selling some index call options against a long futures position or against exposure in the underlying stocks effectively pre-sells a portion of the exposure at the option's exercise price if the market reaches that level by the expiration date of the option. The receipt of the option premium effectively pays the investor for making the decision to sell in advance.

Conversely, the sale of a put option will allow the investor to prepurchase a position in the market at the put option's exercise price. The sale of options are frequently used in asset allocation and trading strategies to automatically reposition the portfolio if certain market levels are reached. Selling call options on 10% of the portfolio's exposure will automatically reduce the exposure by 10% if the market rallies up to the level of the call option's exercise price. Selling put options on 10% of the portfolio exposure will automatically increase the exposure by 10% if the market falls to the level of the put option's exercise price. At that point the investor can replace the option position by selling stocks for a gain and repurchasing the calls or by purchasing stocks at a discount and repurchasing the puts in order to make the shift permanent. The advantage is that the investor gets to keep the option premium for having made the decision in advance. The premium effectively increases the sale price of the appreciated stocks or reduces the purchase price of the depreciated stocks.

The purchase of additional market exposure by buying call options or the hedging of existing market exposure by buying put options can also be thought of as creating automatic changes in market exposure. The purchase of call options allows the investor to increase market exposure as the market rises while the purchase of put options allows the investor to decrease market exposure as the market falls. The options automatically adjust their levels of participation as the market reaches the options' exercise prices and go in the money. The non-linear payoff pattern of an option creates this automatic adjustment feature.

A VALUATION FRAMEWORK FOR
SELECTING DERIVATIVE STRATEGIES

Since the advent of the listed equity option market in the United States in 1973, investors have used options both to reduce risk and enhance return. The majority of investors use options in combination with other securities — option covered-call writing strategies are an example of such a strategy, where options are sold on a portfolio of underlying stocks in order to generate incremental returns. In spite of the fact that options are used in such a fashion, there is no generally accepted framework to evaluate the impact the options have on the return of the overall portfolio. The most widely used option pricing models such as the model developed by Black and Scholes[1] or the model of Cox, Ross, and Rubinstein[2] are geared more to valuing options as opposed to computing the expected return from a combined stock and option position. These models do not help an investor in selecting an optimal choice of option or the optimal structure — i.e., how does an investor choose between the various covered call alternatives?

In this section we outline a framework which can be used to evaluate the combinations of stock and option positions. We do not cover the fundamentals of option pricing as there are a number of books that provide an introduction to this topic.[3] We do, however, briefly cover the assumptions underlying the Black-Scholes model in order to highlight the conditions under which actual option prices may significantly differ from their theoretical Black-Scholes prices. The primary focus of this section is to outline a valuation framework to be used in choosing the optimal trade-off between risk and return when deciding to invest in an option in combination with another security (such as a stock or bond). We focus on covered call or overwriting strategies in our examples, although the framework is applicable to any security and option combination.

The Problem with Black-Scholes

The typical investor has a specific view on the future outcome for an equity security in which he is considering making an investment. Option valuation models, however, take the current price of the stock as given and then price the security using the key assumption that it is possible to combine the option and the underlying security to form a risk-free security. This combination should in equilibrium earn the risk-free rate. These models, as we show using a simple example below, do not allow an investor to estimate the value or expected return from a particular option conditional on the investor's expected return distribution. In order to compute such an expected return it is necessary to compute the actuarial value of the option.

This actuarial value can then be used to compute the expected return from investing in a particular combination of stock and options. We illustrate this below using a simple example for a manager considering using a strategy of selling calls on stock he owns as a means of increasing the return on the portfolio.

---

[1] See F. Black and M. Scholes, "The Pricing of Options and Corporate Liabilities," *Journal of Political Economy* (May/June 1973), pp. 637-657 for the original derivation of this pricing model.

[2] This more general approach to option pricing was first presented in J. Cox, S. Ross, and M. Rubinstein, "Option Pricing: A Simplified Approach," *Journal of Financial Economics* (September 1979), pp. 279-263

[3] See for example R. Clarke, *Options and Futures: A Tutorial*, The Research Foundation of the Institute for Chartered Financial Analysts or J. Hull, *Options, Futures and Other Derivative Securities: 2nd ed.* (Englewood Cliffs, NJ: Prentice Hall, 1993).

Exhibit 24: Expected Stock Return

Current Value	Future Value	Probability	Future Price × Probability
$50	60	0.65	39
	40	0.35	14
Expected Value			$53
Return			6.00%

For example, consider a stock at $50 that can go up or down. This is shown graphically in Exhibit 24, where in a period of say one quarter the stock can move up to $60 or down to $40. Given this set of outcomes, how do we price a call option with an exercise price of $50. The Black-Scholes approach is to first create a riskless position — i.e., a position whose final value is independent of whether the stock price moves up or down. In this simple example, such a riskless position can be constructed by a buying one share of stock and selling two options. On expiration day, if the stock has appreciated to 60 the position will be worth the value of the stock less the value of the two call options (worth $20 at a price of $10 each) for a net position value of $40. Conversely, if the stock moves down, the two options expire worthless, so the net position is again worth $40. Given that this position is guaranteed to have a value of $40 at the end of the quarter, the current value of this position must be equal to $40 discounted at the risk-free rate. If we assume a risk-free rate of 5%, this amounts to $39.50. As the position is equivalent to buying the stock and selling two calls, both calls must be worth $10.50 — or $5.25 per option.

Notice that this does not require us to know the likelihood of outcomes to value options. The key observation in the Black-Scholes model and other risk neutral models is that information about the future outcomes is reflected in the price. From the perspective of a manager proposing to make an equity investment in a security about which he believes to have superior information, this valuation process is not very insightful.

One approach to overcoming this problem is to compute the actuarial return from investing in an option. Suppose in this case that the manager believes — based on his or her internal analysis — that the probability of the stock rising is 65% and the probability of the stock falling is 35% (the probabilities have to sum to one). Given the manager's analysis, the expected return from investing in the security as shown in Exhibit 24 is 6%. Using the Black-Scholes approach, if the manager observed the option selling at $6, he could sell the overpriced call option. However, selling the call would result in the expected return falling to 5.68%. (See Exhibit 25.)

Exhibit 25: Stock + Covered Call (at $6.00) Return

Current Value		Future Value	Probability	Future Price × Probability
$44		54	0.65	32.5
		40	0.35	14
Expected Value				$46.5
Return				5.68%

The expected return is reduced because given the manager's expectations, the expected value of the call is $6.50. This is because there is a 65% probability that the option will be worth $10 and a 35% probability that it is worth zero. Note that this is more than the Black-Scholes value. This actuarial value is the criterion the manager should use in evaluating whether the option should be sold. Indeed, selling the option at a price less than the actuarial value will consistently reduce the expected return from the combined stock and option position *vis-à-vis* the stock position.

This does not imply that the Black-Scholes value is incorrect. However, it does highlight the notion that the Black-Scholes model is not useful when evaluating alternative option strategies given a view (in terms of expected return and risk) on a security. It also highlights the fact that an option's price being above that of the Black-Scholes does not assure that the seller should expect to gain from selling the option. The difference between the Black-Scholes value and the actual market price can only be earned if the seller of the option implements the complete Black-Scholes trade and re-balances the trade to maintain its risk neutrality until the expiration of the option. Transactions costs may often prevent such a strategy from being workable in the presence of limited liquidity and non-continuous markets or some of the other key assumptions underlying the Black-Scholes and other risk neutral models of option pricing as discussed below.

Why Observed Prices May Differ from Black-Scholes

The Black-Scholes model is one of the most widely used models to price securities. However there are key assumptions underlying the model which often result in observed option prices being different from their theoretical values. The factors which affect this usually arise from the violation of one or more of the economic assumptions underlying Black-Scholes. We discuss each of these briefly below.

Perfectly Liquid Markets

In order to construct the riskless hedge which underlies the Black-Scholes pricing model, we have to be able to buy or sell shares of the underlying stock and sell or buy a zero-coupon bond in the proportions required by the hedge. We must be able to trade at precisely the same price as we assumed in estimating the hedge parameters. In reality, when we actually make the purchase or sale, there is no guarantee that we will achieve our target price.

In addition, if the underlying stock is thinly traded the purchase or sale of shares will have a significant effect on the price. In such a case the cash flow of the purchase would not equal the amount required by the Black-Scholes formula.

Constant Interest Rates

The risk-free rate of interest is not constant as assumed by the Black-Scholes formula. In other words, the costs built into the formula are not equal to the actual costs in carrying out the strategy. Whenever this happens it is no longer true that the total cost of constructing the hedge will be equal to the risk-free price.

Continuous Markets

The Black-Scholes hedging strategy works if the investor can continuously rebalance the hedge. This is seldom possible in the presence of transactions costs.

Geometric Brownian Motion

In computing the Black-Scholes hedge, it is necessary to assume that stock prices follow a geometric Brownian motion. In reality we observe serial correlation in stock prices and we also observe that the volatility of stock returns changes over time and often overreacts to new information. Stock returns also exhibit a tendency to "jump" — so Black-Scholes hedge positions will be susceptible to such jump risk.

Short Selling Assumption

The Black-Scholes hedge for an investor who is short call options consists of a bond sold short and a certain number of shares of the underlying security. The short position is used to finance the long position. If this money is not available, an opportunity cost (in terms of borrowing cost or foregone return) has to be incurred. In such a situation, the strategy will not be self financing.

Whenever one or more of these assumptions is violated, we would expect to see the implied volatility on an option being systematically greater than the expected actual volatility. Unless the assumptions are satisfied, however, it is not possible for an investor to attempt to capture the mispricing as he is unable to engage in the Black-Scholes riskless hedging strategy. The valuation approach identified here can then be used to identify the optimal option structure to exploit this mispricing without resorting to an active hedging strategy.

A Generalized Actuarial Model

In the example given above, we illustrated the concept of using an actuarial value approach. Here we outline a generalized approach under the usual assumption that stock returns follow a log normal distribution. We will use the following notation:

$$S_0 \qquad = \text{ initial stock price}$$

$$C_0 \qquad = \text{ initial call price}$$

$$W_0 \qquad = \text{ initial investment}$$

$$D \qquad = \text{ dividends received over the time period of the option}$$

$$S_f, C_f, W_f \quad = \text{ values of the stock, call and investment on the expiry}$$
$$\text{day of the option}$$

$$dS_f P_T(S_f/S_n) = \text{ probability density of stock price changing from } S_0 \text{ to}$$
$$S_f \text{ in time } T \text{ assuming log normal distribution}$$

$$= \frac{dS_f}{S_f \sqrt{2\pi\sigma^2 T}} \exp\left(-\frac{\left(\ln\left(\frac{S_f}{S_0}\right) - \mu T\right)^2}{2\sigma^2 T}\right) \tag{5}$$

$$T \qquad = \text{ time to expiration } (T_{yr} = 1 \text{ year in same units})$$

$$\sigma^2 \qquad = \text{ variance of log of stock price return (ln } (S_f/S_0))$$

$$\mu \qquad = \text{ mean per unit time of stock log price return}$$

Given this distribution, the expected return from an investment in the combination of stock and option is given by:

$$\int dS_f P_T(S_f/S_0) \ln\left(\frac{W_f(S_f)}{W_0}\right) \tag{6}$$

For the covered call position:

$$W_0 = S_0 - C_0$$
$$W_f = S_f - \max[0, S_f - E] + D$$

The integral can be done numerically or approximated analytically. A similar approach handles any complex combination of stock, cash, and options, allowing an investor to identify the optimal security and option combinations. Note that using numerical techniques this same framework can be adapted to handle any arbitrary distribution. For example, the "fat tailed nature of stock price returns" can be taken into account. Transactions costs, including commissions and bid-ask spreads, are also easily incorporated into this valuation framework.

Examples of Actuarial Valuation

We illustrate the benefits of using the actuarial valuation approach to assess alternative covered call strategies — arguably one of the most popular option strategies. In this example, we assume that options on a $50 stock are priced at an implied volatility of 30% per annum. Given this assumption, call options with a maturity of one year on such a stock would take values similar to those shown in Exhibit 26. Our hypothetical investor forecasts the volatility on the stock to be 20% with an expected return of 12%. These forecasts can be derived using a variety of methods based on historical data, a factor model, or scenario forecasting.

Obviously, given this volatility forecast, every option on the stock is overvalued because the implied volatility at 30% is greater than the forecast volatility of 20%. If the investor could trade the stock under the assumptions implicit under Black-Scholes, he could essentially engage in a continuous trading strategy to try and exploit the difference. However, for most investors this is not a feasible alternative — especially if the stock is not actively traded.

The actuarial value approach described above, however, can be used to identify the preferred covered call position. Using equation (6), we compute in Exhibit 27 the expected return from the various covered call positions. Also computed is the standard deviation of the returns associated with each position, as well as the negative semi-deviation. Since selling the call "caps" the maximum return from the covered call position, this results in a non-symmetric distribution, and therefore standard deviation is not an appropriate measure of risk. To accurately capture the risk of loss, we compute the negative semi-deviation. This is a measure of downside risk. The data from Exhibit 27 demonstrate that the sale of an overpriced covered call should not necessarily be expected to generate incremental returns.

Selling of the calls with exercise prices of $52.5 or less actually decreases the expected return. However, it should be noted that the expected risk (assuming that negative semi-deviation is the appropriate risk measure for this investor) of each position is also lower. In contrast, the position with an exercise price of $60 has a higher expected return (15.3% versus 12%) and a lower downside risk (5.5% versus 8.5%) than simply investing in the stock.

Differing expectations for the volatility and return of the security will obviously generate differing expected returns from following this strategy. Using the same example as before, the expected return under the assumption that the investor forecasts volatility to be 25% per annum is recalculated — i.e., closer to the implied volatility of 30%. The resulting returns and risk measures are shown in Exhibit 28.

Exhibit 26: Call Option Prices

Strike Price	Call Price
40.00	13.19
42.50	11.42
45.00	9.80
47.50	8.35
50.00	7.06
52.50	5.93
55.00	4.95
57.50	4.11
60.00	3.40

Prices computed using Black Scholes model using a 30% annualized volatility, a risk-free rate of 5%, three months to maturity, and an underlying stock price of $50.

Exhibit 27: Gain from Alternative Stock Option Combinations
Expected Stock Return = 12% Standard Deviation = 20%

Strike Price	Stock + Covered Call Return (%)	Standard Deviation (%)	Negative Semi-Deviation (%)
40.00	7.8	3.6	2.4
42.50	9.3	4.6	2.9
45.00	10.3	6.3	3.8
47.50	11.4	7.2	3.8
50.00	12.6	8.8	4.3
52.50	13.8	10.2	4.4
55.00	14.6	12.4	5.4
57.50	15.0	13.7	5.5
60.00	15.3	14.8	5.5
Stock Only	12.0	20.0	7.5

Exhibit 28: Gain from Alternative Stock Option Combinations
Expected Stock Return = 12% Standard Deviation = 25%

Strike Price	Stock + Covered Call Return (%)	Standard Deviation (%)	Negative Semi-Deviation (%)
40.00	7.2	6.1	4.4
42.50	7.9	7.8	5.5
45.00	8.6	9.3	6.2
47.50	9.6	10.4	6.4
50.00	10.6	12.5	7.6
52.50	11.4	13.5	7.4
55.00	12.0	15.5	8.4
57.50	13.1	16.7	8.3
60.00	13.6	18.1	8.5
Stock Only	12.0	20.0	10.4

In this case it is only the sale of those call options with an exercise price greater than $55 that can be expected to generate incremental returns. Changes in the expected return for a stock can also have a dramatic impact on the expected return from entering into a covered call position. For example, suppose that the investor has an expected return forecast of 8% with a volatility forecast of 20%. The resulting expected returns from a covered call position are shown in Exhibit 29. With the exception of the option with the lowest exercise price, every covered call strategy has the potential to generate incremental returns and reduce risk. The magnitude of the value added is also substantially greater in this instance.

Exhibit 29: Gain from Alternative Stock Option Combinations
Expected Stock Return = 8% Standard Deviation = 20%

Strike Price	Stock + Covered Call Return (%)	Standard Deviation (%)	Negative Semi-Deviation (%)
40.00	7.6	4.8	3.3
42.50	8.6	5.4	3.3
45.00	9.5	7.2	4.3
47.50	10.4	8.7	4.9
50.00	10.9	10.6	5.6
52.50	11.5	12.2	6.1
55.00	12.1	13.7	6.6
57.50	12.1	15.2	6.8
60.00	12.4	16.6	7.3
Stock Only	8.0	20.0	10.4

In addition to highlighting the use of the actuarial valuation process, the examples in this section also illustrate the importance of forecasting both the mean and standard deviation when attempting to exploit option market mispricing though the use of covered call writing option strategies. In each example presented here, the options were overvalued; however, it was only in the case when the return on the underlying security was low (8% per annum) that the choice of any of the call options would have added value. Without such forecasts with some demonstrated predictive power, it is doubtful that value can be added though a traditional covered call writing strategy considered here.

The implication of the examples presented above is that managers considering the use of option strategies to enhance the performance of their equity portfolios cannot simply rely on using a simple Black-Scholes or risk neutral valuation approach to attempt to add incremental returns to a portfolio. As the analysis in this chapter demonstrates, the observation that the implied volatility on an option is greater than the actual volatility is not a necessary condition to ensure that the sale of the option will generate incremental returns to a portfolio.

More generally, the valuation framework presented here can be utilized as a tool to identify optimal derivative strategies and test the implications of alternative return and volatility outcomes on expected returns. As outlined in this chapter, the potential for modifying the risk and return profile of a portfolio using derivatives is vast. Only by using such a formal valuation framework can managers systematically identify those strategies that efficiently exploit their risk and return forecasts of asset classes or individual securities.

Chapter 13

Implementing Investment Strategies: The Art and Science of Investing

Wayne H. Wagner
President
Plexus Group

Mark Edwards
Director
Plexus Group

INTRODUCTION: THE IMPORTANCE OF THE IMPLEMENTATION PROCESS

"Success in investment management comes from picking good stocks. The rest is just plumbing." This quote from a well regarded money manager highlights one of the key reasons that active managers have failed to keep up with index funds over the past 10 years. Picking stocks is the Holy Grail, and the bulk of a manager's efforts and expenses goes to enhance their forecasting ability. To their credit, Plexus research suggests that active managers do pick stocks that outperform their respective market benchmarks over both a 6 week and a 52 week basis.[1] But, as the quote suggests, managers can become so attached to seeking winners that they become desensitized to the overall goal of maximizing returns.

Investment management can be viewed as a two part process: the information process and the implementation process. The *information process* is the core of stock selection, and is discussed at length throughout this book. The focus in this chapter is the implementation process, or executing investment ideas while preserving the underlying value. The combination of these actions — seeking valuable ideas and implementing them — is what we call the *investing* process. (See Exhibit 1.)

---

[1] W. Wagner, "Picking Good Stocks: Necessary, But Sufficient?" *Plexus Group Commentary #43* (January 1995) and "Decision Timeliness & Duration," *Plexus Group Commentary #46* (November 1995).

Exhibit 1: The Investing Process

Information Value	less	Implementation Cost	equals	Captured Value

The Vanguard S&P 500 fund has outperformed 80% of the active managers over the past decade.[2] But if managers are able to pick winning stocks, why are they losing? The bottom line is that there is more to the investing process than good stock selection. On average, the cost of getting ideas into portfolios exceeds the value of the research. Ironically, this does not have to be true. The problem is that implementation or trading costs have been understated and underestimated, leading to sub-par performance despite better than average ideas.

Industrial America has gone through a difficult process of self-examination that has led to dramatic improvements in productivity. The key to this process is TQM (Total Quality Management). The investment industry is now confronting the same issue. Managers need to look beyond the selection process to the implementation process — from invest*ment* to invest*ing*.

We will first discuss trading, the core of the implementation process. We will then look beyond trading to see how trading strategies fit within the manager's stock selection process.

WHY TRADING IS NOT LIKE PORTFOLIO MANAGEMENT

Equity trading is the action that results from portfolio management decisions. The portfolio manager's process is analytic and hypothetical; trading is in-the-trenches reality.

To the naive, trading can seem like a vending machine — an order to buy goes in, and a trade comes out. But vending machines purchases are expensive and inefficient compared to buying in bulk. To shift the analogy from the retail investor to the large institution, imagine trying to buy 10,000 cases of soda rather than one can. Even if the vending machine could supply that many sodas, the cost would be many times greater than buying wholesale. Similarly, trading strategies that work for the retail investor are inadequate to the task confronting institutional traders. Studies show that roughly two-thirds of institutional managers' orders are more than 50% of an average day's volume.[3] Executing these orders in a single trade can quickly overtax the market's liquidity. For these orders, a manufacturing process is a better analogy than a vending machine. Manufacturing liquidity means finding shares at a price that completes the trade at a price that preserves the value of the idea.

---

[2] Lipper Analytical Services. Ten-year comparison as of December 31, 1996. Comparisons include only managers with 10-year histories.

[3] M. Edwards and W. Wagner, "Best Execution," *Financial Analysts Journal* (January-February 1993).

Trading is fundamentally different from portfolio management in that selecting stocks does not require the cooperation of anyone else. The trader, however, needs somebody to trade with, and thus we move from a deductive exercise to a negotiation process. In a negotiation, one gives something in order to get something. In securities trading, one can trade for either liquidity or for information. Thus a trader is constantly concerned that value is received for value given. This is why large trades occur in successive pieces, each piece revealing only what is necessary to complete that step of the negotiation.

Trading can be thought of as the ongoing choice between trading now for a known price versus later for an unknown, and hopefully better, price. Effective trading requires a multi-step process:

1. Determine the motivation of the trade.
2. Assess market conditions and the liquidity of the stock.
3. Establish the initial trading strategy to assess supply and demand.
4. Probe for liquidity and information.
5. Adapt the strategy to changing market conditions.
6. Appraise the effectiveness when the trading is complete.

Trade Motivation

Jack Treynor[4] has identified three key trading motives: value, news/information, and cash flow. *Value* is represented by the familiar Graham and Dodd process, while information trading reflects the use of new information and changing expectations. *Cash flow* motivations arise from a desire to increase or decrease equity exposure, independent or even ignorant of the prospects for the stocks.

Information value is subject to rapid erosion, and information-based traders are always under pressure to complete trades before the information spreads across the market. This makes information traders time sensitive: their goal is to get the trades done quickly, even if this means paying up for liquidity.

In contrast, *value* trades are seldom timely. Value traders can use time to their advantage, stretching out the timeframe in an attempt to reduce the cost of trading. Value traders are more price sensitive than time sensitive.

Index traders and liquidity traders do not form opinions about the value of individual stocks. However, their buying and selling can exaggerate supply/demand imbalances.

Managers are quite consistent in their approach to investing. Their trade orders will reflect one of these styles for most — but not all — of their trading. The trader's job is to recognize which motivation applies to each trade, and to select a trading strategy that reflects the manager's here-and-now motivation.

---

[4] J. Treynor, "What Does it Take to Win the Trading Game?" *Financial Analysts Journal* (January-February 1981).

Assessing Market Conditions

The next step is to assess current market conditions to determine the expected cost of liquidity for the required size. An actively traded stock is like a supermarket with high turnover and low margins. But not all stocks trade in volume. The greater the desired percentage of the current trading volume, the greater the premium required to create liquidity. The liquidity cost must be added/subtracted from the decision price to determine the expected trading price.

In addition to how much stock typically trades, the trader also needs to consider how frequently the stock trades. Actively traded stocks require little broker intermediation, so there is little spread between the *bid* (the highest advertised buy price) and the *offer* (the lowest advertised selling price). As the frequency of trading drops, the broker is required to act as a middleman, carrying long and short inventories until buyers and sellers can be found. Holding stock creates a risk for the broker, resulting in higher spreads.

Diversity of opinion is another important characteristic of market condition. If everyone wants to sell and no one wants to buy, trading will be impossible. If buyers are now dominating the trading, buying will be difficult and costly, while selling will be easy and inexpensive. Trading tactics will be quite different depending on whether one is *supplying* or *demanding* liquidity.

The trader's first resource in assessing market conditions is the public information sources: ticker tape prints of recent trades and the display of bids and offers, either on the exchange or on the various proprietary trading and information networks.

This is not, however, the full story. All that can be seen here is that which someone else has chosen to reveal. Institutional traders frequently rely on block dealers to locate trading interest that has been quietly expressed but not publicly revealed.

Establish Initial Trading Strategy

At this point the buyside trader has two basic options: he can choose to buy stock directly from a broker (a principal trade), or slowly accumulate stock during the normal flow of the day (a working trade). Each approach carries some danger:

- The payment for immediate liquidity may exceed the value of the information motivating the trade.
- The patient trader risks share prices moving against him before the order is filled.

The art of trading is the balancing of these two risks, performed in the context of the manager's instructions and information.

Probing for Liquidity and Information

Trades occur only when a willing buyer meets a willing seller at a price acceptable to both. The seller may be a broker providing liquidity for a fee, or it may be a natural seller acting as though he believes the *opposite* of what the manager believes. Even though this negotiation may be conducted in private, the market is filled with prying eyes looking for a trading edge. Accumulating stock is a difficult activity to keep hidden in a closely watched market, and knowledge of unfilled trading interest is a most valuable commodity on Wall Street. Other traders try continuously to assess the potential size of the trade and the sagacity of the buyer, and will attempt to buy first and piggyback on likely future behavior. Seeking liquidity, therefore, creates additional risk — and potential cost.

Coaxing out a reluctant seller requires an elaborate give-and-take process to protect the value of the idea. Cagey traders will attempt to get as much information as possible while revealing as little as possible: What does she know that I don't? How big is her trading need? How much is she willing to pay? Everyone wants to be the last person to trade with a big contraparty — certainly not the first.

The buyer may start with *probing* trades to assess available liquidity and possible reactions. If liquidity is available, the buyer has time on his side. But probing may quickly give away the buyer's identity, so the buyer uses a broker to sniff out untapped sources of stock.

We learned in Economics 101 that price changes will attract more supply or demand. In the stock market, however, rising prices will not necessarily induce potential sellers to trade. Rather, rising prices may indicate previously unknown information that leads to a revised opinion, creating hoarding conditions that reduce the desire to sell.

Thus, while it may make sense to slowly trade a liquid stock motivated by a value decision, the same trade in an illiquid stock may trigger competition once other traders detect a short-term buying trend. In this case, the trader may be better served by using broker liquidity and letting the broker assume the time risk.

Adapting to Market Conditions

Every piece of information the trader receives has the potential to create a need for a mid-course correction in the trading strategy. When the assumptions underlying the initial strategy prove incorrect, the strategy must be changed — instantly. This implies that the trader needs a variety of skills to trade different stocks in different conditions — and the ability to switch quickly from one technique to another.

Assess Effectiveness

A critical component of TQM is an on-going process review. In the case of trading, what works when a firm is small may not work as the firm grows. Liquidity demands change, as does the tradable universe of stocks. In addition, the markets themselves are in constant state of change.

Every completed trade provides feedback to the trader, who in turn must constantly adapt to changing demands and changing market conditions. In a broader context, however, we can think of each trade as a manifestation of an ongoing process that involves the manager as well as the trader. The process itself is thus amenable to review and change in a wider context.

A FRAMEWORK FOR MEASURING IMPLEMENTATION

This section describes the process that Plexus clients use to assess the efficacy of their processes. By breaking down each step into definable and repeatable actions, the trader can see where actions add or lose value.

Trading costs are like an iceberg: the real danger comes from the portion that cannot be seen. Commissions are easily observed but represent only the tip of the iceberg. The remaining costs are far more significant, but because they cannot be easily observed, they have been too often ignored. Ignoring the real but hidden costs can compromise performance.

Andre Perold[5] developed a method to assess trading effectiveness in the context of the decisions being implemented. Simply stated, this *implementation shortfall*[6] approach compares the *information return* of the decision on a no-cost basis to the *realized return* on a fully-costed basis. For uncomplicated trades, this amounts to comparing the price at the time of the decision (strike price) with the average execution price. This puts the trading in context: what is the trader paying for liquidity, and does that payment square with the potential gain from executing the trade?

Further elaboration of the implementation shortfall approach allows a manager to disaggregate trading costs into components of commission, intraday impact, interday delay costs, and opportunity costs from abandoned trades. Furthermore, the computations can be made on subsets of the trading database to pinpoint whether problems are more prevalent in large trades, small cap trades, NASDAQ trades, etc.

Consider the following example:

What the ticker tape reveals:

• 30,000 NME bought @ $20.75.

What really happened:

• Manager wants to buy 50,000 shares of NME. The current price is $20.
• The trade desk parcels out an order to a broker to buy 40,000 NME. The price is $20.5.
• NME is bought at $20.75 plus a $.05 commission.
• Price jumps to $21.50, and the remainder of the order is canceled.
• 15 days later the price is $23.

---

[5] A. Perold, "The Implementation Shortfall: Paper versus Reality," *Journal of Portfolio Management* (Spring 1988).

[6] B. Collins and F. Fabozzi, "A Methodology for Measuring Transactions Costs," *Financial Analysts Journal* (March-April 1991).

An accurate assessment of the quality of trading requires knowledge of what really happened:

- What was the idea worth?
- How much did delay on the trade desk cost?
- What was the impact of the trade?
- How much was left on the table when the order was canceled?

Fortunately, modern paperless trading systems readily collect and organize data such as that above. The information provided shows (1) the portfolio manager's desires, (2) the strategies employed by the trade desk, and (3) the resulting executions. Thus we can observe the entire investing process and measure the parts.

THE COST COMPONENTS OF TRADING

Manager and trader actions can now be isolated and analyzed. We can define the actions and calculate the respective costs. When we observe a large number of trades, we can assess the costs within an organization. By gathering this data from many managers, we can assess the industry-wide components of the trading iceberg.

A *commission* is the explicit fee charged by the broker to handle and clear the trade. It is printed on the trade ticket, so it is readily available. In this example, the per share cost is $.05 — typical for an institutional trade.

Price impact is the price adjustment necessary to immediately purchase liquidity. We measure impact as the price difference between the time that the order is submitted to the broker and the actual trade. The broker received the order when the average price was $20.50, and the trade cost $20.75, resulting in a $0.25 per share impact.

Trader timing is the price move prior to contacting the broker. This can be thought of as the cost of seeking liquidity. We measure timing from the price when the order is submitted to the desk until it is released to the broker. The price was $20 when the order arrived on the desk, and the trader gave the order to the broker when the price was $20.50. Timing cost is $0.50 per share.

Opportunity cost is the cost of failing to complete the trade. What about the 20,000 shares that did not get traded? The idea generated a 15% return ($23/ $20) over a 15-day period, but 40% of the order was never completed. On a dollar weighted basis, the manager "lost" $15\% \times 40\%$, or 6 percentage points of potential return. Good ideas are not always easy to come by, and it is as important to learn from what did not trade as it is to review what did trade.

THE ICEBERG OF TRADING COSTS

The example above simply illustrates what the costs are and how they are computed. Exhibit 2 represents nearly 700,000 trades by over 50 different management firms during the second half of 1996. This picture provides a realistic view of institutional trading costs.

Exhibit 2: The Iceberg of Trading Costs (in basis points)

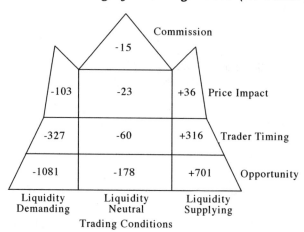

Commissions

Commissions have been under steady pressure since they were deregulated in May 1975. Despite this pressure, commissions have been relatively stable for the services rendered. Full service brokers charge an average of 6¢, while smaller brokers that provide exchange floor access will charge 3-5¢. Automated trades executed via DOT (Direct Order Transmission to the floor) or the Proprietary Trading Systems (Instinet, ITG, AZX, and the Crossing Network) charge 1-3¢. An increasing proportion of trading executed through these lower cost alternatives results in combined rates dropping to 4.5¢.

Price Impact

The next level of the iceberg is shrouded in fog, leaving the viewer aware of its presence but uncertain about its size. Like fog, these costs expand and contract, reflecting changes in available liquidity.

Impact reflects both the dealer spread plus any price movement required to attract additional liquidity to complete the trade. Actively traded stocks will typically be quoted in one eighth increments. As the frequency of trading activity drops, the dealer spread typically rises.

The average impact is 23 bp, or 9¢ per share. Exhibit 3 shows that the most important factor affecting impact is whether or not the trade *supplies* liquidity to the market, *demands* liquidity from the market, or is liquidity *neutral*. A buy order placed into a market where prices are falling will supply liquidity to the market, and should capture a concession. While Exhibit 3 shows the difference between liquidity-demanding and liquidity-supplying orders, it also shows an interesting skew that reflects a high cost when demanding liquidity versus a modest gain for supplying liquidity. This is a typical pattern: traders are willing to supply liquidity for much smaller concessions than they end up paying when put on the other side of the trade. The brokers capture the difference, often described as "vigorish."

Timing

The use of time as a trading tool for the buyside trader was previously discussed. By waiting for natural liquidity to appear at an acceptable price, the trader hopes to minimize direct price impact. This is why most large orders are broken up and worked in more easily digested pieces. Timing cost is the price change that occurs during this waiting period.

Timing is the counterpoint to impact. As time increases, impact should decrease. However, as time increases, so does the potential for adverse price moves. Because trading decisions usually reflect changes in publicly available information, short-term returns are likely to be positive. Consequently, delays to minimize impact leads to higher timing costs, as shown in Exhibit 4.

An information-sensitive trader who fails to find sufficient volume before prices move away will find the timing cost of delay to be very high. Conversely, a value-oriented trader providing liquidity may find that waiting leads to even greater gains than an immediate concession.

Opportunity

The final cost represents the base of the iceberg, never seen but possibly the most damaging to performance. This is the opportunity cost of uncompleted trades.

Money managers are like fishermen in their lament about the "one that got away." However, the manager's lament is legitimate: the most expensive trade is typically the one that never occurred. Exhibit 5 provides some insight into the average percentage of shares that are not completed by order type, as well as the 15-day opportunity effect.

Exhibit 3: Impact and Spread

Liquidity Demanding	Liquidity Neutral	Liquidity Supplying
−103 bp	−23 bp	+36 bp

Exhibit 4: Trader Timing

Liquidity Demanding	Liquidity Neutral	Liquidity Supplying
−327 bp	−60 bp	+316 bp

Exhibit 5: Opportunity Cost

	Foregone Return	% Not Completed
Liquidity Demanding	−1081 bp	13%
Liquidity Neutral	−71 bp	11%
Liquidity Supplying	+701 bp	10%

Exhibit 6: Definitions, Computations, and Experienced Cost

Cost	Definition	Measurement	Experienced Costs
Commission	Explicit fee charged by a broker for services.	Provided for listed trades.	−4.5¢
Impact	Cost of immediate execution.	The difference between the average execution price and the price at the time the order is revealed to the broker.	−8¢
Timing	Cost of seeking liquidity.	Price change between the time the order goes to the trade desk and when it is released to the broker.	−23¢
Opportunity	Cost of failing to find liquidity.	15 day return for unexecuted shares.	−71¢
Total	Difference between costless and fully costed returns	Weighted sum of the above	−38¢

There are two primary reasons for unexecuted orders. Either the trader cannot locate the shares to complete the trade, or the stock has moved out of the range that the manager is willing to pay. On a day to day basis, traders are quick to complete trades when the volume appears at an acceptable price — but as the timing costs show, they are not as willing to step up when a premium is required. Consequently, opportunity costs tend to be large. Exhibit 6 summarizes the definitions, computations, and cost experiences.

Conclusions about Trading Costs

Managing trading costs can be compared to squeezing a balloon: pushing in one side results in a distortion elsewhere. The commission, the most visible element of transactions costs, can be — and has been — driven down, but often at the cost of higher impact. Similarly, trade impact can be reduced by simply refusing to trade in high impact situations. In both cases, the trader diverts visible costs into less observable areas. This cannot be done without compromising investment performance. Thus the goal is to focus on total implementation costs, not simply trading costs.

This leads us to a functional definition of best execution: *best execution is that procedure most likely to capture the potential investment return.*

CASE STUDIES

In the remainder of this chapter we go beyond trading and explore the implications of different trading strategies within a manager's selection process. These are followed by some practical trading recommendations that we make to all desks.

Case Study #1: Momentum Manager Mismatched with Cautious Trader

Manager pattern: Manager reacts to news and price momentum to generate buying decisions. After the decision, the prices continue to appreciate.

Selectivity is excellent: decisions appreciate 6% over the six weeks after decision.

Trader pattern: Exhibit 7 shows the trader is sensitive to impact, and executes trades over several days. The table below reveals that although impact is low, timing costs run away as prices move while orders sit on the trade desk: when all costs are considered, the trader pays much more than other desks when faced with similar orders.

Recommendations: The trader's perspective focuses on creating zero impact with her trading. However, using a realistic cost benchmark of −115 bp rather than zero impact allows for more aggressive, and subsequently lower cost, trading.

Results: Within three quarters, timing costs had dropped to −65 bp while impact rose to −40 bp (Exhibit 8). Most importantly, total costs dropped from −190 bp to −117 bp. This case study perfectly illustrates the importance of controlling the total cost, instead of focusing on one component.

Case Study #2: Capturing an Insufficient Concession when Providing Liquidity

Manager pattern: Manager's buy decisions are deep value — almost contrarian. The more price drops relative to the fundamentals, the more likely this manager is to buy. Typical trade is very early, well in advance of the eventual price bottom.

Exhibit 7: Comparison of Cost Components — Minimizing Impact: Case Study #1

	Timing	Impact	Comm.	Total	Benchmark*
Trading G/L	−175 bp	−3 bp	−12 bp	−190 bp	−115 bp

* Benchmark costs are determined by averaging the costs for similar trades executed in the previous six months by all manager in the database. Over 700,000 trades are used to derive the benchmark equations.

Exhibit 8: Comparison of Cost Components — Minimizing Total Costs: Case Study #1

	Timing	Impact	Comm.	Total	Benchmark
Trading G/L	−65 bp	−40 bp	−12 bp	−117 bp	−115 bp
Change	+106 bp	−27 bp	—	−73 bp	—

Exhibit 9: Comparison of Cost Components —
Capturing Available Opportunities: Case Study #2

	Timing	Impact	Comm.	Total	Benchmark
Trading G/L	+35 bp	+11 bp	-14 bp	+35 bp	+90 bp

Exhibit 10: Comparison of Cost Components —
Taking More Time to Probe: Case Study #2

	Timing	Impact	Comm.	Total	Benchmark
Trading G/L	+112 bp	+11 bp	−11 bp	+115 bp	+90 bp
Change	+77 bp	—	+3 bp	+80 bp	—

Trader pattern: Exhibit 9 shows the trades are executed quickly, often at the best price of the day and at much better prices than the manager's decision price. However, there is no need to trade quickly given the repeating experience of subsequent weakness. Relative to other desks, this trader was providing a large concession to demanders of liquidity.

Recommendations: This case shows the opposite problem to the first case — fast trading in the face of weak returns. The trader should scale in gradually, letting the sellers come to him and making them pay for the privilege of liquidity. This is a case where probing trades to determine the level of buyer interest would be beneficial.

Results: Within three quarters, 95% completion was stretched out from 2 days to 5 days (see Exhibit 10). Timing gains rose to +112 bp while impact fell slightly. Total gains rose to +112 bp, slightly better than the benchmark.

Case Study #3: Over Reliance On Low Cost Brokers

Manager pattern: Manager used a quantitative model to generate lists of "alternate" trades. Model uses a timing overlay. Selectivity is good, with stocks rising 4% over six weeks.

Trader pattern: Trader believes strongly in using low cost proprietary trading systems to maintain anonymity and keep impact and commission costs to a minimum. (See Exhibit 11.) Trader takes pride in the low commission costs, avoiding the spread, and leaving no footprints in the market. Unfortunately, less than half the orders are completed, and there is evidence of strong adverse selection: stocks purchased appreciated 0.5%, while the untraded stocks went up 6.5%. The best model selections were left on the table. Performance suffers.

Exhibit 11: Comparison of Cost/Return Components — Low Cost, Low Return: Case Study #3

	Timing	Impact	Comm.	Total	Benchmark	Percent Traded	Net Returns Traded	Unex.
Trading G/L	-91 bp	+27 bp	-4 bp	-68 bp	-62 bp	48%	55 bp	655 bp

Exhibit 12: Comparison of Cost/Return Components — Higher Costs, Higher Return: Case Study #3

	Timing	Impact	Comm.	Total	Benchmark	Percent Traded	Net Returns Traded	Unex.
Trading G/L	−51 bp	−10 bp	−6 bp	−67 bp	−62 bp	76%	110 bp	73 bp
Change	+40 bp	−37 bp	−2 bp	−1 bp	—	+28%	+55 bp	+582bp

Recommendations: The problem with over-reliance on crossing networks is that there is no guarantee of finding the desired liquidity through these routes. As a result, trading stretches out over many days while prices moved upward. The manager's good selection and timing ability dissipates.

Results: This trader learned that passive trading is but an arrow in a quiver, and effective trading requires the use of all tools to find and capture liquidity at an acceptable price. (See Exhibit 12.) Expanding broker use and monitoring incompletes at the end of each day leads to better prioritizing of the next day's trading. Within three quarters, completion rates rise to 76%, trading costs are flat, and realized returns rise to +110 bp despite weaker underlying decisions. More costly trading leads to better capture of investment ideas.

FOUR PRACTICAL TRADING RECOMMENDATIONS

In each of the case studies, the trader and the manager firmly believed they were doing a good job. The truth is that they were! The problem is not how they did their job, but how they *defined* their job, and how they defined their objective. By focusing on a part of the process, they missed the big picture. Once they were able to see and accept the wider viewpoint, the solutions were straightforward and improvement was rapid.

   In closing, we would like to present four general recommendations that come from the practical experience of working with institutional trade desks.

Recommendation #1 — One Trading Strategy does Not Fit All Situations

Case Study #3 shows the problem of over reliance on passive trading. No matter how consistent a manager is, occasional trades will not fit the normal pattern and require special treatment. Not all orders should be traded with the same sense of urgency. Many managers sell stocks to fund new purchases, and sell decisions often contain less short term value than do buy models. As a result, the sells will often move up with the buys. An effective desk needs to offset trading costs generated by liquidity demanding trades with trading gains when providing liquidity. *Know why the manager wants to trade, and plan accordingly.*

Recommendation #2 — Prioritize and Make Contingency Plans

The worst tactic is to trade the minimal costs trades first, and wait to work orders with little available liquidity or with higher levels of competition. Instead, the desk needs to rank orders by urgency based on both motive (information-based trades are more urgent than value-based trades) and on current levels of supply and demand (an imbalance will often signal short-run information that may not be publicly available). *Do the hard trades first.* In addition, the desk needs to have a process alert when stocks move into higher urgency categories.

Recommendation #3 — Build Expected Costs into Portfolio Decision Making

Identifying potential buys and sells is a critical part of the money manager's job, and manager stock picks do add value. The problem is the number of decisions where costs exceed the return. As assets continue to grow, the problem is compounded. Knowing the expected exit cost of each holding can help the manager determine both the desired size and desirability of trading. Knowing the cost of acquiring new positions puts the value of the decision in proper context. *Strive to capture return, not minimize costs.*

Recommendation #4 — Rationalize Broker Use

One of the first lessons in business is to make vendors and customers dependent on you while not becoming dependent upon them. The same holds true for the trade desk. By concentrating business with a few brokers, the trader becomes important enough to the broker to make a difference. The trade desks with the best consistent results are those that concentrate brokerage, and make sure their brokers know what is expected of them. *Trust, but verify.*

Not all brokers are equal in skill. All brokers can take a simple trade to the floor of the exchange for simple market or limit order execution. Trades that require significant size relative to the trading volume require a broker who has the skill, inventory, and integrity to handle the order and protect the customer's interests. *Use the commission to buy the needed trading services.*

CONCLUSION

Remember the Dali painting "Lincoln in Dalivision?" At first glance your eye sees a seemingly random pattern of color. When you step back, you see the likeness that was there all along. To effectively evaluate an investing process, you need to look at each component in detail, then step back to understand how each piece fits together into the big picture.

Searching for alpha within the investment management shop may be the most overlooked obvious idea in investment management since risk measurement. When managers widen their horizons beyond stock picking and analyze how their decisions thread into portfolios, they can capture risk-free, recurring returns. The secret to improving invest*ing* is to watch the handoffs and trade-offs.

Small improvements accumulate to make big differences in total performance. Since managers' track records are tightly bunched near the average, these improvements can raise a manager's ranking half a quartile or more. A good invest*ing* process is a crucial part of, and natural complement to, a good invest*ment* process.

Index

A

@RISK, 123, 124
Above-average growth prospects, 147
Above-average stock returns, 186
Above-market multiples, 147
Absolute returns, 187
Active versus passive indexing comparison, 67-85
  quantitative solutions, 80-84
Active management, 54, 55, 77. *See also* Risk-controlled active management; Traditional active management
  pitfalls, 80
  risk-controlled approach, 67
Active managers, 37, 82
  performance, 67
  underperformance reasons, 78-80
Active quant, perspectives, 67-85
  quantitative solutions, 80-84
Active-management process, 55-56
Actuarial model, 230-234
Actuarial valuation, examples, 231-234
Actuarial value, 227
Additive growth model. *See* Deterministic additive growth model; Trinomial additive growth model
Alpha, 24, 52-57, 59-61, 62, 64, 66, 84, 155, 181. *See also* Law of One Alpha; Transporting alpha
  searching, 249
  strategies. *See* Portable alpha strategies
American Stock Exchange, 42
Anomalies, 73, 77, 82. *See also* Low-risk anomalies
Appreciation, exchange. *See* Income/appreciation
APT. *See* Arbitrage Pricing Theory
Arbitrage. *See* Stock index arbitrage
Arbitrage pricing relationship, 212
Arbitrage Pricing Theory (APT), 22
Arbitrage-related strategies, 60. *See also* Index arbitrage-related strategies
Arnott, Robert D., 104
Arrow, Kenneth J., 7
Asness, Cliff, 67
Asset deployment, 143
Asset management, 61
Asymmetric hedges, downside protection, 216-221

B

Back-office employees, 47
Backtest, 104
Balkanization. *See* Segmented market
Bankruptcy, 76, 119

possibility, 118
probability, 117
Barings, 7
BARRA E2 model, 91
BARRA E2 fundamental factor model, 92
BARRA factor model, 96, 100, 101, 104
BARRA HICAP universe, 92
BARRA optimization model, 101
BARRA organization, 127
BARRA risk model, 130
Bayesian strategies, 68
Beginning-of-month factor, 74
Benchmark model, 51
Benchmark returns, 10
Benchmark-accountability, 19
Benchmarks, 10, 99, 128, 138, 141. *See also* Ideal benchmarks; Manager; Manager-specific stock-matching benchmark; Mid-cap benchmarks
  construction. *See* Customized benchmarks
  selection, 41-43
Bernstein, Peter, 67
Best-revision portfolio, 187. *See also* Second-best-revision portfolio
Beta, 52, 73, 124, 211. *See also* Capital asset pricing model; Residual beta; Residual market beta
Bid, 238
Bid-ask spreads, 231
Bid/asked spread, 47, 48
Bid/offer spread, 48
Binomial dividend growth models, 116
Binomial growth model, 117
Binomial growth stochastic model, 116-118
Binomial stochastic DDMs, 116
BIRR. *See* Burmeister Ibbotson Roll and Ross
Black, Fischer, 73, 227
Black-Scholes, 232
  approach, 228
  formula, 230
  hedge, 230
  positions, 230
  model, 227, 228
  observed prices, 229-230
  prices, 227
  pricing model, 229
  problem, 227-229
  riskless hedging strategy, 230
  trade, 229
  valuation approach, 234
  value, 229
Book value, 146
Book/price (B/P)

ratio, 91, 169, 170, 174, 175, 177, 179
  variable, 27
Book-to-price ratio (B/P), 27, 30
Book-value-to-price ratio, 124
Borger, David R., 163
B/P. *See* Book/price; Book-to-price ratio
Breadth, 34, 35
Break-even point, 216-218, 220
Broad-based equity index, 2
Broad-based stock index, 104
Broker liquidity, 239
Broker/dealer, 96, 115
Brokers. *See* Low cost brokers
  usage, rationalization, 248
Brownian motion, 230. *See also* Geometric Brownian motion
Bull market, 31
Burmeister, Edwin, 88
Burmeister Ibbotson Roll and Ross (BIRR)
  macroeconomic factor model, 97, 98
  model, 88, 98, 99
Business activity. *See* Real business activity
Business cycle risk, 88. *See also* Short-term business cycle risk
Buy-and-hold passive vehicle, 79

C

Call options, 225.
  buying, 221-222
  selling, 214-216
Call spread, 221, 222
Capital asset pricing model (CAPM), 22, 68, 84, 85, 110, 111, 152-156
  beta, 73
Capital gains, 43
Capitalization bets, 141
Capitalization distribution. *See* Style
Capitalization indexing. *See* Medium capitalization indexing; Small capitalization indexing
Capitalization market, 132
Capitalization weighting
  advantages/disadvantages, 135-136
  break points, 135
Capitalization-weighted indexes, 134
Capitalization-weighted median, 153
Capitalization-weighted portfolio, 135
Capitalization-weighting, 134
CAPM. *See* Capital asset pricing model
Cap-weighted benchmarks, 152
Cap-weighted portfolio, 136

Cash drag, 206
Cash equitization, 206
Cash flow, 74, 108
    motivations, 237
Cash flow/price (CF/P) ratios, 169
Cash holdings, 155
Cash management. *See* Index
    futures/enhanced cash manage-
    ment
Cash portfolio, 204
Cash reserves, 60, 61
Certainty-equivalent return, 17
Chattiner, Sherman, 114
Christopherson, Jon A., 127, 131,
    134, 137, 142, 143, 153, 155
Clarke, Roger G., 201, 227
Client equity portfolios, 96
Client needs, 12-14
    broad-based   engineered
        approach, 12
    opportunity expansion, 13-14
Client risk-return goals, 20
Coggin, T. Daniel, 104
Cognitive errors, 7-8, 74, 82
Collar, 216, 219-221. *See also* Zero
    cost collar
Collins, B., 240
Commissions, 241, 242
Common stock, 108
Companies, growth-oriented group,
    167
Complex equity market, profit, 21-
    35
    coherent framework, 24-25
Complex systems, 21
Complexity. *See* Disentanglement
    profit, 34-35
Compound growth rate, 112
Conditional decision making, 133-
    134
Confidence intervals, 119-122
    obtaining, Monte Carlo simula-
        tion usage, 122-124
Confidence risk, 88
Confirmation bias, 8
Connor, Gregory, 87
Consistent growth, 147
Constant growth models, 112. *See
    also* Deterministic constant
    growth models
Constant interest rates, 230
Consumer-oriented industries, 147
Contingency plans, 248
Contrarian managers, 146
Core-like holding, 9
Cost experiences, 244
Country-selection ability, 75
Covered call, 214
    alternatives, 227
    position, 232, 233
Cox, J., 227
Credit risk, 206
Cross-held shares, 42
Cross-holdings, 42
Crossing Network, 242

Cross-sectional analysis, 91
Cross-sectional results, 197
Customized benchmarks, construc-
    tion, 127-142
Cyclical growth, 167

D

Daiwa, 7
Daniel, Kent, 76
de Silva, Harindra, 201
Debt-to-asset ratio, 91
Debt-to-equity ratio, 91
Decision making. *See* Conditional
    decision making; Portfolios
Default, 76
DeMakis, Drew D., 81
Derivative strategies selection, valu-
    ation framework, 226-234
Derivatives, usage. *See* Equity port-
    folio management
Descriptors, 91
    influences, 92
Designated Order Turnaround
    (DOT). *See* SuperDOT
    Box, 48
Deterministic additive growth
    model, 113
Deterministic constant growth mod-
    els, 110-113
Deterministic dividend discount
    models, 108-115
Deterministic geometric growth
    model, 111-113
Direct Order Transmission (DOT),
    242
Discount rate, 109-112
Discounted Markov dividend
    stream, 121, 122
Discounted value, 120-124
Discriminant model, 179
Disentanglement, 25-33
    complexities, 32-33
Distress risk, 76
Divecha, Arjun, 128, 130
Diversified portfolios, 184, 185, 209
    nondiversified portfolios compar-
        ison, 197-199
Dividend discount models (DDMs),
    25, 30-32, 105, 107-125. *See also*
    Binomial stochastic DDMs;
    Deterministic dividend discount
    models; Generalized Markov
    growth stochastic DDMs; Sto-
    chastic DDM
    assumptions, 124-125
    factor models, comparison, 105
    introduction, 107-108
    stocks, 32, 33
    value, 30
Dividend increase, 116
Dividend omission, 76
Dividend stream, 107, 113. *See also*
    Stochastic dividend stream; Sto-
    chastic dividend stream
Dividend yield, 124, 142

Dividends. *See* Historical dividends
Dog stocks, 37
Dollar changes, 88
DOT. *See* Designated Order Turn-
    around; Direct Order Transmis-
    sion
Downside risk, 209

E

EAFE benchmark, 83
Earnings growth, 5, 22
Earnings model (E-MODEL), 115
Earnings momentum, 147
Earnings-estimate revisions, 183,
    199
Earnings/price (E/P), 169-171, 174,
    175. *See also* Value-like E/P
    ranking, 170
    ratio, 177
Earnings-to-price ratio, 92
    projection. *See* IBES earnings-to-
        price ratio projection
Economic sectors, 192
Economic-sector portfolio, 200
Edwards, Mark, 235, 236
Efficient market hypothesis (EMH),
    71, 74, 76, 84, 85
    paradigm, 78
Efficient markets, 38, 67, 72-73
    catch-22, 72, 83
Electronic crossing network, 48
Electronic trading, 33
    network, 48
EMH. *See* Efficient market hypothe-
    sis
E-MODEL. *See* Earnings model
Endowment effect, 7
Engineered management, 10-12
Enhanced cash management. *See*
    Index futures/enhanced cash
    management
Enhanced equity indexing, 51-66
Enhanced index, 81
    program, implementation, 63-66
    strategy, 60, 64, 66
Enhanced indexing, 55-56, 66
    nature, 52-54
    strategies. *See* Stock-based
        enhanced indexing strategies;
        Synthetic enhanced indexing
        strategies
    types, 56-63
Enhanced-indexing process, 56
E/P. *See* Earnings/price
Equal weighting, 135
Equal-weighted average score, 179
Equal-weighted basis, 134
Equal-weighted returns, 172
Equal-weighted sector-neutral port-
    folios, 185
Equity index. *See* Broad-based
    equity index; International equity
    index
    swap transaction, 205

Equity indexing. *See* Enhanced equity indexing
Equity management approaches, taxonomy, 54-56
Equity market. *See* Complex equity market
Equity market architecture, 1-20 objective, 19-20
Equity portfolios, 199 management, derivatives usage, 201-234
factor-based approach, 87-106
Equity returns. *See* Target equity returns
Equity strategies. *See* Value-based equity strategies
Equity style, definition/importance, 143-161 types, 145-148
Equity style classification, fundamental factors, 163-182 introduction, 163-164 size dimension, 164-165
Equity style management, 101-104
Estimation errors, 45
Estimate revisions, 189 usage. *See* Portfolios
Estimate-revision portfolios, 198
Ex post returns, 53 selection, 174
Excel spreadsheet, 123
Excess returns. *See* Expected excess return; Portfolio expected excess returns; Risk-adjusted excess return
Excess volatility, 74
Exercise price, 212-221, 226
Expectational inputs, 169
Expectations. *See* Growth; Homogenous expectations; Quasi-rational expectations; Value
Expected excess return, 97
Expenses, 78, 80
Exploitation, 59
Exposure profiles. *See* Risk
Extended market indexes, 42

F

Fabozzi, Frank J., 87, 104, 107, 131, 240
Factor analysis, 87
Factor approach, advantages. *See* Style
Factor models, 100, 101, 152-156 approach, limitations, 137 comparison. *See* Dividend discount models inputs/outputs, 97-99 return performance potential, 104-105 types, 87-97. *See also* Fundamental factors models; Macroeconomic factor models; Statistical factor models

Factor-based approach, 180. *See also* Equity portfolio management
Factor-based model, 104, 181
Factor-based style classification, 173, 181
Fair price, 110
Fair values, 72
Fama, Eugene F., 73, 74, 76, 79, 153, 160, 174
Fee options. *See* Performance-based fee options
Fees, 78, 80
Fence, 216, 219-221
Financial statements, in-depth examinations, 4
Finite life general model, 109-110
Fixed income techniques, 61
Fixed-income security selection, 64
Fixed-rate coverage, 91
Foresight tests, 104
Framing information, 11
Frank Russell Company, 145
French, Kenneth R., 73, 76, 79, 153, 160, 174
Frictionless markets, 68
Friedman, Jacques, 67
Fund management, 140
Fundamental factor models, 91-92, 101-104
Futures, 205-212 buying applications, 206-207 contract, 49, 201, 206, 207, 211. *See also* Synthetic futures contract fair value, 61 selling applications, 207-209 usage. *See* Hedge ratios

G

Gambler's Fallacy, 7-8
General model, 108. *See also* Finite life general model
Generalized Markov dividend growth models, 116
Generalized Markov growth stochastic DDMs, 116, 118
Geometric Brownian motion, 230
Geometric growth model, 117. *See also* Deterministic geometric growth model; Two-phase geometric growth model
Global coefficient, 75
Goldman Sachs Asset Management (GSAM), 96 factor model, 96, 101
Gordon, Myron J., 111
Gordon model, 111
Graham and Dodd process, 237
Grinold, Richard C., 5, 15, 34, 35, 53, 81, 128, 130
Grossman, Sanford, 72
Group-optimal portfolio, 71
Growth. *See* Consistent growth; Cyclical growth; Earnings

growth; Large-cap growth; Long-run economic growth; Small growth; Turnaround growth companies, 168 definition, 165-180 expectations, 165 index, 170, 175 managers, 147, 151, 176 market segment, 24 measures, 96 models, 113-115. *See also* Binomial dividend growth models; Deterministic additive growth model; Deterministic constant growth models; Deterministic geometric growth model; Generalized Markov dividend growth models; Three-phase growth model; Trinomial additive growth model; Trinomial geometric growth model; Trinomial Markov growth model phase, 113 rate, 171 stocks, 166-168. *See also* Out-of-favor growth stocks; Value/growth stocks
Growth at a price managers, 148
Growth-based managers, 147
Growth/value spectrum, 147

H

Hagin, Robert, 183
Haughton, Kelly, 153
Hedge ratios, futures usage, 209-212
Hedges. *See* Asymmetric hedges; Black-Scholes
Hedging. *See* Market exposure costs, 83
Higher-risk portfolios, 16, 17
High-growth investing, 152
High-yielding stocks, 71
Hindsight bias, 76
Hirshleifer, David, 76
Historical dividends, 111, 119
Homogenous expectations, 73 assumptions, 71-72
Hull, J., 227
Hurley, William J., 107, 115, 121

I

Ibbotson, Roger, 88
Ibbotson-Sinquefield Small Stock Index, 157
IBES earnings-to-price ratio projection, 92
IBM, 135
IC. *See* Information coefficient
Ideal benchmarks, 139
Illiquid markets, performance. *See* Indexing
Illusion of control, 76
Illusory correlation, 76

Implementation shortfall, 240
Implied repo rate, 206, 209
Income/appreciation, exchange, 214-216
In-depth research, 6
Index approach. *See* Weighted style index approach
Index arbitrage. *See* Stock index arbitrage
Index arbitrage-related strategies, 59-60
Index fund, management. *See* Midcap index fund; Small-cap index fund
Index futures/enhanced cash management, 59-62
Index program, implementation. *See* Enhanced index program
Indexes. *See* Extended market indexes; Small-cap indexes; Style Indexes/portfolios, 174
Indexing, 54-55. *See also* Active indexing; Enhanced equity indexing; Medium capitalization indexing; Small capitalization indexing
    anomalies, 74-76
    behavioral arguments, 76-78
    case, 68-78
    definition, 38-41
    empirical arguments, 73-76
    empirical evidence, 70
    illiquid markets, performance, 39-41
    long-run performance, 38-39
    nature. *See* Enhanced indexing strategies. *See* Stock-based enhanced indexing strategies; Synthetic enhanced indexing strategies
    theoretical arguments, 71-73
        assumptions, 71-72
    theoretical case, 68-70
    verdict, 78
Industry sector, 124
Industry weights, 42
Industry-based model, 82
Industry-related events, 27
Industry/sector concentrations, 57
Inflation, 88
    risk, 88
    shock, 88
Information coefficient (IC), 5, 34, 35
Information process, 235
Information ratio (IR), 15-18, 35, 52-56
Information value, 237
Initial trading strategy, establishment, 238
Instinet, 48, 242
Institutional money manager, 135
Institutional research, 160
Institutional traders, 236
Institutional trading costs, 241

Intel, 32
Intended bets, 159
Interest rates, 74, 88, 109. *See also* Constant interest rates
International equity index, 204
Investing, art/science, 235-249
    process, 249
Investing process, 235
Investment analysis, 21-35
    coherent framework, -25
    introduction, 21-22
Investment decision-making, 1, 7
Investment decisions, 78, 79
Investment horizon, 4
Investment ideas, 247
Investment management, 1-20, 87, 235
    architecture, 2-4
    fees, 56
    objective, 19-20
Investment managers, 180
Investment philosophy, 150
Investment process, 84
Investment return/risk level, 5
Investment returns, 76, 244
Investment strategies, implementation, 235-249
    implementation process, 235-236
    measurement framework, 240-241
    opportunities, 243-244
Investment strategy tools, normal portfolio usage, 138-141
Investor confidence, 88
Investor overreaction, 77
IR. *See* Information ratio
Iterative techniques, 45

J

Jacobs, Bruce I., 1, 2, 4, 11, 13, 14, 17, 21, 24-26, 28, 31, 32, 87, 91, 97, 104, 105, 124
January effect, 74
January seasonal, 27
Japanese equities, 181
Jenson, Michael C., 73
Johnson, Lewis D., 107, 115
Joint hypothesis, 73
Jones, Robert C., 67

K

Kahn, Ronald N., 5, 15, 34, 35, 53, 81
Kahneman, Daniel, 6, 76
Keynesians, 72
K-factor model, 97
Khanna, Vinti, 67
Kimball, Judith, 1, 21
Krask, Mitchell C., 25
Kreichman, Steven B., 115
Kritzman, Mark, 128

L

La Porta, Rafeal, 78

LaBerge, Natalie, 155
Labor-intensive methods. *See* Traditional active management
Labor-intensive research, 23
Large Company Growth, 178
Large Company Value, 178
Large Growth, 163, 164
Large Value, 164
Large-cap counterparts, 157
Large-cap domestic market, 84
Large-cap domestic stocks, 74
Large-cap growth, 3, 9, 81
Large-cap managers, 149
Large-cap portfolios, 12
Large-cap stocks, 3, 32, 39, 74, 80, 154
Large-cap styles, 151
Large-cap universe, 150
Large-cap value, 9
    stocks, 3, 24
Large-capitalization portfolios, 54
Large-capitalization stocks, 49
Large-stock portfolios, 32
Law of One Alpha, 24
Leinweber, David J., 104
Levy, Kenneth N., 1, 2, 4, 11, 13, 14, 17, 21, 24-26, 28, 31, 32, 87, 91, 97, 104, 105, 124
LIBOR. *See* London Interbank Offered Rate; Short-term LIBOR
Liew, John, 84
Linear payoffs, 202-212
    patterns, 201
Linear return combinations, 87
Lintner, John, 68
Lipper Analytical Services, 236
Lipper Growth and Income Indices, 79
Lipper Index, 79
Lipper large-cap fund universe, 70
Liquid markets. *See* Perfectly liquid markets
Liquidity, 242. *See also* Broker liquidity
    demand, 238
    problems, 135
    provision, concession, 245-246
    supply, 238
Liquidity-demanding orders, 242
Liquidity/information, probing, 238-239
Liquidity-supplying orders, 242
Local-market regression, 75
Loftus, John S., 51
London Interbank Offered Rate (LIBOR), 202, 205. *See also* Short- term LIBOR
    returns, 61
Long call/short put combinations, 60
Long-call/short-put options combinations, 60
Long-only portfolio, 14
Long-run economic growth, 88
Long-run steady-state geometric rate, 114

Long-short balance, 14
Long-short portfolios, 14
Long/short portfolios, 61
Long/short strategies, 61
Long-short strategy, 104
Long-term bond yield changes, 88
Long-term investment horizons, 158
Long-term trend-line growth, 150
Long-term performance, 38
Long-trend trends, 8
Loss aversion, 7
Low cost brokers, overreliance, 246-247
Low P/E managers, 146
Low-P/E effect, 74
Low-risk anomalies, 77
Low-risk effect, 77
Luck, Christopher G., 104

M

MacBeth, James D., 74
Macroeconomic factor models, 88-91, 104
Macroeconomic models, 98
Macroeconomic variables, 88
Malkiel, Burton G., 70
Manager mixes, 128
Manager pattern, 244-246
Managers. See Growth; Market-oriented managers; Small-capitalization managers; Value
    cooperation, amount, 140-141
    credit, 139-140
    ideal portfolio, 140
    normal habitat, 129
    performance benchmarks, 128-129
    universe misfit, 133-134
Manager-selection decision, 83
Manager-specific conditional weighted benchmark, 130
Manager-specific factor benchmark, 130
Manager-specific stock list method, 137
Manager-specific stock-matching benchmark, 130-137
Mark to market, 206
Market beta. See Residual market beta
Market capitalizations, 42
Market conditions
    adapting, 239
    assessment, 238
Market cycles, 182
Market exposure
    automatic expenses, 226
    creation, 221-222
    hedging, 207
Market factor sensitivity, 96
Market factors, 90
Market index, 88. See also Extended market indexes
Market indicators, 129
Market portfolio, 71

Market prices, 78
Market psychology, 108
Market timing risk, 88
Market-like risk levels, 9
Market-like sector exposures, 136
Market-like weights, 10
Market-normal managers, 148
Market-oriented group, 151
Market-oriented managers, 147-148, 155
Market-relative returns, 183, 187, 189
Market-selection decision, 83
Markov dividend stream. See Discounted Markov dividend stream
Markov processes, 115
Markov property, 115
Markowitz, Harry, 68, 82
Markowitz efficient frontier, 69
Mathematical strategies, 58
Maturity phase, 115
May, Catherine, 114
McMurran, Greg M., 201
Mean reversion, 62
Median breakpoint, 153
Medium capitalization indexing, 37-49
    introduction, 37
    summary, 49
    trading considerations, 47-49
Medium-cap bias, 152
Medium-cap sectors, 49
Medium-cap stocks, 47, 152
Medium-capitalization indexes, 43, 46, 48
Medium-capitalization sectors, 49
Medium-capitalization stocks, 42
Mencken, H.L., 34
Mezrich, Joseph J., 88, 90, 98, 104
Michaud, Richard, 125
MidCap 400 Index, 42
Mid-cap benchmarks, 42-43
Mid-cap index fund, management, 44-47
Mid-cap portfolios, 152
Miller, Paul, 183, 184
Misra, Diane, 67
Model risk, 59
Moldovsky, Nicholas, 114
Momentum manager, 244-245
Momentum measures, 96
Monetarists, 72
Money management firm, 131
Montana Power, 119
Monte Carlo simulation, 119, 121, 122
    usage. See Confidence intervals
MSCI-EAFE Index, 74, 83
Multifactor approach, 173-175
Multivariate modeling, 11
Multivariate models, 11
Multivariate regression, 26
Mutual funds
    active returns, 79
    risk-adjusted analysis, 84

N

90/10 strategy, 226
NASDAQ, 42
    trades, 240
Near-term business dynamics, 188
New York Stock Exchange, 42
News/information, 237
Noise, 26, 73
    reduction, 27-28
Non-benchmark-constrained traditional portfolios, 19
Noncap-weighted normal portfolio, 136
Nondiversified portfolios, 184, 185
    comparison. See Diversified portfolios
Non-dividend-paying stock, 22
Non-linear effects, 209
Non-linear payoffs, 202, 212-226
Non-linear probability, 142
Nonmarket risk, 147
Non-simultaneous pricing, 63
Non-symmetric distribution, 232
Normal portfolios, 127-142. See also Noncap-weighted normal portfolio; Poor man's normal portfolio; Style-weighted normal portfolio
    construction, approaches, 129-131
    creation
        issues, 137-138
        process, 129-131
        reasons, 139
    definition, 127-128
    management questions, 139-141
    measurement, communication, 138
    usage. See Investment strategy tools

O

Obsolescence, 59
O'Donnell, Mark, 88, 90
Offer, 238
Opportunity, 243-244
    cost, 241
Optimization, 45-46
Options
    payoff profiles, 212-214
    selling. See Call options
OTC. See Over-the-counter
Out-of-favor growth stock, 23
Out-of-favor industries, 146
Out-of-favor issues, 7
Out-of-favor stocks, 139
Overconfident investors, 78
Over-confident optimists, 77
Over-confident pessimists, 77
Over-the-counter (OTC), 16
    market, 42
    stocks, 48
    swap market, 83
Over-trading, 82

P

Pagels, Heinz, 21
Passive investing, 71, 72
Passive management, 136
Passive style indexing, 57
Payoff matrix, 214, 219
Payoff patterns, 226
Payoff profiles, 201. *See also* Options
Payoffs, 3. *See also* Linear payoffs; Non-linear payoffs
Passive benchmarks, 70
Passive indexing, comparison. *See* Active indexing
Passive management, 9-10
P/E. *See* Price/earnings ratio
Pension funds. *See* Tax-exempt pension funds
    consultants, 84
Perfectly liquid markets, 229-230
Performance. *See* Indexing; Long-term performance
    attribution, 165
    benchmarks. *See* Manager
    measurement, 165. *See also* Style patterns. *See* Style
    potential. *See* Factor models
    profile. *See* Stocks
Performance-based fee options, 56
Perold, A., 240
PIPER database, 81
Policy portfolio, 138, 139
Poor man's normal portfolio, 136
Portable alpha strategies, 81, 83
Portfolio characteristics, 152
    analysis, 136. *See also* Style
Portfolio distribution, 222
Portfolio expected excess returns, 99-100
Portfolios. *See* Large-cap portfolios; Long-only portfolios; Long- short portfolios; Manager; Normal portfolios; Policy portfolio; Small-cap portfolios; Value-based portfolios
    comparisons. *See* Diversified portfolios; Stocks
    constructed returns
    estimate revisions, usage, 186-188
    p/e ratios, usage, 184-186
    value scores, usage, 188-192
    construction, 8-9, 33-34, 174
    construction-based techniques, 57-58
    decision making, 248
    effectiveness, assessment, 239-240
    engineering, 11-12
    evaluation, 33-34
    exposure assessment, 100-101
    management, 237. *See also* Equity portfolio management
    comparison. *See* Trading

optimization, 8
performance, 14
risk, 8, 12
risk-return profiles, 8
selectors, 188
substitutes, 202
tilting, 101
trading, 33-34
weights, 15
Portfolio-based approach, 180
POSIT, 48
Post earnings announcement drift, 74
PPI. *See* Producer Price Index
Predictability, 30-32
Pre-tax risks/returns, 71
Price impact, 241-243
Price movement, 211
Price/book, 142
Price/earnings, 133, 142
Price-earnings ratio, 124
Price/earnings (P/E), 133, 188, 189, 192, 199
    approach, 191
    continuum, 25
    diversified portfolio, 197
    inclusion, 10
    levels, 24
    multiple, 144
    portfolio, 185, 186, 189, 197, 198
    quintile. *See* Stocks
    ratio, 23-26, 33, 34, 91, 137, 144, 146, 150, 183, 184, 186, 191
    threshold, 57
    securities, 184
    stocks, 24, 33, 186, 192
    threshold, 57
    usage. *See* Portfolios
Price/sales ratios, 146
Price-to-book ratios, 150
Price-to-book value, 146
Pride in Ownership syndrome, 7
Principal components analysis, 87
Principal trade, 238
Private-party transactions, 202
Probabilities, 71
Probability distribution, 107, 108, 208. *See also* Returns
Probing trades, 239
Process discipline, 81-83
Process review, 239
Producer Price Index (PPI), 105
Professionally-managed assets, 70
Proprietary trading, 246
Proprietary Trading Systems, 242
Protective put, 216-220
    spread, 216, 218-219
    strategy, 216, 221, 222
Pure returns, 26, 30
Put/call parity relationship, 224, 225

Q

Quant. *See* Active quant
Quantitative strategies, 58
Quasi-efficient market, 74

Quasi-rational expectations, 74
Quintile portfolio, 197
Quintile returns, 192
Quintile stocks, 191, 192, 196, 200
Quintiling, 26

R

Range forward, 216, 219-221
Real business activity, 88
Realized return, 240
Real-time monitoring, 34
Rebalance interval, 172
Rebalancing frequency, 172
Reebok International Limited, 98, 99
Regression, 142. *See also* Local-market regression; Single-variable regression; Univariate regression
    coefficient, 91
REITs, 38
Replication, timing, 46-47
Repo rate. *See* Implied repo rate
Residual beta, 98
Residual market beta, 90
Residual risk, 12, 15, 16, 18, 148
Return differential, 155
Return on equity (ROE), 133, 142, 150
Return pattern analysis, 136. *See also* Style
Return performance potential. *See* Factor models
Return revelation, 28-30
Return/risk level. *See* Investment return/risk level
Return/risk ratio, 5
Returns, 73. *See also* Benchmark returns; Ex post returns; Investment returns; Pure returns; Target equity returns
    long-term rates, 41
    probability distribution, 222-226
Returns-based approach, 181
Returns-based framework, 51
Returns-based tools, 52-54
Return-variable relationships, 33
Reweighting, 172-173
Risk. *See* Model risk
    aversion, 17
    control, 11, 57, 78-80, 81-82
    exposure profiles, 99-100
    factor exposure, 97
    factors, 100
    indexes / indices, 91, 92, 100
    levels. *See* Market-like risk levels
    measures, 96
Risk Attribute Model (RAM), 88, 90, 97-98, 100, 104
    factor model, 98
Risk neutral valuation approach, 234
Risk-adjusted analysis. *See* Mutual funds
Risk-adjusted excess return, 52, 73

Risk-adjusted net excess return, 80
Risk-averse investor, 15
Risk-aversion level, 16, 19
Risk-controlled active management, 51
Risk-controlled managers, 81
Risk-free rate, 61, 97, 98, 119, 227, 228
Risk-free recurring returns, 249
Risk-free security, 227
Risk-return continuum, 15-19
Risk-return goals. See Client risk-return goals
Risk-return profiles, 8, 13, 15
Risk/return profiles, 10
Risk-reward posture, 84
Risk/reward trade-off, 69
Risk-seeking, 7
Risk-tolerance levels, 19
Rochester G&E, 119
ROE. See Return on equity
RogersCasey, 81
Roll, Richard, 88, 129
Rosenberg, Barr, 127, 153
Ross, Stephen A., 88, 227
RSC system, 142
Rubinstein, M., 227
Russell 1000, 132, 133
    Growth Index, 153, 154
    index, 74
    Value Index, 153, 154, 160
Russell 2000, 39, 41, 46, 154
    Index, 83
Russell 2500, 39, 41, 42
Russell 3000, 2, 131, 133, 138, 155
    Growth Index, 79
    index, 129, 134
    Index, 148-150
    Value Index, 79
Russell Manager Research, 142
Russell MidCap Index, 42, 43, 152
Russell Style Universe, 155

S

Salomon Brothers, 88, 97-98, 100, 104, 115
    model, 88, 90
Samak, Vele, 88, 90
Sampling. See Stratified sampling
    timing, 46-47
Sauter, George U., 37
Scenario factors, 98
Scenario score, 98-100
Scholes, Myron, 73, 227
Schlarbaum, Gary G., 183
Screening rules, 130
Second-best-revision portfolio, 187
Second-best-value-score portfolio, 189
Sector allocation, 141, 150
Sector bets, 173
Sector weighting, 134
Sector representation, 173
Sector-neutral portfolios, 197

Securities
    choice, 131-133
    in-depth analyses, 5
    losers, 13
    universe, 131
    weighting, 134
    winners, 13
Security price, 213, 218
Security pricing, 32
Security selection. See Fixed-income security selection
Segmented market, integrated approach, 22-24
    Balkanization, 22
    out-of-favor segment, 23
    self-imposed barriers, 22
Segment-specific model, 24
Selection strategies, sector-by-sector comparison, 192-197
Selective perception, 76
Semi-deviation, 232
Sharpe, William F., 68, 130, 142
Sherrerd, Jay, 183, 184
Shiller, Robert J., 7, 74
Short selling, assumption, 230
Shorter-term risk, 159
Short-sale candidates, 99
Short-term business cycle risk, 88
Short-term LIBOR, 61
Short-term overreaction, 32
Short-term price fluctuation, 172
Short-term tracking error, 47
Short-term Treasury bill changes, 88
Short-term trends, 181
Sierra Pacific, 119
Single-variable regression, 26
Size effect, 74
Size/style quadrant, 182
Slovic, Paul, 76
Small cap trades, 240
Small capitalization indexing, 37-49
    introduction, 37
    summary, 49
    trading considerations, 47-49
Small Company Value Index, 181
Small Growth, 164
Small growth, 168
Small-cap company, 23
Small-cap counterparts, 152
Small-cap funds, 39, 41, 83
Small-cap growth managers, 148
Small-cap index fund, management, 44-47
Small-cap indexes, 9, 43
Small-cap investing, 41, 152
Small-cap managers, 39, 149, 150
Small-cap market segment, 24, 32
Small-cap market-oriented managers, 148
Small-cap markets, 39
Small-cap portfolios, 9, 12, 32
Small-cap sectors, 49
Small-cap stocks, 3, 5, 29, 32, 41, 47, 154
Small-cap styles, 5

Small-cap value managers, 148
Small-cap years, 41
Small-capitalization characteristics, 156
Small-capitalization indexes, 43, 46, 48
Small-capitalization managers, 22, 148
Small-capitalization portfolios, 148
Small-capitalization sectors, 49
Small-capitalization segments, 38
Small-capitalization stocks, 37, 41, 43, 49, 157
Sorensen, Eric H., 88, 90, 98, 104, 114, 115
S&P500. See Standard & Poor's 500
Spread. See Protective put
Standard deviation, 29, 53, 90, 120, 232
Standard & Poor's 500 (S&P500), 2, 9, 30, 37-39, 42, 43, 46, 49, 54, 60, 62, 67, 70, 99, 100, 101, 105, 129, 134, 155-157, 212, 221
    fund. See Vanguard S&P500 fund
    futures, 60
    contract, 60, 210, 211
    Index, 42, 49, 70, 78, 80, 83, 210-212
    fund, 70
    index, 60, 127, 131, 205
    futures, 59
    MidCap 400, 43, 165
    futures contract, 49
    return, 79
    SmallCap 600, 43
    SmallCap Index, 43
    stocks, 60, 62
Standard & Poor's 600 (S&P600), 43
Standard & Poor's Corporation, 164
Statistical factor models, 87-88
Stiglitz, Joseph, 72
Stochastic DDM, 107, 110, 115-124. See also Binomial stochastic DDMs
Stochastic dividend stream, 107
Stochastic models, 107. See also Binomial growth stochastic model
    application, 119
Stochastic process, 115
Stock index arbitrage, 59
    opportunity, 60
Stock list model, limitations, 137
Stock pickers, 37
Stock picking, 4
Stock prices, 197, 217-219
    appreciation, 216
    behavior, 30
Stock-based approach, 51, 63
Stock-based enhanced indexing strategies, 57, 63
Stock-based method, 58
Stock-based strategies, 51, 56-59, 63
    issues, 58-59

Stock/manager selection/review
process, 182
Stocks. *See* Growth; Price/earnings
ratio; Value; Value/growth
classification, 170-171
P/E quintile, 197
performance profile, 175-176
returns, 105, 186
sources, 25
sector-neutral portfolio, 189
selection, 23, 63
sub-universe, 131
Stock-selection ability, 75
Stock-selection process, 183
Stock-selection systems, 82
Stratified sampling, 44-45
Strike price, 212
Style. *See* Equity style
bets, 101. *See also* Unintended
style bets
biases, 158
classification. *See* Equity style
classification; Factor-based style
classification
descriptions, 144
diversification, 159-160
drift, 176
evidence, 148-151
factor approach, advantages, 180-
182
historical perspectives, 151-152
index returns, 130
indexes, 137, 152-156
management, applications, 156-
159
performance measurement, 156-
158
management strategy, 106
managers, 22
map, 180
metric, 177-180
performance patterns, 150-151
portfolio characteristics, 148-150
analysis, 142
capitalization distribution, 149
economic sectors, 150
growth characteristics, 150
valuation characteristics, 150
portfolio comparisons, 180
return pattern analysis, 141-142
weights, 136
Style-based model, 82
Style-diversified choice, 159
Style-oriented manager, 181
Style/size exposure, 173
Style-weighted normal portfolio,
136-137
Subrahmanyam, Avanidhar, 76
SuperDOT, 48
Supply/demand imbalances, 237
Supply-siders, 72
Swaps, 202-205
contract, 204
seller, 202-204
tenor, 202

Synthetic enhanced indexing strategies, 59, 63
Synthetic futures contract, 224
Synthetic strategies, 59-63
issues, 62-63

T

Tangency efficient portfolio (TEP),
69
Target equity returns, achievement,
158-159
Target price, 230
Target value profile, 181
Tax-exempt pension funds, 71
Taxes, 70
assumption, 71
laws, 22
Tax-loss selling, 28
Terminal price, 110
Thaler, Richard H., 6
Three Mile Island, 27
Three-factor model, 79
Three-phase growth model, 113-115
Thum, Chee, 88, 90, 98, 104
Tilting. *See* Portfolios
techniques, 57
Tilts, 57
Time horizon, 60, 150, 157, 159
risk, 88
Time series data, 88
Timing, 243. *See also* Trader timing
costs, 243, 244
Total Quality Management, 236,
239
Tracking error, 44, 45, 52-56, 58-64.
See also Short-term tracking
error; Zero tracking error
Trade motivation, 237
Trader pattern, 245-246
Trader timing, 241
Trading. *See* Electronic trading
case studies, 244-247
cost components, 241
costs, 33, 71, 190, 241-244. *See
also* Institutional trading costs
assumption, 71
conclusions, 244
effectiveness, assessment, 239-
240
industry-wide components, 241
partner currencies, 88
portfolio management comparison, 236-240
price, 238
recommendations, 247-248
services, 248
strategy, 248. *See also* Initial trading strategy
Traditional active management, 4-
9, 59
labor-intensive methods, 6
Traditional management, segment-
oriented focus, 24
Transaction fee, 48

Transactions costs, 43, 46, 47, 59,
68, 71, 85, 104, 229, 231
Transporting alpha, 204
Treasury bills, 105
returns, 142
Trend, 176
Treynor, J., 237
Trinomial additive growth model,
118
Trinomial geometric growth model,
119
Trinomial Markov growth model,
118-119
Trittin, Dennis J., 131, 142, 155
T-statistics, 53, 79, 81
T-tests, 81
Turnaround growth, 167
Turn-of-the-month effect, 74
Turnover costs, 59
Turnover ratios, 191
Tversky, Amos, 6, 76
Two-phase geometric growth
model, 114
Two-phase model, 113, 114

U

Uncertain dividend stream, 107
Undervalued stocks, 139
Unexpected information, 68
Unintended biases, 159
Unintended style bets, 159
Unintentional bets, 101, 137
Univariate regression, 26, 28
Unweighted medians, 133
Up-front money, 201
U.S. equity market, 2, 143, 221
U.S. stock market, 42
U.S.-domiciled companies, 42
Utility industry effect, 27
Utility-maximizing agents, 68

V

Value
benchmark, 13
definition, 165-180
expectations, 165
investor, 144
managers, 135, 145-146, 168
market segment, 24
measures, 96
model, 175
scores, usage. *See* Portfolios
stocks, 168-170. *See also* Large-
cap value
trades, 237
Value Line Industry Review, 118
Value-based equity strategies, 183-
200
conclusion, 199-200
introduction, 183-184
Value-based portfolios, 185
Value-benchmark-like return, 13
Value-biased managers, 147
Value/growth, 58

stocks, 171-172
Value-like E/P, 179
Value-score approach, 191
Value-score portfolios, 198
Vanguard S&P500 fund, 236
Variable-return relationship, 25, 32
   nonlinearities, 32
Variables/factors combination, 174
Volatility. *See* Excess volatility
Volatility-based strategies, 59, 62
Volatility-based synthetic strate-
   gies, 62

W

Wagner, Wayne H., 235, 236
Weighted medians, 133
Weighted style index approach, lim-
   itations, 138
Weighting, 172-173. *See also* Capi-
   talization weighting; Re- weight-
   ing; Sector weighting; Securities
   alternatives, 135
   rules, 130
   schemes, 134, 135
Williams, C. Nola, 143
Williams, John B., 108
Williamson, David, 114
Wilshire 4500, 42, 46
Wilshire 5000, 2
   Index, 164, 166, 176
Wilshire factor model, 96
Wilshire Growth Indexes, 176
Wilshire Institutional Services/
   Equity Division, 164
Wilshire model, 91
Wilshire Small Value Index, 173
Wilshire Style Indexes, 176, 181
Wilshire Top 750 Index, 164-166
Wishful thinking, 76
Working trade, 238

Y

Yao, Yulin, 118, 119
Yield managers, 146

Z

Zero cost collar, 219, 220
Zero tracking error, 53, 64
Zero-coupon bond, 229